HISTORY OF THE TANGKHUL NAGAS

HISTORY
OF
THE TANGKHUL NAGAS

By
A.S.W. Shimray

AKANSHA PUBLISHING HOUSE
NEW DELHI-110 059 (INDIA)

AKANSHA PUBLISHING HOUSE
R 37-B, Vani Vihar, Uttam Nagar
New Delhi-110059

History of the Tangkhul Nagas

First Edition, 2001
ISBN 81-87606-04-5
Reprint 2022

[The responsibility for the facts stated, conclusions reached etc. is entirely that of the Author. The publisher is not responsible for them whatsoever.]

PRINTED IN INDIA

Published by M.P. Mishra for Akanksha Publishing House, Delhi, and Printed at Mehra Offset Press, Delhi.

Dedicated

to

my beloved parents

CONTENTS

PREFACE

In the early stage of my academic career, it was my plan to write the chronology and history of my clan (Shuingtuidang) and produce a book on it during the life time of my father who was well versed in our oral history. I had feared that if this was not done, it would slip the memory of our clan. However, before things were set into order and completion, I had to leave it on account of insurgent Naga political upheavals.

Later, when I joined the discipline of history, I felt the importance of doing research on the history of the Tangkhul Nagas and the institution of the Awunga (chief) which is permanent hereditary post in the Village State, which will serve as written history for the use of future generations. The history of the Tangkhul Nagas and the institution of the Awunga are closely linked with the origin, migration and settlement of the Nagas at present Naga Homeland. Therefore, writing history of the Thangkhul Nagas without touching the Village State is incomplete and mere wastage of time and energy. Because, in the Village State, the Institution of Awunga is supreme having wide range of functions—social, economic, political, cultural and religious life of the Tangkhuls in particular and the Nagas in general. This requires to be conducted during the life of surviving Tangkhul elders who are the only custodians of oral past history, customs, culture and religion of the people.

The Nagas do not possess written records of their past. A few books had been written on the Nagas, and that too, mainly by non-Nagas. These are social and anthropological studies in nature. Therefore, they failed to appreciate and understand the deeper and real life of the Nagas. The indigenous writers also had not done in-depth research with regard to the Institution of the Awunga and the Village State. The Awunga had to run the Village State according to Riyan (unwritten constitution) and Mayorin (unwritten law) of the Tangkhul Nagas which are based on their customary culture. Again, the customs and culture of the Tangkhuls had the elements of their religious principles. Therefore, it is expedient that a deeper research in all areas of the total life of the people is conducted. In this area, foreign writers had failed miserably. As such, it is the interest of the author to carry out a thorough investigation of the work.

The present study covers the period from the antiquity of Naga history to the present day. For, the history of this region makes a quick jump from antiquity to modern times. Again, to have reconstructed this work from original written material was not possible since the Nagas had no script. Drawing materials from questionnaires given to the Awungas was difficult due to lack of response by them. Reason for this may be, because, many of them are illiterate. Secondly, they took the questionnaires with some hesitation; some were even suspicious of the intention of what was being asked to them. Answers to the questionnaires, therefore, came from the Tangkhul Nagas, many of them were not Awungas. They appreciated the nature of enquiry and gladly responded to the queries.

This source, and the use of oral traditions and also secondary materials already available are found of very useful to reconstruct this portion of history in the absence of other sources. It has now become possible for the Nagas to write their own history. Traditional institutions are undergoing rapid changes.

During this research work, a number of people and well wishers lent out their helping hand without which the work would not have taken its shape. I apologise for not being able to acknowledge them individually. However, my close and constant associates who helped me produce this book can not escape the pen of the author. First, I thank the Principal of Patkai Christian College for granting me study leave and financial assistance. I thank Dr. P.S. Dutta, then Assistant Director, ICSSR, North East Region, Shillong, for a study tour grant. My profound thanks goes to Dr. Joseph Thomas, his successor, who helped me secure study grant from the Indian Council of Social Science Research, New Delhi. He was my patron in the production of this book by finding proper publisher, without which it would be an arduous and costly job. I am much indebted to the Indian Council of Social Science Research, New Delhi, for granting partial Financial Assistance without which the research might have been difficult. My special thanks are to Joseph F. Khongbuh for secretarial assistance.

I am also grateful to the authorities of Assam and Manipur States Archives for allowing me access to their holdings. I am indebted to village chiefs and respondents to the questionnaires for their prompt response. I am extremely indebted to my father, A.S. Hongvaileng and my brother, A.S. Vashi who have been well acquainted with Naga traditions, oral history, customs and culture who provided historical data from oral history, folklores and mimeographs.

Finally, I wish to put on record my highest thank and gratitude to my teacher and mentor, Dr. David R. Syiemlieh, at North Eastern Hill University, for his able guidance of this research work. He was the editor and took the initiative for the publication of this book. The untiring care and devotion which he rendered for the success of this venture can never be measured in terms of time, labour and material assistance. Thanks are also due to Shri M.P. Misra, Director, Akansha Publishing House, New Delhi for readily agreeing to publish the book.

A.S.W. Shimary

GLOSSARY

Akhang	- The Shan/Burmese name for the Nagas.
Akekao	- Sema village chief.
Ang	- Konyak village chief.
Aguang	- Kabui village chief.
Awou	- The principal religious official of Sema village.
Awunga	- Tangkhul village chief.
Chipee	- Demon (of the Tangkhuls).
Chochomi	- Sema village elder; councillor.
Chumphut	- New rice eating festival.
Dao	- A Naga knife of different sizes and Shapes.
Dharshat Phanit	- Festival to begin harvest.
Ekyung	- Lotha village chief.
Erongpa	- Village chief of the Mayon Nagas.
Eyong	- Religious official of the Upper Konyak village.

Hao	- Originally the Tangkhuls called themselves, and other Nagas 'Hao'. The Meiteis call the tribals 'Hao'.
Hambu	- It is a warrior class, leader of war and expendition of the Upper Konyaks.
Hong/Hung	- Early titles of Tangkhul village chief.
Hangva	- Tangkhul village council.
Hara-Khayang	- Egg divination.
Kapa-Khayang	- Bamboo slit divination.
Khang	- Kachin term for footprint.
Kazeiram	- The Tangkhul believed the land of death.
Kazingram	- Tangkhul for Heaven.
Kasa-Akhava	- Master of Creation/Creator.
Kharing-tuk	- War of hostage.
Kemevo	- Angami village priest/religious leader.
Kokto	- Ruler of the souls of the dead/the king of dead.
Kongsang	- Beads over the chest of woman.
Khureng	- Village chief of the Anal Nagas.
Khokhugu	- Village chief of western Rengma.
Khekho-ong	- Village chief of eastern Rengma.
Khawung	- Tangkhul village state.
Laa Khanganui	- Tangkhul singing and dancing competition.
Lambu	- A Meitei peon.
Leingapha	- A Tangkhul village fair held during the Luira-Phanit (New Year Festival).
Liphan	- Dining table made of bamboo and cane.

Longshim	-	Bachelor's dormitory.
Lam	-	It is a priestly class of the Khiamnungans.
Longshang	-	Highest sub-clan of the Sheev clan.
Longwang	-	Clan representative in the village council of Upper Konyak.
Luira-Phanit	-	Tangkhul New Year Festival.
Lungning	-	Magic stone grown hairs of animals.
Maharaja	-	Title of Meitei ruler.
Mayonrin	-	Tangkhul for law.
Maran-Kasa	-	Tangkhul Feast of Merit.
Putir	-	Village priest of the Aos.
Pareiyar	-	Group of Tangkhul housewives formed as a working group.
Petchi	-	A class of Khiamnungans who performed both secular and religious functions.
Pukreila	-	Woman peace-maker.
Riyan	-	Unwritten Constitution of the Tangkhuls to run the village State.
Samsangva	-	A Tangkhul goddess of cultivation with long and luxurious hair.
Shar	-	Tangkhul day where work is prohibited. Also a taboo where they are prohibited to do, to speak, and so on.
Shara	-	Priestess of the Tangkhuls.
Shiyan-yanza	-	Customary law of the Tangkhul.
Sugong	-	Maram village chief.
Sheev	-	The ruling class of Khiamnungan village

Sungba	- Ao village chief of the Mongsen group.
Shang	- Exogamous Tangkhul clan.
Tang	- Block or Division of village settlement of Tangkhul.
Tarung	- Totem.
Tangkhul Long	- Tangkhul Tribal Council.
Tatar	- Councillor of Ao village.
Thai	- Second topmost clan of the Sheev.
Thisham	- Tangkhul festival celebrated in honour of farewell to the souls of the dead.
Ungr	- Ao village chief of the Chongli group.
Uzumbok	- Another name of Tangkhul called by the Burmese on the basis of tangkhul coiffure.
Varivara	- A Tangkhul name for God.
Wungnao	- Tangkhul village chief, but when the village clan-chiefs have a sitting with the Awunga separate from the Hangva members, they are known as Wungnaos. They settle issues of serious matters which the village council could not solve.
Yarra	- A Tangkhul festival of age-group.
Yarthot	- Tangkhul age-working group.
Zeithing	- Iron-shod walking stick of Tangkhul women.

1

INTRODUCTION

Origin, Migration, Settle ment and Nomenclature of the Nagas

The Nagas are a mongoloid race living in the heart of the rightangular centre of China in the north, Myanmar in the east, Bangladesh in the south and India in the west. They are the largest of the tribes of the region. It is beyond doubt and argument that the Nagas are the most ancient people in the area they are inhabiting. No legend, tradition and history tells that the land had been inhabited by any other people or race before the advent and settlement of the Nagas in the area. However, since the Nagas do not have a written history of the past, this led the people to question about the origin, migration and settlement of the Nagas. This, again, has resulted in a serious identity crisis of the Nagas. This question is an issue before the modern generation, particularly, to the scholars, writers and historians. Attempts to solve this problem have not been satisfactory and this has led us to go for deeper research to trace the origin of the Nagas.

The absence of written past history of the Nagas has not discouraged the author to construct the history of the Nagas, especially their origin, migration and settlement in their present habitation. Although the Nagas do not have any written account of their past, they are endowed with rich legends, traditions, folksongs etc., which are the most important sources of information for the construction of the early Naga history. Again, another important source of the Naga history is the oral tradition handed down from generation to generation. Indeed, culture, customs and traditions stand as unwritten history of mankind in early days before the development of written scripts.

In fact, no society was born with a script in the beginning. Rather, it was the result of the progress and development of human civilization. After much experience, they could devise the art of writing. Unfortunately, the Nagas did not possess any script and consequently, Naga history has mostly to depend on the oral traditions, culture, customs, folklores etc. In this connection, a Naga teacher quotes from Jan Vansina, "Oral tradition should be central to the students of culture, ideology, of society, of psychology, of arts, and finally, of history."[1] The same is true to the students of history of the Nagas today. Therefore, we have to construct history of the Nagas mainly basing it on a critical assessment of oral tradition.

Origin

The origin of the Nagas is shrouded in history. A systematic study on the Nagas is a matter of recent past, and it was mostly done by western anthropologists, ethnologists, administrators and some Christian missionaries, which was latter, followed by Indian scholars. However, none of them gives the correct picture of the Nagas and their history as Horam remarks, "As a matter of fact, no single writer has yet found himself equal to the task of correctly portraying the Nagas—historically, socially, politically and psychologically."[2] Today, there are a good number of Naga scholars who are equally interested in finding their ancient history, especially their origin, migration and settlement.

Several theories are forwarded by scholars having different ideas about the origin of the Nagas. G. A. Grierson gave his view with regard to the racial origin of the Nagas. According to his observation: "The Naga group comprises a long series of dialects which are mutually different much from each other. They are, on the whole, more closely related to Tibetan than to Burmese."[3] Gangmumei Kabui, a noted Naga historian at Manipur University mentions that some Indian philosophists led by Dr. S. K. Chatterjee advocate that the Kiratas of the ancient past were the Indo-Mongoloids and that the Nagas of North-Eastern India belong to this group. B. S. Guha also has the same view. But according to Gangmumei, this theory does not stand to reason since the Nagas do not have any racial affinity with the larger Indian population—traditionally, culturally and linguistically. Racially also, the Nagas had never identified themselves with the Indian population.[4] M. Horam, another Naga scholar in Manipur University refutes the racial mixture of the Nagas with the Aryan culture of Bengal. He writes:[5]

> The racial origin of the Naga tribes is baffling complex. All attempts to connect them with the rest of India, especially with the aborigines of India as well as with the Aryan culture of Bengal have not helped in making the confusion less confounding.

Though the Indian population at large are the immediate neighbours of the Nagas, there is a wide difference between the religion, culture, language, tradition and physical feature of the Nagas and Indians. The Nagas who are Mongoloid are more akin to the Mongoloids of Burma, and further east, and towards south east Asia.

The linguist G.A. Grierson classed the Nagas in the Tibeto-Burman group and this theory has been supported by many scholars of the Nagas and non-Nagas. According to Y. L. Roland-Shimmi, "The Sino-Tibetan languages can be classified into two parts (i) Tibeto-Burman, (ii) Siamese-Chinese. All the Naga dialects are included in the former group".[6]

The study of the physical feature of the Nagas is another determining factor of the origin of the Nagas. The Nagas bear similar features of the Mongoloids which is immediately recognised at a glance. Here T. C. Hodson, an authority on the Naga tribes of Manipur wrote that, pure Mongolian cast of countenance would be observed in the face of the Nagas,"[7] J. H. Hutton, an anthropologist and another great authority on Naga tribes of Naga Hills has written, "They have been connected with the head- hunters of Maley and the races of the southern seas on the one hand and traced back to China on the other."[8] The fact cannot be denied that people of the same race have similar physical characteristics such as colour, facial features and perhaps, some culture, custom and tradition. The distance of time of separation and geographical location cannot wipe it out completely. These features are found in Naga society as well as in the societies of Tibet, China, Burma and the people of South East Asian countries. In this connection, Sipra Sen remarked:[9]

> The tribes of Manipur belong to Tibeto-Burman group of Indo-Mongoloid people. They are generally medium to above medium stature, mesocephalic head, every prosopic broad flat round face, broad high chick-bone, flat platyrrhine to leptorrhine nose, brownish, yellow-skin narrow Mongoloid oblique eyes with limbs. They are strong and sturdy. The Naga tribes of Manipur has all the affinities with the Naga tribes of Nagaland and have some affinities with the tribes of South East Asian countries.

When this researcher conducted several field works,"[10] one of his respondents, R. K. Luikham said that Hao city, now, known as Xian in China was the last settled city from where the Naga people, particularly the Tangkhuls migrated to their present habitation. Ramyo Luikham is of the opinion that, according to Chinese history, their tribesmen migrated towards south west in between 200 B.C. and 500 A.D. It is believed that the Nagas were among the major tribes during the construction of the Great Wall.

Summing up all these evidences—oral, tradition and written evidences one may come to the conclusion that the Nagas belong to Tibeto-Burman family of the Mongolian race. In the extreme past, their ancestors might have lived in Mongolia, which in course of time, during their migratory stage, they came to China. In search of suitable settlement, at last, they moved out of China and came to this present homeland.[11]

Here, I may be permitted to narrate an interesting incident. In 1972, I was in China for twelve months. On arrival, we were invited to an entertainment where a Chinese film called 'Red Detachment' was screened. It depicted the condition of China during the old regime where landlords and privileged class of people oppressed the poor and down-trodden society. In the film, on the birthday of a landlord called Nam Pathe, he forced the villagers to perform dance and other entertainments to make his birthday a grand one. The village girls appeared on the stage with their traditional costumes which was quite similar to that of the Tangkhuls. When the visitors expressed surprise at what they viewed, one Chinese officer asked them whether such costumes were worn in Nagaland. We answered, "Yes, but why?" There he said that the Nagas emerged from China. This further cleared the doubt concerning the origin of the Nagas.[12]

While discussing the racial origin of the Nagas, there comes another important and equally interesting topic. The discovery of racial origin without finding the original homeland is incomplete. So the question, now, is what was the original birth-place of the Tibeto-Burman race, particularly of the Nagas. This issue is another complicated problem again. Because no tradition of the Nagas carries any particular name of a place of China from where they dispersed. Again their myths and legends are not supported by history though they cannot be outrightly rejected. Further, the interpretation of myths and legends are different from tribe to tribe, especially in relation with the geographical location which they refer to in their legends. Therefore, any attempt to study Naga migration into their present homeland stated above must be drawn from oral tradition either still unwritten and those that had been put into writing such as Naga folktales in the ethnographical accounts. We start this discussion by quoting at length from G. A. Grierson:[13]

> Tradition and comparative philology agree in pointing to the North Western China between the upper courses of the Yang-Tse and of the Huang-Ho as the original home of the Tibeto-Chinese race. Further, India and Assam have been populated by successive waves of Tibeto-Chinese invaders, each advancing in turn down the courses of one or more of the principal streams, the Brahmaputra, the Chindvin, the Irravadi, the Salvin, the Menam and the Makong and driving its predecessors nearer to the sea-coast or into the mountain fastness which overlook the valley.

Both R. R. Shimray and M. Horam give affirmation to the statement of Grierson. Shimray referring to Smith to some extent, and Marshall, mentioned that the early home of the people of Eastern Asia was in the upper reaches of the Huang-Ho or the Yellow river of China and from this centre, the Nagas followed the movement of the early tribes of Indo-China towards the south.[14] According to Horam, there were four waves of migration from China, and the Nagas belonged to the first group, the Konyaks being the oldest settlers."[15] He further said that, first they started from China towards the south and entered into their present habitation crossing Tibet and NEFA, now called Arunachal Pradesh. Horam, therefore believes that the route was through South East Asia, then via Tibet and crossing the Himalayas, the tribe settled in the hills which now take their name. He believes that, subsequent Naga migration did not take the route mentioned above. The Naga tribes such as the Tangkhuls, Semas, Rengmas, Angamis and Lothas, having left South China, entered the present homeland from south and south east directions. What is interesting is that despite two distinct routes, the various migrating Naga tribes should have finally settled in close proximity to each other.

Again, the Nagas have their own myth and legend which tell of their origin and migration, and occupation of their present homeland. Although absolute authenticity of their myth and legend is in question, and sometimes there can be exaggeration in their bearing, we cannot reject them altogether. Because, unquestionably, there are certain information that may be drawn from such traditions. In support of the view of such oral tradition, the statement of R. C. Majumdar is important. He opined, "Tradition naturally begins with myth."[16] The same is true with the legends and myth of the Nagas. Unfortunately, there are slight variations in the interpretation of the myth and location of the origin where they referred to in the myth. But its basic principle and authenticity may be accepted with some reservations.

From the mythical and legendary point of view, the Nagas emerged from the bowel of the earth. Almost all the Naga tribes have this theory of cave-origin. Mizo-Chin- Kuki tribes of Tibeto-Burman family also have the same cave-origin theory similar to the Nagas. According to the Maikhel theory, Angamis, Semas, Rengmas and Lothas came out .from the hole of the earth in Maikhel-Tungam area in present Mao Sub-Division of Senapati District in Manipur. A group of Tangkhuls also claim this theory. However, the Aos said that they came from Lungterok (six stones), perhaps, a hole near Chungliyumti. This theory is shared by the Phoms, yet they do not reckon themselves to be Aos.

Some Naga tribes of Manipur, like the Marings, Anals, Mayong, Monshangs, Lamkangs etc. have their tradition of coming from caves, which according to them, are located in south east of Manipur. Referring to reports of Dr. Brown (1668-69), T. C. Hodson recorded basing on the confession of the Tangkhuls that they came out of the earth called Murrungphy in a hill about four days journey towards north-east of Manipur valley.[17] The theory that the Tangkhuls came out of the earth is reflected by a Tangkhul folk-song. The song goes: [18]

O Katata kashang-shang.
Na Kachi eina shokli?
O Marilungvali shok
O Chili mashok-akha
O Kazing sirali kanganalo,
Laga unghang serlu.

[O thou traveller
Whence thou cometh?
O I come through the deep holes and rocks
If not cometh from that,
O listen to the stars and sky
And come thou all to report.]

This Tangkhul folk-song must explain the early origin of the tribe. Since oral tradition is handed over from generation to generation, it just might be that this tradition relates to the settlement of an ancient group of people along the Nanpan river in the Yunan province of China. Recent research has shown that along this river, there flourished an ancient settlement of man. One connection that may be drawn to the people referred to above and kindred peoples in South East Asia is that a design of a drum has been found in China which had similar designs even today among tribals of South West China, among the people of Indo-China, South East Asia and the Kachin-Naga and Chin-Mizo-Kuki tribes. This evidence, Chinese scholars point out, might have been the birth place of many of the tribal people mentioned, and in particular, the Naga tribes of whom the Tangkhuls are a branch.

Migration

Now, the question may be asked what were the nature and circumstances that led the Nagas to migrate from their original homeland? What were the routes and directions of their migration? Here again, there is no certainty as to how, when and why the tribes left their original home in China to migrate in search of a suitable place for settlement. That there was a migration from somewhere in Yunan province of China, there is no doubt. The migration could have taken place due to the pressure of increasing population and the inability of the land to sustain the population. There might have been a migration also due to oppression by certain sections of the community on others. Horam is of the opinion that there were four ways of migration of what constitutes the Naga tribe. The first wave of migration was that of the Konyaks who came from South West China passing through Tibet, Nepal and Arunachal Pradesh. The other three waves of migration of diflerent period of times entered into the areas dominated by the Nagas through Burma. Other related groups such as the Chin-Kuki, whose migration is outside the scope of this study, might also have had similar background of their migration. Eventually, they settled in adjoining Chin-Kuki hills of what is today Mizoram, Tripura and Chin Hills of Burma.

Authorities of Naga history, Keane, Horam and Shimray have mentioned in the course of their migration, the tribes who are now known by the name Naga, and who at the stage of migration did not called themselves by this name, just might have reached a huge expanse of water. Where this might have been is not sure. That the Nagas have a tradition of sea-shell and the sea-shore may be taken that having reached an expanse of water in the south, the migratory tribe turned north again. R. R. Shimray explained this in a long quotation given below.[20]

> From hypothesis that the Nagas must have come from the sea-coast or at least seen some islands or the sea is strengthened by the life-style of the Nagas and the ornaments being used till today in many Naga villages. The Nagas being left undisturbed for such a long time, have retained the culture of the most ancient times till today. Their fondness of cowrie shells for beautifying the dress, and the use of conch shells as ornaments (precious

> ornament for them), and the fact that the Nagas have many customs and way of life very similar to that of those living in the remote parts of Borneo, Sarawak, Indonesia, Malaysia etc. indicated that their ancient abode was near the sea, if not in some island. The long war drum hewn out of huge log also feature very much like the canoes so common with the islanders. It is also a fact that the Nagas ate almost all living sea creatures.

The dispersal into the present areas of settlement of all those related tribes must have followed the northern marches and having arrived at their present homeland, the migration stopped. There is another interesting theory with regard to the migratory movement of the Kachin-Nagas and Chin-Kuki-Mizos; and this theory is based on the traditional/legendary accounts of the Chinese, Kachins, Tangkhuls and Chin-Kuki-Mizos. Though the traditional/legendary account of Chin-Kuki-Mizos is outside the purview of this topic, it, may be useful to see some links between them and the Nagas.

According to Gao-Daxian, during the oppressive and cruel rule of *Yin* and *Shang* dynasties in China (3000 B.C.) ten people of Hao tribe with the equal number of women escaped to Hainan island and occupied the Five-Finger Mountain. One of them named Li went out for hunting and chased a doe. The poor animal being unable to escape turned around. When the hunter pointed his arrow and ready to shoot, the doe turned into a beautiful girl. Then they married and got five sons—Meifu-Li, Ziao-Li, Oi-Li, Detou-Li and Local-Li. Out of this five Li-brothers emerged five big Li-tribes who are living today in Hainan Island, South West Chinese provinces and in Indo-China countries."[21] The present Kachin-Nagas and Chin- Kuki-Mizos are the off-shoot of Li people. Migration of these tribes and their settlement at present occupied areas are discussed in the following legendary account.

According to Kachin legend/tradition,"[22] Meifu-Li, the first son of Hunter-Li, had a son named *Jingpo* meaning 'a man'. He came back to Yunan province in search of new land for settlement. He was followed by his nephew, Lengdo, a descendant of Xiao-Li of the Hunter-Li. Jingpo and Lengdo lived in the territory between the Salwin and Mekong rivers for sometime. But since the land had been occupied by other Li tribes, they were compelled to leave the place, and thus crossed the Salwin river. At last they found their settlement at the mountain region of *Phuangchuang*[23] east of the Hmaikha river in Kachin State in Myanmar.

The settlement at Phuangchuang mountain is regarded as the gathering place as well as the place of separation of the ancestors of the Kachin-Naga and Chin-Kuki-Mizo groups. The name, *Phuangchuang*, is still well remembered by the Kukis and sing in praise of it during their festivals. The Kachin tradition says that, when Jingpo lived at *Phuangchuang* with his nephew, Lengdo, the former married a girl and got two sons by her. In course of time, when the two sons grew up, the elder one implored the father that they should go and find a new settlement. Because, Lengdo, though younger by family geneology, was older than the two sons of Jingpo in age; and he had the mind to find a new land of his own so that he might be the owner of his own discovered land. As Jingpo's elder son knew it, he thought of finding a new land before Lengdo could do it. This idea was further incited when Lengdo and Jingpo's elder son saw a vast area of plain between the Chindwin and the Irrawadi during their hunting expedition.

At first, Jingpo could not agree to the request of his elder son. However, fearing that Lengdo might find a new land before his son could do, he granted the request on the condition that the elder son should stay with the parents according to their custom. The younger son might go and settle in the discovered land, at all if that should be occupied.

The next morning, Jingpo provided *taro* and pea both for seedling and victual for the journey, ginger to ward off the evil spirit and a crowing cock for omen divination.

According to Kachin-Naga custom, if the cock- flapped its wings and crowed in the new-discovered land, it was taken as a good omen, favourable to live there. People would enjoy peace, prosperity and be victorious in war. Further, Jingpo blessed them with prayers for the success of the journey and safe return of Lengdo and his son to *Phuangchuang* again. After that, he sent them off.

The two cousins, Lengdo and the elder son of Jingpo, started their journey and crossed the Nmai-Hka and Hrana-Hka by making bridges of canes and destroyed them lest the enemy follow them from behind. Crossing the Mali-Hka, they turned towards the west, and reached a high mountain called Zibyu-Tuang from where they could see the Irrawadi valley in the east, and the Chindwin valley in the west. They were extremely happy to find such a fertile valley, good for their settlement. But Jingpo's son claimed that the new land should go to his name since he was the elder by way of family geneology, which Lengdo did not protest. Everything was found favourable for them to live there. Then, they started homeward journey towards Phuangchuang again.

During the absence of the two cousins, the younger son of Jingpo became restless and repeatedly asked his father to leave Phuangchuang and follow his brother. But under no circumstances, his father could consent him since they could not trace the direction and footprints of Lengdo and his elder son. Further, they could not leave the aged mother alone at the Phuangchuang camp. The younger son, then realising that his mother was a hindrance from following his brother, committed matricide one night. Then Jingpo and his second son started to trace the footprints of Lengdo and his elder son. When they found any footprint, they shouted to each other *'Khang, Khang'* meaning "foot-print, foot-print."[24] Eventually, after crossing the Mali-Hka, they met Lengdo and his elder son, and they all returned to Phuangchuang again.

However, soon it was discovered by the elder son, that the death of his mother was by the violent act of his younger brother. But his father sternly warned him not to take revenge on his younger brother lest the family be made extinct.

But when they were living at Phuangchuang, again, the elder son asked his father's permission and blessing to go and occupy the new land, otherwise, Lengdo would do it and become the owner of the fertile land gifted by nature. Reluctantly, his father accepted the request on the conditions that his younger brother should not be banished; he should not assimilate to other people and he should keep close contact and maintain the custom and culture of their .forefather. Taking oath to keep all those terms and conditions before their father, Jingpo's elder son and Lengdo started for the new homeland. Thus, Phuangchuang was the place of separation between the Kachins and the Nagas. The descendants of the second son of Jingpo are known as Chingphaws or Kachins, and they are regarded as younger brother or descendants of the younger brother. Jingpo and his second son continued to live at the original camp of Phuangchuang. In course of time when the population of their descendants increased, they occupied the whole north-eastern Burma (Myanmar) now called Kachin State, three provinces of China-Yunan, Sichuan and Guangxi and in some pockets of Assam and Arunachal Pradesh in India. At present, there are more than twenty tribes of the Kachins. In this connection, G. A. Grierson remarked:[25]

> In Burma, they are called Kachins . . . . The Kachins called themselves Chingpo or dialectically Singpo. In Western dialect, this word is said to mean 'man', but not so, according Dr. Cushing, on the Burma side, which is only meant, a Sing-pho .... The Sing-phos or Kachins are a numerous race, covering a large area, from Upper Assam across north Burma beyond the Chinese boundary into Yunan.

However, their traditions, customs and culture are all the same though their habitation covers a large area which involves three main Asian countries. Slight variations could be observed in their life-style when they try to suit their environments under different governments and due to the influence of modern civilization in different degrees. But the basic character remains unchanged wherever they may be. The researcher which travelling through Burma and China witnessed all these features.

Later Jingpo's elder son and his cousin Lengdo occupied Zibyu-Tuang and settled down together for a long period of time. However, the possession of the land went to the name of Jingpo's elder son. According to the legend of the Kachins, Zibyu-Tuang means Goose-Berry Mountain in Burmese and was a very fertile land suitable for all kinds of vegetations, blessed with different kind of faunas and floras.

When the population of the two cousins increased at Zibyu-Tuang, Lengdo wanted to find a new land again for his own and to live separately from the elder son of Jingpo. Getting permission on the condition that their relationship should be maintained and honour the descendants of Jingpo's son as elder ones, Lengdo, with his family members moved towards the south. The descendants of Jingpo's elder son are, today, known as the Nagas; and the descendants of Lengdo are the Chin-Kuki-Mizos. Now their habitation lies in the south of Naga Homeland which are some portion of Burma (Chin Hills) and some portion in India including present Mizoram. Therefore, Zibyu-Tuang mountain is regarded as the place of separation between the Nagas and Chin- Kuki-Mizos which led to the emergence of two distinct races.

After a long period of time, the descendants of Jingpo's elder son also increased in number and they required more land for their settlement. So they occupied the Chindwin river valley in the south-west of the mountain. However, when the population kept increasing, they dispersed to different parts of present Naga Homeland. They are none other than the Nagas who are the descendants of the first son of Jingpo, the son of Meifu-Li, the first son of Hunter-Li of Hainan Island in Guangdon province of China. Therefore, even today, the Kachins say that the Nagas are the off-springs of the older brother of their progenitor. Hence, they are related in blood and origin.[26]

Mass dispersal of the Nagas is believed to have taken place from Zibyu-Tuang. Some of them occupied the Chindwin river valley and some others moved straight to the West and occupied the Patkoi ranges. Still some other groups crossed the Patkoi and went further West which those groups claimed that they came direct from the east."[27] However, most of the Naga tribes claimed their migration from south-east direction which no doubt is from Samsok. It is most likely that the Naga migration could have been under several waves and directions within a period of times.

Though mass distribution of the Nagas seems to have taken place from Zibyu-Tuang and the Chindwin Valley, these two places can be taken as the Tangkhul settlements despite the fact that some other Tangkhuls were also on the move as well. Because, the Tangkhul settlement in the east of the Chindwin river adjoining the territory of the Kachin had been found in the writings of the Europeans. A good number of the Tangkhuls are still living in northern Burma today. But surprisingly, most of them had been assimilated to Shan culture and Buddhism. Therefore, in some places, especially in the Chindwin Valley, their cultural identity had been completely changed. However, the writing of Grant testified the presence of the Tangkhuls even across the Chindwin and three villages of the Tangkhuls in Thaungthut State and several places of northern Burma.[28]

> The people of Maungkan, Tazou, Kawya and other village on the Chindwin north of Homalin dress as Burmans, talk: Shan and called themselves Shans, but confess that they

are the Tangkhul Naga descent came from the mountain to the West.

Elwin also wrote describing the eastern frontier of the Tangkhul inhabited areas adjoining the territory of the Kachins.[29]

> The country lies immediately north east of Manipur Valley, commencing from it and extending north east for about eight days journey, from that, east, to a great distance until the country of the Singhphu is reached.

Actually, there lies no other tribe in between the territories of the Tangkhuls and the Kachins. The Kachins are the immediate neighbours of the Tangkhuls in the east. Again, the Tangkhuls living in those places preserve their ancestral articles such as sea-shells, conch-shell, bead and other ornaments which can survive against the ravage of time in order to prove their identity. Thus, the Kachin frontier in the east is the beginning of the Tangkhul settlement in Burma, extending as far as the eastern frontier of Senapati District of present day Manipur. Indeed, a good number of Tangkhul villages had been merged to former Mao Sub-Division. In the south, the whole Kabaw Valley adjoining Chin Hills state, Shan state in south east as far as Somra Tract in the north is the territory of the Tangkhul settlement. Former Samsok palace of King Phaipanong of Kabo-Khari clans was the palace of the Tangkhul Naga Kingdom. Regarding the people of the state, Grant wrote:[30]

> The people of the state (Thaungthut, or Thap or Samsok) mostly called themselves Shan like its ruler, but it is probable that they have very little Shan blood, and are mainly of Naga or Chin descent. . . . There are also three villages of Tangkhul Nagas.

The merger of Somra Tract to Burma was a matter of very recent occurrence. It so happened that a Kuki Lambu (peon) of the Meitei *raja* exploited the Tangkhul villages of Somra Tract by collecting taxes without proper authorisation of the *raja*. This provoked the villagers. He was executed by the villagers. This led to a serious war between the Somra villagers and Meitei-*raja*. At first, the Tangkhuls inflicted heavy casualties on the Meiteis. But later, the Meiteis got the upper hand, and the chief of Somra Khunjao was captured where he died in the custody of Meitei *raja*. The tradition says that, being tired of controlling the people of the Tract, the Meitei *raja* sold it to Ava king at a price of 700 silver pieces. There are twelve villages of the Tangkhuls in the Tract still maintaining old life-style of the Tangkhuls. However, the Tangkhul of Pansa and neighbouring villages had undergone complete change due to lapse of time and their close association with the other Naga tribes there.

The migration of some of the Tangkhuls from Zibyu-Tuang and the Chindwin Valley to present Ukhrul District in Manipur State is another point of great interest. Some of the descendants of Jingpo's elder son occupied the Chindwin Valley. But owing to occasional flood of the river in the basin, and constant attack of mosquito-bites which consequenced malaria, the people looked for a safer place where they could be free from all these dangers. A good number of them shifted towards the Highland of Patkoi ranges under the leadership of Kabo-Khari and Chaphang which out of these two leaders emerged two big clans bearing these names of their patriarchs. They established their home at Hongkha-Muja, a twin village, of Mayo-Kachui[31] ranges where Kabo-Khari was the chief, and Chaphang was second to him. It is said that, Hongkha-Muja was not only the political centre of Kabo-Khari Awunga, but it became a great commercial centre which is called Leingapha in Tangkhul (to be discussed later) of the surrounding areas. The greatness, beauty, dignity and glory of Hangkha-Muja is still well ascribed in the folklores of the Tangkhuls.

It became another transit camp of future migration of the Tangkhuls. It is believed that the institution of the Tangkhul Awunga had been well established during their stay at Zibyu-Tuang and the Chindwin Valley. It is proved by the construction of several fortifications with stone boulders, and the war between several chiefs for supremacy. The chieftainship of Kabo-Khari and Chaphang over their clans was the continuation of the existing chieftainship at Zibyu-Tuang and the Chindwin river Valley. Some established palaces and forts of early ruling Tangkhul chiefs are still existing in Upper Chindwin District (Burma).

However, the settlement of the Tangkhuls at Hongkha-Muja on Mayokachui could not be their permanent place of habitation. For their political ascendency, commercial convenience and prosperity, they looked for a better place, which the choice was ultimately to go down to a suitable place in the plain area. So they turned towards the west and entered into a valley which today is called Kongkan-Thana. But originally, it was called Phaipa meaning 'vast valley', During their settlement at Phaipa, a son was born to Kabo-Khari. Then he called his son Phaipanong meaning 'Son of vast valley 'Later he succeeded Kabo-Khari, his father. When Kabo-Khari became a powerful ruler, he dominated the whole Valley and called it Kabo-Valley after his name. The Valley continues to be called after Kabo-Khari.

According to tradition, when they were moving up and down in search of suitable place for settlements,, the sun was already below the horizon. So they discussed to repose the night there. But when they could not find water, they released their sow (a female pig) to search water. After sometime, she came back, smeared with mud. Tracing the footprint of the pig, they found a small spring which quenched their thirst. Further, they found that the place was suitable for them to live. Since then, it became a new settlement of the people.

However, the spring which their pig found could not produce much water, sufficient for them. So they enchanted their python to work and increase the amount of water of the spring.[32] Than the whole night, the python wallowed and rolled about in the spring that when day dawned, they found a big lake producing enough water instead of a small spring. Around this lake, King Kabo-Khari established his palace and called it Samsok."[33] But originally, the name of the place was called by the Tangkhuls Songshuingreng, meaning 'land of mass settlement', in a Tangkhul dialect. Song means clan, mass; Shuing, settled, planted, fixed; reng, land, place.

Since their settlement of Songshuingreng, later called Samsok, it was probable that, there was no thirst for a new homeland. Rather, it became a great political, social and commercial centre of the people around it. Its prosperity and happy life attracted the jealousy of the neighbouring states, that the Moguong King of the Shans attacked Samsok which led to the dispersal of a good number of the Tangkhuls. Later Burmese King of Pagan attacked Samsok and occupied it. He appointed a chief over Samsok with the title - Sawbwa (pronounced Zoba) as governor.[34] Since the time of the Ava rule, the Burmese were known by the name 'Mii-Sowba" in the tongue of the Tangkhul meaning 'Man-Sowba' or 'Sowba-Man'.

But before the occurrence of these incidents, there arose a dispute between Phaipanong, successor of Kabo-Khari, who was also the ruling monarch of the whole group in Samsok, on the one side, and Hongmalai, the chief of Chaphang clan, on the other. As a matter of fact, Kabo-Khari of the royal clan, ruled over the group 'since the establishment of their home at Hongkha-Muja. But it so happened that when they shifted from Hongkha-Muja of Mayokachui to Kabo valley, Hongmalai of Chaphang clan took the lead. By virtue of his leadership in the movement, he claimed to be the owner and master of the newly discovered land, and ultimately the throne of Samsok kingdom. The tradition said that Hongmalai was a clever and farsighted chief whereas Phaipanong was a righteous and kind-hearted king. As the dispute for kingship dragged on, at last, it came in the minds of both Hongmalai and Phaipanong to end the quarrel once and for all. Here Chaphang-Hong (Chaphang Chief) Hongmalai suggested that they should go to the pond/lake and call out the python. Whoever was the real king would be responded by the python. Since the creation of the lake, the python had been living inside the pond. It was in the company of the group throughout their migratory journey under the guardianship and custody of Chaphang-Hong. Perhaps, he was the priest of the group and incantation to the python was uttered by him only.

At the pond, Hongmalai the Chaphang-Hong uttered words of incantation and threw a handful of rice calling the python to appear on the surface of water. But there was no response of the python and the water in the pond remained undisturbed. As he failed to call out the python, it was time for Phaipanong to do his part. He cut a small trunk of a tree called/Khamkhui-thing' in Tangkhul, and removed its skin at places to make it half-stripped and speckle. Then he threw it into the pond. No sooner had the stick been thrown into the water, the python appeared on the surface of the water and placed its head on it. Phaipanong, then called the creature to come at the edge of the pond where he bound it with the sling of basket. In this way, the dispute of kingship between king Phaipanong and king Hongmalai was settled and they continued to live together at Samsok for a long time after this incident.

But later, Chaphang -Hong had to leave the place again with a group of Tangkhuls and some of whom became the settlers of present Tangkhul area. No writer has recorded the reason of leaving Samsok. R.R. Shimray also could not establish why Chaphang-Hong left Samsok. He wrote, "The reason for their leaving Samsok is not clear."[35] However, the Tangkhul tradition is very clear about the departure of Hongmalai of Chaphang-Hong, his queen and .a group of people under him. Hongmalai's son married the daughter of Phaipanong, and according to Tangkhul custom, Hongmalai had to pay bride-price for his daughter-in-law to the father of the girl which he wanted to settle it as early as possible. Because, being the chief of his clan, he wanted to be free from dishonour of delaying the payment. Despite his repeated approach to know the amount of the bride-price, Phaipanong becalmed him not to bother for that, but to be patient and wait for sometime.

In course of time, one day, when negotiation for the bride-price was going on, Phaipanong asked Hongmalai to give the pond which the python had made, as the bride-price. Hongmalai, out of his rash-mind, offered it without hesitation. Since then, the ownership -of the lake went to Phaipanong and Hongmalai had to pay a heavy price again for his thoughtless act.

The python which was under the guardianship of Hongmalai could not remain inside the pond after its ownership passed to Phaipanong. So, the anger of the python caused Hongmalai sleepless night. Further, he could not eat or drink with peace of mind as he enjoyed before. Being tortured day and night, at last, Hongmalai, the Chaphang-Hong, had to leave Samsok along with his python and a group of people yet to find another suitable place again. From this group of people, different Naga tribes emerged and they occupied the hill countryside whereas those who remained in Samsok valley (Kabo-Valley) submerged under the influence of Shan culture and Buddhism. The fact that the Tangkhuls migrated from Samsok is evidenced by the Tangkhul folk-song, an English version of which is:[36]

Oh whence cometh thou originally?
Oh we originate from Samsok in Burma,
We call and gather all our kindred at Shokvao,
We make fire at Meichailung,
We distribute at Ru-Ngatak,
Oh Hungphun chief, the eldest,
Oh Ronra Shimray your tributes are everywhere,
Au. . . . Oh

Chaphang-Hong took his wife, Queen Anungkhungla and the python with him and moved towards the north, followed by a group of people. First, they halted at a place now called Nampisha in Ukhrul District of Manipur State. It was the first camp for Chaphang-Hong and his followers when they settled in present Tangkhul inhabited area. There again, the python performed a miracle and caused to issue a spring of water called Kengza which is today located at Nampisha village.

From Kengza, Hongmalai continued his journey further north and sojourned at Daming, a nice place in present Ningchao village. Hence, it is called Ningchao-Daming today. But miraculously when they were sleeping at night, the python, already displeased with rash act of Chaphang-Hong caused a big landslide from the point where Queen Hungkhungla's iron stick was fixed. The earth on the other side of the stick was taken down to the stream below, but the stick remained intact. Today, it. is popularly spoken that, the big landslide was effected by the displeased python of king Hongmalai.

Since the python was not pleased with the place, as they believed, they proceeded further again, and late in the evening, they reached the foothill of Malungdung, a hillock in Bungpa-Khullen village. They sought for a shelter there for the night, but owing to non-availability of water, dispute arose among the people. However, Chaphang-Hong invoked the python to cause a source of water. Accordingly, the python let out a spring of pure crystal water that it is called Mathingkung. Local tradition has compared the utility of this water to the milk of a woman. Further, it was said that in ancient time, when womenfolk washed their hair with this water, it produced luxurious hair the tip of which reached the heels of women. This fountain of water was comparatively small, but surprisingly enough, there was no change of volume throughout the year. Neither dry season reduces the amount of water, nor rainy season increased the size of the spring - it was a constant water. Therefore, the people of ancient composed a song in praise of "Mathingkung'. The song, composed in praise of Mathingkung by the ancestors of the Tangkhuls goes in this way:

Bungpa Mathingkung, Bungpa Mathingkung, aprongye,
Sungza prongma leiyang sayang leihaosa,
Sungza prongmaya, sungza prongmaya,
Khungkhuileng Sachingna ching
Leiyang Sayang leihaosa.
Sachingna chingye, Sachingna chingye,
Khungkhuileng rachong khaleo,
Rachong khaleoya, Mathingza Khiningchang?
Leiyang sayang leihaosa.

Khiningchang leida, khining leida, Mathingza?
Sungzato rung, leiyang sayang leihaosa,
Sungzato rungya, Sungzato rungya,
Aungkhungla, khining phaning?
Leiyang sayang leihaosa.

The gist of the song is that, the spring of Bungpa Mathangkung is smaller than the fountain of a woman's breast. But it satisfied men and animals. Why they hanker for it and what thought comes in the mind of Aungkhungla?

Later, this Mathingkung was named Aungkhungla-Zashu after the name of Queen Aungkhungla of Chaphang-Hong. It can be interpreted as "Aungkhungla's Spring which does not run dry. " The song is very popular even today among the present day generation, and is sung on festive occasions and other ceremonial functions.

On the following day, Hongmalai and his followers went up the top of the hill, Malungdung for geographical study in view of finding a suitable place for their settlement, leaving their woman-folk and children at the camp of the foothill. On top of the hill, they released a pig to find water, and found a spring of water. But in the evening when they returned to their camp, to their disappointment and schock, they found women and children weeping and wailing. Because, the injured python coiled around the body of the Queen as it was wroth with Hongmalai for offering the lake to Phaipanong as bride- price; and they saw this miserable condition of the queen at the camp. Therefore, they invoked the python with the words: "Thou has been our companion since the days of our ancestors, and we shall remain companions forever. So release thy queen, now." They repeated these words three times, but there was no positive response from the python. They then took their sword and cut the serpent to save the queen. But the serpent escaped with a huge landslide leaving the queen and the people. This marked the separation between Chaphang-hong and the serpent for all, and there was no mention ever made that Chaphang-Hong adopted a python or serpent again in the future.

But another story says that, when the household of Chaphang-Hong prepared food and drink, first they served the python before they tested as per tradition. However, the new daughter-in-law of Chaphang-Hong, being unaware of all these things, prepared rice-beer without first offering it to the python. This hurt the python and out of rage, it punished the queen and brought disaster in the house.

According to Tangkhul legend, Chaphang-Hong Hongmalai (Chaphang-King Hongmalai) was the first to settle into the land of present Tangkhul inhabited area in Manipur State, and the Tangkhuls of this region are his descendants. After his separation from Phaipanong, king of Samsok, he was unquestioned and undisputed king of the group he led to Tangkhul area, and the Tangkhuls regarded him as their king. Thus, he took the responsibility of governing over his subject people. Therefore, it is not denying to the fact that, since the days of old, the Tangkhuls belonged to a royal family. The word Hong or Hung, later used as Wung is, the word used to the 'king' and therefore, Chaphang-Hong Hongmalai means Chaphang-king Hongmalai. He was the king of Chaphang clan, and only next to King Phaipanong of Samsok.

But tradition, again, mentioned that during Hongmalai's march in present Tangkhul area, the legs of games killed were sent to him from Samsok. By Tangkhul custom, the legs of animals killed is always the portion of the elder one. So this question still remains unsettled that if Phaipanong, the Samsok King, were the elder, why the leg-portion of the animals killed should go to Hongmalai, the Chaphang-Hong, who was second to Phaipanong. In this respect, some Tangkhul elders are of the opinion that the offering of legs to Chaphang-Hong might be the work of his own clansmen who remained at Samsok with Phaipanong.

Sometime later, the migration of Chaphang-Hong and his group was followed by another waves of migration from Samsok at different periods of time. It was due to the invasion of the Shans and Avas from the south. The event is explained by K.Y.L. Roland. [37]

When a greater power of the south attacked the UNG tribe, the latter had to flee towards the mountain. This is testified by the tradition of KAMO-KHOKOK -' 'As Samsok Valley experienced severe warfare, people ran helter skelter". Because of war, the Hung tribe moved northward and occupied Somra Tract; and thus the entire Hung tribe who were then living in Ningthi Valley fled to Ango-Ching. The long ranges of the Patkai mountain served as the bulwark of the Hung tribe against the attack of enemy.

However, the entire Tangkhul population did not flee Samsok and Chindwin Valley. A good number of them continued to live under the yoke of foreign suzerainty; sometimes, under the Shan rulers, and in some other occasions, under the Zawbwa of the Burmese kings. In course of historical process, the culture and identity of these Tangkhuls came under the influence of Buddhism and Shan culture. But recently, there started a movement of national awakening by the Naga tribes of Burma to whom the strong arms of military junta of General Ne-Win dealt with severely. Since then their tribal and inter-tribal festivals, gatherings and conferences had been completely stopped.

To continue the movement of Chaphang-Hong again, from Malungdung-Mathingkung camp, Hongmalai proceeded to a place called Sampui village today where he and his group sojourned there for sometime. But they did not remain there .for long. They moved again in a south-west direction and made another camp at Khampi.[38] How long did they stay there could not be ascertained, but as a mark of their establishment of a habitation, they heaped up a mount of stones which still remains even today. Since then, it became a place of historical event in the migration of the Tangkhuls. It is assumed that Hongmalai and his group lived there longer than the preceding camps before they reached the vicinity of Imphal valley.

It is surmised that king Hongmalai and his group were looking for a plain area and that none of the camps they sojourned could serve a permanent dwelling place for them. Therefore, they moved down towards imphal lowland. But to their disappointment, the lowland of Imphal valley was submerged under water. Both tradition and history said that, in early days, the valley was covered by water; and so human habitation was not possible due to the presence of water. As J. Roy remarked:"[39]

> According to the geologists, Manipur, Cachar, Tripura, Garo Hills and a considerable portion of Bengal were under water. . . . Though the sea receded from the area, the valley portion of Manipur remained under water for a long time. . . . The Manipur purana also refers to this fact.

However, when water receded and dry ground appeared at the edge of the valley, people living in the hills around the valley, came down and occupied it gradually. No doubt, Lotak lake is the remaining portion of water in the valley.

Then, they moved by the edge of the lake for sometime looking for suitable place. But they found that it was swampy, not proper for them to settle down. So they turned towards the north and divided into two groups. One group moved towards north-east and the other, towards the north."[40]

The group which followed north-east direction occupied present Ukhrul District, and they became the Tangkhuls; and those who went straight towards the north, later dispersed from the historical place called Maikhel, three miles east of Tadubi Sub-Divisional Headquarters, in Senapati District of Manipur State. A party of the dispersed group entered Ukhrul District and joined with their kindreds who occupied the land already via north-east direction. It is no wonder that those who followed north-east direction occupied southern and eastern Tangkhul areas, whereas those who came from Maikhel occupied western and north Tangkhul areas. There are slight variations in the life-styles of the two groups.

How long the Nagas lived together at Maikhel is another point of those unsettled matters. Neither legends nor folklores of the Nagas tells about the length of period they lived there. However, Maikhel as the last place of mass dispersal is popularly accepted by the Nagas; and several historical facts and monuments testify and confirm this point. Before their dispersal from Maikhel, they were only one Naga group, perhaps, the Tangkhul tribe. The fact is that they were the group of people led by Chaphang King Hongmalai out of Samsok, who was the king of the Tangkhul Nagas. But when they were separated one another and scattered at different places, different Naga tribes emerged out of different groups and clans. This is what we see several Naga tribes today. The group of Tangkhuls coming out of Maikhel moved straight towards east and occupied the extreme east of Senapati District, where several Tangkhul villages are located. From there again, they spread in western and northern Tangkhul areas which are nearest to them.

But why did the Nagas should separate and scatter at all is another question of interest. If they belonged to one clan or group or tribe, they should have been contented to be one and live together at a place to make themselves a bigger and stronger group of people. In course of time, with the increase of population, a straight land cannot accommodate the growing population. The problem of economic difficulties arises, and so naturally people look for wider area of land for a better economic sustenance. Visier Sanyu opines:[41]

> We have seen over a period of time, more fertile land and the subsequent growth of population, and search for sustenance split the early Nagas tribes into various settlements of Semas, Lothas, Rengmas, Tangkhul, Zeliang, Chakhesang, and so on.

R.R. Shimray defended the Ma khelian theory of the dispersal of the Nagas and said that this theory has been supported by various Naga tribes and historical facts, stone monoliths and sacred trees planted at Maikhel as a sign of their separation.[42] On one stone monolith called Tamaratu meaning "Stone of Departure' engraved with the figures of man, animal and bird, had been erected at Maikhel. It also bore what is believed to have been a Naga script, but the ravage of time has washed it away. A wild apple tree was also planted at present Sajouba village, two miles up from Maikhel, when people separated from Maikhel, as a sign of their departure. Therefore, in olden days, whenever any branch of the sacred tree was broken, the Angamis, Eastern Angamis, Semas, Rengmas and Lothas observed a solemn day, which day people called "Genna', where any form of works was forbidden. Regarding the distribution of the Nagas, Gangmumei Kabui wrote:"[43]

> . . . the Zeliangrongs of western Manipur have a tradition that they came out of a mythical cave known as Taobhei. They migrated to Makhel, then to Ramting Kabum, a village in a deep gorge, then to Makui Longdi, then they dispersed towards three regions, the south, west and north.

The tribes such as the Angamis, Semas, Rengmas and Lothas point their origin from the south where there was a flat-stone near Maikhel. But there are three historical flat-stones, and it is difficult to specify which was the particular stone from where the Nagas separated. One stone is at

Tabufu two miles from Maikhel; the second one at Futhufu, five miles away from Maikhel, and the third one at Khezha-Kenoma, ten miles away from Maikhel. The aforesaid Nagas claim to have originated from Khezha-Kenoma village. But the fact is that, the Khezha-Kenoma itself also separated from Maikhel. The Semas claimed that they originated from a hole of the earth pointing to Tukabo which means to Mount Japfii, where the source of the Doyang river situated. Indeed the source of the Doyang river starts from Maikhel village. The other tradition says that, the Semas separated from Swemi village, a Tangkhul village in Ukhrul district, now called Chingjaroy.

Other Naga tribes like Changs, Yimchungers, Khiamnungans etc. also point to the south from whence they came, though they do not mention Maikhel as the place of their origin. The Aos claimed that they emerged from Lungtorok: (six stones) near Chungliyumti. Phoms have the same origin with the Aos, but they do not identify with the Aos. A group of the Konyaks claimed their origin from the north, which Horam noted:"[44]

> . . . for instance the Konyaks of Tamlu point to the north as the original place from where they migrated southwards while a few Konyak villagers who claim that they came from the south.

The Tangkhul who followed north-east direction gathered together at a place called Shokvao meaning they called their fellows together.[45] From this place, they scattered again; perhaps one group occupied southern Tangkhul, and the other went north-ward via Ukhrul, as far as Longpi village, finding their settlement elsewhere enroute. The other Tangkhuls who went straight to the north entered Ukhrul District from the west after their mutation from Maikhel. Whereas some of them settled down in the adjoining territory of Senapati District and Ukhrul District, the rest went as far as Phungcham village which was another point of distribution of the Tangkhuls. This group of people dispersed to the north and west of Ukhrul District. However, their chief, perhaps, the Hungpum Hung, moved towards the south of Phungcham village and made his abode at present Hungpum village. In course of time, with the increase of population, they got mixed up and scattered in different parts of the entire Tangkhul area. But eastern Tangkhul could have been already occupied by some of the group of Chaphang -Hong during their migratory journey across eastern Tangkhul.

Tradition says again, that a section of the Tangkhuls lived at Imphal for sometime. But due to heat, mosquito and swampy soil, they moved up the hill country. This is proved by the erection of stone monolith found at the heart of Imphal town standing even today. The people of Ningthi village also came up from Imphal valley, and at long last, they found their settlement in their village having passed through Hungpum Leishan of present Hungpum village.

Another wave of migration occurred-from Samsok kingdom, after the departure of Chaphang-Hong and his group due to invasions of the Shans and Burmans at different periods of time. They followed the tract of the early emigrants. But without proceeding further, they found their settlement among the eastern and southern Tangkhuls. No doubt, they brought the culture of the Shans and Burman, and spread among the early settlers that, Hodson, an authority of the Naga tribes of Manipur remarked: [46] "The different style of houses built by the Tangkhuls who have come up from the Kabo Valley shows evidence of Burmese influence." The type of houses of eastern and southern Tangkhuls is all the same to the housing of the Kachins and Shans of northern Burma.

Assessing all the sources of the migration of the Nagas discussed above, we can safely conclude that, the migration of the Nagas from their original homeland to present Naga Homeland took place over a period of times by different waves of migration and from different direction, to find them again living together at a compact area.

Settlement

After a long march over many generations from South Western China, a group of the Tibeto-Burmans found their habitat in the heart of the neighbouring countries—in what is present day China in the north, Burma in the east, Bangladesh in the south and India in the west. There are a large number of related tribes of the Tibeto-Burman race who occupied the above mentioned region of which the Nagas are the biggest group. The group of people called NAGA is also divided into several tribes and sub-tribes - some big and some small - but every tribe and sub-tribe has its own occupied region the size of which depends on the size and population of the tribe concerned. However, the Nagas have their own compact area of settlement covering a vast territory. But Naga inhabited territory had been divided into small administrative units, first by the British colonial rule for their administrative convenience to serve the purpose and interest of colonialism. Some portions of Naga inhabited areas are partitioned into different states of India like, Assam, Arunachal Pradesh, Nagaland and Manipur. An equally large portion of the area is the home of Nagas under Burma. Still another big portion, perhaps, the biggest of the three, remains as Naga Homeland—neither under the control of India nor Burma, it is not under the control of China either—though boundary demarcation indicates they are under the countries referred to.

It is no wonder that the knowledge of the people on Naga Homeland (the territory of Naga inhabited area) is so limited that the extent of Naga country is still in dark obscurity. Since a big portion of Naga inhabited area remains unsurveyed; even during British rule, no clear and detail record of their territory had been laid down. Therefore, Alexander Mackenzie rightly remarked: [47]

> Our knowledge of the Naga tribe though of late years fast extending is still very incomplete.... And finally, with regard to the inhabitants of this huge tract, 'We are equally in the

> dark; and indeed to such an extent, does our ignorance go that we cannot even safely suggest any limit at all to the country occupied bv the Naga race. . . .

Therefore, Mackenzie roughly concluded the extremities of the Naga inhabited area with the water sheds of the Irrawadi in the east and of the Brahmaputra in the west. But northern and southern frontier remained undemarcated.

Settlement of the Tangkhuls

Regarding the habitation of the Tangkhuls, popular belief is that present Ukhrul District in the north east of Manipur state is the only area where the Tangkhuls are living. But as much as the Naga inhabited area had been partitioned and divided under different administrative units, so also the territory of the Tangkhul inhabited area. In fact, the so-called Indo-Burma international boundary line passes in the midst of Tangkhul country. The creation of an administrative unit by the name of Ukhrul was exclusively the work of the British colonial power. A good number of Tangkhul villages have been merged to present Senapati District of Manipur; and still a greater part of Tangkhul area remains in Burma. Beginning from Samsok (Songsuingreng as the Tangkhuls call), Thaungthut state in Burma, in the south, it goes as far as Pansa and Somra Tract in the north; and in the east, it has its frontier with the Kachins, is the territory inhabited by the Tangkhuls. Despite the assimilation of the Tangkhuls to Shan and Burman cultures and adoption of Buddhism, Grant Brown spotted the presence of the Tangkhuls within the area mentioned above. Merger of Somra Tract to Burma was of recent occurrence though the date cannot be ascertained.

At present, Ukhrul District is regarded as the settlement of the Tangkhuls. According to 1971 Census, Ukhrul District has an area of 4,409 sq. km. with a population of 51,101 Tangkhuls. But the Tangkhuls living elsewhere in Manipur came up to 57,851. There were 168 Tangkhul villages in

Ukhrul District alone. However, if the Tangkhul inhabited area of Manipur state and Myanmar (Burma) are amalgamated together, it will be the biggest area of all the Naga tribes with its united population. But since no complete survey of the Tangkhul inhabited area has been done, the exact area cannot be established.

Dating the Immigration and Settlement

Due to lack of written history of the Nagas, it is difficult to tell the definite period in which the Nagas migrated from South-Western China to their present occupied Naga Homeland. Though there are several legends, traditions and folklores of the Nagas which tell of their origin, migration and settlement, this part of periodising has not been mentioned. However, in relation with the foreign accounts, artifacts, relics and monoliths of the Nagas, we can establish the date of migration and settlement of the Nagas in Naga Homeland.

First, according to Gao-Daxian, a reporter of the journal, *China Reconstruct*, October 1981, some 3,000 years ago, during the reign of Han Dynasty in China, the minority people of South-Western provinces of China fled the country for fear of oppression of their rulers. This included ten men and ten women who escaped to Hainan Island of Guandong province of China, and settled down there. Latter, the descendants of a hunter called Li or Lee (also known as Hunter-Li) occupied the Finger-Mountain of the Island. Some returned to China mainland and some others scattered to South East Asian countries which included Kachin-Nagas and Chin-Kuki-Mizos. Therefore, this date can be roughly taken as the date of the first migration of the Nagas which brought them to their present homeland.

In this connection, R.R. Shimray forwarded several references and he wrote:[48]

> Capt. Steel was the first European to find the evidence of Stone Age Culture in Nagaland after the examination of

> some brightly coloured stones produced from a NAMSANG Naga in exchange of a few grains of opium. S. E. Pearl, an authority of Naga culture, also writes in his book: "On Some Traces of Kol-Mon Anam in the Eastern Nagas" that the use of polished stone-celts shows traces of Naga culture of the Neolithic Age. The recent discoveries of a pebble chopper at MACHI village, Maring Naga area and the Khangkhui cave materials at Ukhrul District by 0. K. Singh have proved that there is unmistakable evidence of Paleolithic culture in Naga Areas. Hutton, an authority on Naga culture has also recorded that the smooth stone-tools from Nagaland preserved at Oxford and Cambridge Universities are regarded by many writers as evidence of a rich Neolithic culture in that area.

Summing up the evidences discussed above, Shimray concludes that, after roaming in the Irrawadi valley .and South East Asian countries, in the Neolithic 'Age, the Nagas might have reached the legendary hole in bronze age (3100-2000 B.C.) or early iron age in 1200 B.C. and made their settlement in Naga Homeland.

Several historical evidences also tell of the early settlement of the Nagas. According to Poireiton Khunthokpa, an ancient account of the Meitei text deals with the adventures and colonisation of Poireiton.[49] When the coloniser came to Manipur hills, he found the Kabui, Tangkhui, Anal tribes etc. had already been living there. Further, Gangmumei Kabui referred the Ningthourol Lambuba, an ancient chronicle of Manipur that the first Poireiton (colonising adventure) took place in the first century A.D., and the Poireiton slipped on the mossy place that he called it Anal meaning slippery. This is now a village in Chandel District in Manipur, and the tribe living in the area is called the 'Anal". Machung Zirnik, in harmony with the above points tells of the early settlement of the Nagas. He wrote: [50]

> We learned, though, from 'A Short History of Manipur" by Jhalajit Singh (p. 17) that when in 33 A.D. Poireiton came

to Manipur, he also visited the Tangkhuls. From this historical account, we can safely accept the proposition that the Hundung village had been there in and before the year 33 A.D. that is before Poireiton visited Manipur in 33 A.D.

Moreover, several mentions on Nagas had been made and the country they are living in by various writers. There are several accounts left by the Greek adventurer of Egypt, Ptolemy in 150 A.D.; Hiuen Tsang, a Chinese pilgrim 645 A.D.). The *Assam Buranji* mentioned the struggle between the Ahoms and the Nagas in early 12th Century A.D. Lastly, the European writers came and studied the people and the land of the Nagas. Though they had not given a definite date of the Naga migration and settlement, they agreed that the Nagas are the earliest settlers of their present habitat. It is not denying the fact that Imphal valley was occupied by the Tangkhuls. But due to heat and mosquitoes, they shifted to the hills, as the tradition says. However, several stone monoliths had been erected during their settlement in the valley. Regarding the antiquity of the Nagas, Roland gives several evidences:[51]

> As for monoliths, they still exist at many villages. Some of the most numerous of these, supposed to be the work of certain tribes, can be seen on almost every peak of the Ango Range or the Patkai as the Assamese called it. Though at the present time, the longer portion of this range is uninhabited, the Nagas, possibly, the Neolithic men of the Eastern Naga Hills had settled there for years before they spread all over these hills.

So we can safely conclude that the Nagas are the earliest settlers of their present occupied territory and that they settled there in the Neolithic Age. No legend, folklore and history ever mentioned about the settlement of any other tribe in this region; and also there is no evidence given that at any time, the Nagas had dislodged any particular people from the present Naga Homeland. Though there were later some sporadic establishment of the Kuki villages, their advent in Naga Homeland is a matter of recent years - in late 19th century only. Since then, the Kuki immigration is still continuing. Many European writers also mention the late coming of the Kukis in Manipur, Nagaland, Assam and other North-eastern states. Today, the presence of the Kukis in the Naga inhabited areas has led to the emergence of ethnic crisis which the tension is increasing day by day.

Nomenclature

The origin of the name NAGA is a mystery to scholars. Again, this nomenclature does not find any place in the legends, traditions and folklores of the Nagas either. This is one of the most difficult problems for the Nagas in general and historians, anthropologists and others, to solve as to how the name 'NAGA' was given to the particular race among so many tribes of the Tibeto-Burman origin living side by side with them. Several theories had been propounded by scholars, writers, anthropologists and administrators with regard to the appellation of the tribe NAGA'. But none of them can bring satisfactory solution of the problem. However the Nagas share a common idea in this matter in one hand; and the non-Naga writers have different explanations, which they themselves also do not agree one another, on the other hand. However, all writers - Nagas and non- Nagas - agree at this point that, the name 'NAGA' was given by the foreigners, not by the Nagas themselves. Nevertheless, the Nagas have a good ground to tell why they had been called by the said name; and this seems to be the most acceptable theory of all.

Some are of the opinion that the word 'NAGA' came from Sanskrit 'Nag' of snake Nag-worship cult. But the Nagas never happened to be snake worshippers. Some others say that they live in the mountains difficult to access. But none of these theories holds water. The third theory says that, the word 'NAGA' COMES FROM 'Nangta', naked, and applied it to the Nagas living in the hills with scanty cloths. This argument is true to some extent, because some Nagas are scantily clothed though a good number of the Nagas have their own cloths with beautiful fashion of patterns. Again this theory is not acceptable the reason being very simple and clear. Refuting this theory, Horam wrote :[52]

> That the Nagas are scantily clothed is true but why they alone should have been singled out as 'naked men' when the same, if not greater, degree of nudity is found not only among some other neighbouring hill tribes, but also among the South Indians, particularly the Andhras, Malayaylis and Tamils.

In this connection, Verrier Elwin gave a strong argument of disagreement to the theory of paucity of cloths, he wrote:[53]

> . . . but there seems little foundation for this etymological derivation, as the term has never been known applied by the Bengalis to either the Khasis or Garos with whom they are far better acquainted than with the Nagas; and besides, the Garos especially are habitually accustomed to a greater degree of nudity than any of the Naga tribes with whom we are acquainted.

In view of these reasons the naked Naga theory of the nomenclature of the Nagas may be rejected. But, to the Nagas, the word NAGA has a deep meaning and is the authentic information with regard to the naming of this particular people lonely by the name referred to. In this connection, the view of Hokishe Sema may be worth mentioning in this rather long quotation:[54]

> The nomenclature 'Naga' is given to this tribe by the outsiders.... Here it may be added that the term 'Naga' was given to this people even before they migrated from Burma. Hence this name does not derive from the place - Nagaland - where they live. . . . On the other hand, their hesitation gets the name from their nomenclature. . . . In Burma, the Naga tribes are called 'Na-ka', which in Burmese means people or men or folk with pierce ear-lobes. . . . Most of the Naga tribes migrated to India from Burma, therefore, the

name 'Naka' or 'Naga' was given to them even before they reached India. Moreover, it was from the Burmese that the British first came to know about the Nagas soon after their earliest war with 'Surma during 1706 to 1826.

This theory is the most acceptable and authentic information with regard to the origin of the word 'NAGA'. Modern Naga writers also agree to this view of nomenclature; and the Nagas accepted it without reservation. It is no wonder that in early days, all Nagas-men and women, young and old-pierced their ears,"[55] and they were fond of decorating their ears with ear-rings of metals, feathers of birds and other ornamental articles.

However, the Shans and Burmese call the Nagas Akhang. This word has its own derivation and meaning. During the migratory stage, Jingpo's first son and his nephew, Lengdo left their camp which was at Phuangchuang in search of new place for settlement. Later they were followed by Jingpo and his second son tracing the footprints of elder son and Lengdo. Whenever any footprint was found, they shouted each other 'Khang Khang" meaning 'footprint'. Since then, the descendants of Jingpo' s elder son who are now called the Nagas, are called AKHANG by the Shans and Burmese. This name is still in vogue among them even today. However, some Naga tribes of eastern Nagaland (Burma) called themselves by other name called KAKHANG. But this could be the corrupt name of AKHANG which they have their own way of vocabulary. But, neither of these two is used as official name of the Nagas by the Burmese. Before the advent of the British in Naga Homeland, the Nagas knew each other by their tribal names only. Although they knew that they belong to the same origin and race, the name Naga which is commonly used today was unknown to this people. But when the British came and studied about the people and their land, they found that this particular race has the common origin and features. So the name 'NAGA' was given to all the tribes which share the common characteristics given above; and the name became popularised among them since then. This common name has enhanced and strengthened national consciousness and integrity of their people. However, it must be admitted that the origin and nomenclature of the name 'NAGA' is a field of study and research that continues. Detail and deeper research on the topic is still required. It will be some time before an acceptable answer to the problem is found. But, before this could be achieved, the above "*piercing-ear-iobes*" theory may be accepted as the origin of the name NAGA.

Tangkhul

In this study when emphasising the history of the Tangkhuls, mention may be made of the origin of this name Tangkhul. Originally, the Tangkhuls called themselves HAO. Their traditional songs, dresses and other day to day articles they used were also known by these names: Hao-la means Hao-Song; Hao-Kachon, Hao-cloth; Hao-Sari, Hao Dress; Hao-Kuiret, Hao-coiffure; and so on. This bears the evidence that HAO was the original name of the Tangkhuls. In this nomenclature, some say that the name HAO came from 'Ho-Ho' a tone the Tangkhuls used in harmony in two-three groups when they were singing, dancing, or even carrying heavy loads and other merry makings. But this "Ho-Ho' explanation does not give enough weightage with regard to the origin of the name Hao.

Some others are of the opinions that, in early days the Tangkhuls came from HAO-city which today is called XIAN in China.[56] Hence, they had been called HAO. But others said that, according to legend discussed earlier, Meifu-Li, who was the progenitor of the Nagas belonged to the Hao tribe of China, and so this tribal name was carried by the Nagas, particularly by the Tangkhuls. These theories may be accepted as the most appropriate one with some reservation. As a matter of fact, Hao was the earliest name ever used to the Tangkhuls. But this name was used in two ways. In narrow sense, Hao was used to the Tangkhuls only, whereas, in wider sense, it was used to all the Nagas irrespective of different tribes. Even in the tongue of the author, the Kukis are also called KHACHA-HAO. The Meiteis called 'Hao' to all tribals regardless of the Nagas, Kukis, Mizos and other peoples of close affinity. Then it can be considered and accepted that Hao was the original word of appellation used on the tribals of Tibeto-Burman origin.

From the discussion given above, it is found that the Tangkhuls called 'Hao" to the Nagas in general, and the Tangkhuls themselves in particular. However, some are of the view that, referring T. Lukham's books, Okthot Mayonsa and English-Tangkhul Dictionary, the original name of this particular tribe was known by the name WUNG or WUNGMI before they settled down in present habitat. No doubt, in remote past, the Tangkhul were known by the name HONG or HUNG or WUNG. According to their concept, the Tangkhuls belong to a regal .family since remote past. So in early days when they occupied the Ango Range called Mayo Kachui (Patkai range), the establishment of wungship under Kabo-Khari (out of whom a clan bearing the name emerged) and Hongmalai, had been well in existence. The Awungaship was also carried and continued to exist at Samsok in Kabo-Valley. From there, the Chaphang-Hong separated and led out a group of people as their leader of which the present Tangkhuls are his descendants. In Tangkhul HONG, HUNG and WUNG may roughly be translated in English as King. As they belong to the family of Chaphang -Hong, the tribe was known by HONG or HUNG or WUNG. But surprisingly, this name is not in use today, neither by the people themselves, nor in official transaction. Though the name is very much alive, it is more or less in oblivion.

It may be noted that, reference had been made to Samsok King and Chaphang-Hong. Apparently, at that period of time, there were only two Tangkhul leaders whose position may be set to closely resemble the position of kingship

However, after their settlement in Tangkhul Hills fragmenting into villages in the Tangkhul inhabited areas, and with the increase of their villages, the institution, though hereditary, may not be defined as kingship. The term chieftain would be more appropriate in this context.

Again, the Burmese have another term of calling the Tangkhuls by way of their (Tangkhuls') coiffure. Observing the hair-style of the Tangkhul, Hodson remarked:[57]

> The Tangkhul men wear the hair in a curious manner, which is to a large extent distinctive of the tribe. They cut the hair closely at the sides, leaving the broad crest, which varies in width from five to six inches down the middle of the skull.

Actually, this form of coiffure is not found in other Naga tribes who maintain more or less the same form of hair-style, considerably different from the Tangkhuls. Because of this peculiarity of hair-style, the Burmes called the Tangkhuls 'UZUMBOK', crested head (people). However, this name is not known to the Tangkhuls except in referring to Tangkhuls in Burma early this century. It is a strange name to the Tangkhuls of Manipur who have no use of the word.

The question then remains how the term 'TANGKHUL emrged if they had been called by various names given above. According to some, the word '*Tangkhul*' came from the name of a person called 'TANGKHU' who was well versed in war-dance and skillful in the art of using sword and spear. Another version says that, to the Tangkhuls, Thang' (sword) and 'Ta' (spear) are unseparable items of their daily use. Hence, they are called 'Tangkhul' meaning village or people of 'Thang-Ta' - sword and spear. Another version is that the Tangkhuls are generous, full of hospitality and liberal who provided food and drink to their guest. Therefore, their Meitei counterparts called them 'Tangkhul' - 'Atangba' meaning rare, unique;. and 'Khul' means village - there is no village as liberal and generous as these people. However, none of these theories can given conclusive and satisfactory explanation to the derivation of the name 'Tangkhul'.

The most acceptable explanation with regard to the origin of the name, 'TANGKHUL has been well explained by A. S. Vashi Shimray.[58] According to him, when Phaipanong of Kabo-Khari clan and Hongmalai of Chaphang clan established a Naga settlement at Samsok, the Nagas had a close trade and commercial relationship with the people of Burma. The Tangkhul tradition says that, the prosperity of the Nagas attracted the Avas since early days along the river ports of Thaungthut and Taunghai. Later, the trade centre shifted to Samsok for both the Nagas and Burmans.

The Nagas exported precious stones like gems of different colours, jades, diamonds in plenty (available in the Chindwin river and its tributaries) cotton, sesamum etc. in exchange of iron from the Avas (Burmans). The demand of iron by the Tangkhuls was so high that the Avas brought in a large quantity. As for the Nagas, iron was everything. They used it for agricultural implements, war weapons, bride price, purchase of land etc. that, it was no doubt, a medium of exchange in the early life of the Tangkhuls. Realising the high demand of iron by the Tangkhuls, the Avas made it available in large quantity at Taunghai which in the tongue of the author called the place 'RASHERENG' meaning 'land of iron cutting'[59] It was at this place that they imported iron from the Burmans for their domestic uses.

Since then, the Avas (Burmans) called the Nagas 'ATHANGPI' or "THANPI' meaning 'Iron-man' or 'Iron-People' . Because, they had much use of iron as the Burmans had known them which in Burmans, 'Than' means 'iron' in English. Later on, Samsok state fell into the hands of the Burmese king and it became a vassal state. However, at a time, the influence of the Ava.king in northern Burma became so weak that the Meitei raja once attacked Samsok and subdued it. Then the Nagas of Samsok whom the Burmese called Thanpi was adopted by the Meiteis again. Therefore, the village which they lived was known by the name 'THAN-KHUL' meaning Than-Village in Meitei language. Therefore, the name 'TANGKHUL' is derived from Than-Khul, a combination of Burmese 'Than' (iron) and Meitei 'Khul' (village). This is the most appropriate theory and explanation of the origin of the name Tangkhul group of people by the Meiteis, since the time of which the name TANGKHUL is in existence and, the people are known by it.

Tangkhul–Meitei Origin and Separation

We have seen that many of the tribal groups in the present day North East India have a common past. It is interesting that both the Tangkhuls and Meiteis also are descendants of the same progenitor in the distant past. Oral tradition of the Tangkhuls say that the ancestors of the Tangkhuls and the Meiteis were brothers, the former being the elder brother and the Meitei, the younger brother. The Meitei elders who are familiar with the tradition of origin and separation of the Tangkhul-Meitei agree that in the remote past, the ancestors of the Tangkhuls and Meiteis belonged to the same parents. According to tradition, the Meitei procreator emerged from the Hundun Awunga, which will be discussed later in more detail. Very recently, following the footsteps of his predecessors, Maharaja Churachand; his successor Maharaja Budhachandra, and Ningthourel Parei-Hanba Okendrajit also went up to Hundung Awunga, Wungnayo Thawaijao and performed the same ceremony of the Tangkhul-Meitei oneness. (Refer to Appendix II for report).

The younger generation of the Meiteis, however, do not accept this tradition despite it still being a popular fact. The reasons for rejecting this tradition, are that with the conversion of the Meiteis to Hinduism, any link with such a tradition and past would go against the new faith and the theories of Meitei origin as explained within the Hindu traditions. For this, they invented several theories in order to override the historical facts and traditions, and try to explain their origin as different than the traditions. This sentiment of separate origin of the Meiteis is mostly found among the intellectual class of today. Some among the Meiteis claim their origin from west as the descendants of Arjun, one of the five Pandavasi; whereas, some others are of the view that the Meiteis are a branch of TAI people of Thailand, i.e. `Meitei' is a derivation from Mei-Tai meaning Tai people. Again, the Meiteis,' almost all of them being Hindus claim their origin from the Aryan Hindus. While it is not the opinion of the present researcher to make any point of argument for, and against all these theories, it is of interest to see how legend, tradition and history have undergone rejections on the origins of the Tangkhul-Meitei and their separation. That the Meiteis were originally residents of the surrounding hills before their conversion to Hinduism is conjectured by T.C. Hodson:[60]

> Should it be a correct view that the valley of Munipore was at no very distant period almost covered entirely by water, the origin of Munniporis from the surrounding hill tribes is the proper and only conclusion to be arrived at. I think it that when only a small part of the valley skirting the hill was capable of cultivation, the hillmen bordering it used to descend and cultivate the little land there then was, returning to their homes in the hill after reaping their harvests; as, however, land increased, some few of them settled permanently in the plain gradually increasing in numbers. The various tribes thus settling in different parts of the valley would in time came into contact, and after a struggle for supremacy amalgamate.

Though those different tribes of Imphal valley might be the off-shoot of different tribes of hills around them, it is accepted that, the Meiteis, particularly the ruling - family (Meitei Ningthouja) were the descendants of the Hundung Awunga (chief). According to tradition, the Awunga of Hundung village, which is 5 miles from Ukhrul town, was the elder brother; and th Raja of the Meiteis, the erstwhile princely state of Manipur, was the younger brother. The separation of the brothers is explained in the tradition as follows. The younger brother who found the promise of the plain insisted on his brother to let him go and settle in the valley. Hence, their separation. However, the younger brother, now Meitei, keeping the Tangkhul custom and tradition, used to send the due share of his elder brother, chief of Hundung village out of his products and games he killed. As such, brotherly relationship between the Tangkhuls and Meiteis continued and exchange of gifts was practised. However, when the Meiteis embraced Hinduism, their relationship had been severed. After a breach of relation for many centuries, it has been revived again. Horam informs:[62]

> The Tangkhuls specially have very strong reasons to believe that they and the Meiteis were once very close to each other. Hundung is a Tangkhul village. The chief of the village and the king of Manipur were brothers. This relationship was maintained till very recently, i.e. till the abolition of the princely states. There used to be an exchange of gifts and the Hundung Chief, being the elder brother of the Meitei King, was consulted often on several matters and shown due respect.

The separation of the two brothers and their future relationship are discussed in more elaborate form. The younger brother, who had been fascinated by the fortune of the valley all through those days lost contact with the elder brother. Fearing that he might be in danger of the enemies and ferocious animals, the elder brother went in search of him and at last found in the valley. But the younger brother refused to accept food and drink offered by his elder brother that he might separate and live apart in the valley. Because, he feared that any acceptance of food and drink from his elder brother would bring connection between the two; and he would be obliged to serve the elder brother according to Tangkhul custom. But the temptation of tobacco was so strong that he could not resist, and accepted it from the hand of his elder brother unwittingly. This brought him under the obligation to pay homage to the elder brother whether they live together or separate. Then at the persistence of the younger brother to settle in the valley, the elder brother conceded it and they separated peacefully on the condition that brotherly relationship should be maintained and there should be exchange of gifts between them as a sign of their relationship.

However, before they separated each other, the elder brother performed some rites and ceremonies, and offered sacrifices for the peace, prosperity and success of his younger brother, and let him go to live in the plains. Then the younger brother asked the elder to give him a cult so that he might perform rites and ceremonies, and worship the deity to begin the year and close it, and to carry out cultivation according to change of season. Accordingly, the elder brother took out a leather in which old Naga scripts[63] were written, and copied it into a bamboo bulb, and gave it to his younger brother. There he mentioned, the changing of season and year, and performance of festivals to mark the beginning and close of the year. The deity whom he had to worship was called goddess SAM SANGVA (Goddess of Jungle or Forest) of the Meiteis. To close the year, perhaps, the dedicatory festival, has to be performed which is known as YU-HONGBA after the harvest. But to begin the new year, it was marked by the celebration of LAI-HARAOBA festival. It is the rejoicing festival of gods and goddesses of the Meiteis.

In Meitei Lai-Haraoba festival, a number of war dances are performed. They are Thang-Haiba, Ta-Khao-Shaba (dancing with Tangkhul sword and spear) and Lirung Kappa (archery or arrow shooting) etc. These cultural and religious dances were handed over by the elder brother to the younger brother on the day of their separation.

Another festival that illustrates close connection between these peoples is the LAI-HARAOBA festival. It enacts the TANGKHUL SABA which means acting a Tangkhul, or faking a Tangkhul or representing a Tangkhul. In this sense, the actors and actresses have to appear on the stage with Tangkhul costume: daos (sword), spears, shields, head-gear, beads, necklace, sling-basket etc. and act the Tangkhul way of talking and living. Without Tangkhul-Saba, the Lai-Haraoba festival is never a complete one, and failure of performing of this scene, they incur the wrath of deity who bring disease, sickness and calamities to the people.

Again, there are several important evidences supporting the Meitei origin as limited with the Tangkhuls. For instance, at a corner of the palace of the former Meitei Rajas, there was always a construction of a pig-shed which is a typical Naga way of making a house. The frontal structure of the coronation hall of the Meitei Raja was decorated like those of the Angamis, Maos and the Tangkhuls. Further, at the coronation, the *Raja and Ranee* had to appear in Tangkhul costumes to validate the ceremony. Once in a year, according to custom and traditional practice, they were required to sit on the throne in Tangkhul costumes even for a short-while. In early days, they were escorted by two or three Meitei armed guards in Tangkhul war dress and weapons. By custom and culture, all these had to be strictly observed by the Meitei Raja.[64] This was even practised after the conversion of the Meiteis to Hinduism. The due share of the elder brother, known as LOIPOT was also sent to the chief of Hundung village. All these evidences referred above testify the origin of the Meiteis to be the same as the Tangkhuls. In the legend and tradition of the Nagas, there is no mention of the Meiteis coming from outside Manipur.

Tradition says that when the two brothers separated, the younger brother formed a new clan which was known by the name 'SHONGVAI" meaning the one who has become or formed a clan. Ho vever, the relationship continued for centuries again. History tells us that it was Raja Garib Niwaz who first made a breach with the established Meitei and Tangkhul relation.[65]

When the principles of Hinduism had taken sufficient roots with the Meiteis, the relation between the plains and the hills was adversely severed. Because, by religious doctrines and practices of Meitei Hindus, they had nothing to do with others, especially, with the backward Nagas. This led to the separation of the peoples of the plains and the hills. Then, the plain Hindus were known by the name MI-TEI - Mi, man; Tei, other or separated. This terminology is found in the dialects of the Angamis, Eastern Angamis, Maos, Tangkhuls and other Naga tribes. Since then, the name Meitei came into existence. The theory that the progenitors of the Tangkhuls and Meiteis emerged from one ancestor is found in the SANA PUYA, the Royal chronicles of the Meitei Raja. According to Puya, Kangba had three sons. They were Thangal, Hungbum (Hundung) and Meitei. Whereas, the Thangals found their settlement in present Thangal area, the Hundung Awunga and his brother, now, the Meiteis, proceeded as far as Hundung village, again from there they separated each other. [66]

Maharaja Churachand, king of Manipur traced back the origin and re-established the relationship between the Meitei Raja and Hundung Awunga. In honour and memory of this historic event, he erected a memorial stone in front of the house of Hundung Awunga on which his footprints were engraved. This example was followed by Maharaja Budhachandra, Raja of Manipur. A similar stone with his footprints engraved on, was erected on 11th November, 1945 - by the side of the first one. The last occasion known as PAREIHANBA meaning revival-revival of the Meitei Tangkhul oneness, was held in Imphal and celebrated in 1992 MERA HAOCHONGBA at Kangla.[67] A joint procession of Hundung dance troupe, Tangkhul Hao Arts and Cultural Council members, Hao National Inat Thousillup members and Kangla Defence Party was taken out in Imphal town. This was a great and important landmark: in the history of the re-union of Meitei-Tangkhul after a long breach of separation.

The Pareihanba celebration in imphal being over, Maharaja Okendrajit Preihanba, with a Dance Troupe of 300 strong and a number of Meitei brothers and sisters proceeded to Hundung Thawaijao village where A. S. Wungnaoyo Zimik, Awunga of Hundung village offered a warm welcome. The same Pareihanba celebration was held with the erection of the memorial stone of the Meitei-Tangkhul oneness. Maharaja Okendrajit Preihanba delcared it in the presence of Hundung Awunga, Thangal chief and thousands of the participants of dignitaries and the people of both the plains and hills. As a token of the Pareihanba, the Maharaja presented one female buffalo to Hundung Awunga, and there was exchange of gifts between the two brothers as it was practised before their one time separation: There was a great rejoicing to all for the great occasion of the reunion again.

NOTES & REFERENCES

1. Sanyu Visier, "Nagas in History", Nagas 90, p. 5.
2. M. Horam, *Naga Polity,* p. 1.
3. G. A. Grierson, *Linguistic Survey of India,* Vol. III, Part I, p. 72.
4. Gangmumai Kabui, *Genesis of the Ethnoses of Nagas and Kuki-Chin,* p. 10.
5. M. Horam, *Naga Polity,* pp. 33-34.
6. Y. L. Roland Shimmi, *A Comparative History of the Nagas: From Ancient Period Till 1826,* p. 50.
7. T. C. Hodson, *The Naga Tribes of Manipur,* p. 6.
8. J. H. Hutton, The Angami Nagas, p. 8.
9. Sipra Sen, *Tribes and Castes of Manipur,* p. 20.
10. During field work, the author conducted interview with a variety of people, retired I.A.S. Officers and social workers, with a prepared

questionnaire. The above-mentioned interview was held at Ukhrul on 19th October, 1993.

11. At present, a portion of Naga inhabited area became the 16th state in India Union called Nagaland. The author prefer to use Naga Homeland as the territory inhabited by the Nagas in India and Burma.

12. In 1971, the Nagas sent a "Good-will Mission" to China to strengthen diplomatic relations between the Nagas and Chinese. The present author was one of its members.

13. G.A. Grierson, *Linguistic Survey of India*, Vol. [illegible], Part I, p. 42.

14. R. R. Shimray, *Origin and Culture of Nagas*, pp. 12 - 13.

15. M. Horam, *North East India, A Profile*, pp. 162-164.

16. R. C. Majumdar, *Ancient Indian History*, p. 68.

17. T. C. Hodson, *The Naga Tribes of Manipur*, p. 10.

18. R. R. Shimray, *op.cit.*, p. 18.

19. R. R. Shimray, *op.cit.*, p. 18.

20. R. R. Shimray, *op.cit.*, p. 13.

21. Gao-Dazian belongs to Li nationality of Hainan Island of Goungdong province of China. He is/was a reporter of Hainan island to the magazine 'China Reconstruct'. This legend/tradition of 'Li people" was published in the magazine, *China Reconstruct*, Vol. XXX, No. 10 of Oct. 1981.

22. Jingpo was the progenitor of the Chingphaws. This particular tribe is called by different spellings, like Jingpho, Singpho. Now, they are called Kachins.

    When A. S. Vashi Shimray conducted field work for his book, 'Naga Kingdom' (unpublished), he made an interview with an old man named Haw Daw, Chief of Saw Law village (a Kachin) in Mitkyina District of Kachin State in northern Burma. The old man narrated this story as the origin of Kachin-Naga and Chin-Kuki-Mizos. Thus this information was collected from the manuscript of Vashi.

23. According to the tradition of the Kachins, Phuangchuang is regarded as the oldest village in Kachin State, situated in north east of Mitkyina town, capital of Kachin state.

24. The word 'Khang, Khang' was used by Jingpo and his second son meaning 'foot-print, foot-print' to call each other when they found the foot-prints of Lengdo and Jingpo's elder son. Later the descendants of the elder son, who are today called 'Naga" were known by the name Akhang' in early days. Even till today, the Shans and Burmans call the Nagas, 'Akhang".

25. G.A. Grierson, *Linguistic Survey of India,* Vol. III, Part II, p. 499.

26 In 1972, when the present researcher crossed Kachin State on his way to China, the Kachin independent undergrounds welcome him and his party warmly. In course of their discussion, the Kachin village elders and underground leaders narrated the story of the origin of the Kachin-Nagas and claimed that both the Kachins and Nagas are brothers bifurcated from the same parents.

27. R. R. Shimray, Origin and Culture of Nagas, p. 39; S. C. Sardeshpande, The Patkoi Nagas, p. 10.

28. G.E.R. Grant Brown, *Burma Gazetteer,* Upper Chindwin District, pp. 3, 17, 24, 85.

29. Verrier Elwin, *The Nagas in the Nineteenth Century,* p. 482.

30. G. E. R. Grant Brown, *op. cit.,* p. 85.

31. Mayo-Kachui is tangkhul name to Patkoi ranges. The Meiteis called it Ango-Ching. In Tangkhul, 'Mayo' means lovely or charming and 'Kachui" means, height or highland. It is, indeed, a lovely highland of the ranges with charming view of the Chindwin Valley in the east and Kabo-Valley in the west. Even at the lapse of time, the old habitation at Hongkha-Muja is still clearly seen with the trees and bamboos they had planted.

32 Kachin-Naga and Chin-Kuki-Mizo had their tradition of association with Python since their migration from remote past. This tradition has a close relation wi h the story of Gao-Daxian who said that the tribes of Hainan island were born by a monkey and brought up by a serpent.

33. The Burmese called Samsok by different names, such as Thap, Thaungthut, Taungthut, Thaungdut and Hsaungsup, whereas the Meiteis called it Samjok, Samshok etc. different from the Tangkhul original name of Songshuireng.

34. G.E.R. Grant Brown, *op. cit.,* p. 9.

35. R. R. Shimray, *op. cit.,* p. 29.

36. R. R. Shimray, *op. cit.*, p. 23.

37. The above paragraph is a translation from K. Y. L. Roland' s book, *Tangkhul Naga History*, pp. 12, 13, from Tangkhul into English, HUNG-tribe means to Tangkhui, and KAMO-KHOKOK means to the great warriors of southern Tangkhul Nagas. Ningthi Valley is the Chindwin Valley and Ango-Ching is the Patkoi mountain called by local people.

38. Sampui village is now two miles from S.D.O. Headquarters, Kamjong and Khampi is 8 miles from S.D.O. Headquarters of Phungyar, both in Ukhrul District, in Manipur State.

39. Jyotirmoy Roy, *History of Manipur*, p. 3.

40. R.R. Shimray, *op. cit.*, pp. 24-25.

41. Visier Sanyu, *The History of Village Formation Among the Angami Nagas*, p. 57.

42. R. R. Shimray, *op. cit.*, p. 26.

43. Gangmumei Kabui, *Genesis of the Ethnoses of Nagas and Kuki-Chin*, p. 31.

44. M. Horam, *North East India, A Profile, p. 163.*

45. R. R. Shimray, *op. cit.*, p. 38.

46. T. C. Hodson, *op. cit.*, p. 42.

47. Alexander Mackenzie, *The North-East Frontier of Bengal*, p. 77.

48. R. R. Shimray, *op. cit.*, p. 16.

49. *Poireiton* means colonisation. According to Roy, the word 'Poireiton' might have been originated from the word 'Purohito' (*History of Manipur*, p. 22) which could be the colonisation of the priests in Manipur. See also G. Kabuis "Genesis of the Ethnoses of Nagas and Kuki-Chin," pp. 13, 14.

50. A. S. Machung, *Bakshimi Ground History*, p. 1.

51. Y. L. Roland; *A Comparative History of the Nagas*, p. 59.

52. M. Horam, *Naga Polity*, p. 23.

53. Verrier Elwin, *op. cit.*, p. 24.

54. Hokishe Sema, *Emergence of Nagaland*, pp. 2, 3; R. R. Shimray also expressed a similar view in his book, Origin and Culture of Nagas, p. 41.

55. Yet another version of the nomenclature "Naga" may be drawn from Naga tradition itself. According to tradition, when the tribe was oppressed by the ruling dynasties of China fled the land. So as to identify themselves as coming from the same progenitor, the people pierced their ears-Na-Ka.

56. During the field work of the researcher, it had been explained by Ramyo Luikham of Ukhrul, a retired IAS Officer, of 65 years of age. Reference to this is also made in Maiya Gachui, Hao Mi-un Ngashan Kala Tangkhul Khararchen, *(History of Tangkhuls)*, Goodwill Press, Imphal, 1980; K. L. Sira, *Hao Khararchen*, Published with the assistance of the Government of Manipur.

57. T. C. Hodson, *op. cit.*, p. 27; G. E. R. Grant Brown also makes mention of it in p. 3.

58. A. S. Vashi Shimray, "The Naga Kingdom" (MSS) made available with reservation, p. 53.

59. Iron was cut into different sizes to suit the purposes of price and purchase, and for the convenience of the material they required for making various articles of sizes.

60. T. C. Hodson, *The Meiteis*, p. 7.

61. The legend says that when the two brothers were living at Hundung village, their sow wandered from home to bring forth a litter. The younger brother traced the tract and at last found the sow with litter pigs in the valley. He remained there for days to look after the pig, and found the land favourable to him. Since then, he separated from his elder brother who remained at Hundung village.

62. M. Horam, *op. cit.*, pp. 42-43.

63. According to tradition, after copying the scripts in a bamboo bulb, the leather was left uncared that a dog devoured it. Therefore, the Nagas lost their script for all whereas the Meiteis have the original Naga script called "Ariba Mayek' meaning 'Old- Script' .

64. T. C. Hodson, *The Naga Tribes of Manipur*, pp. 8-12; T. C. Hodson, *The Meiteis*, pp. 4-12; R. R. Shimray, *Origin and Culture of Nagas*, pp. 33-37; James Johnstone, *Manipur and the Naga Hills*, pp. 82-85; M. Horam, Naga Polity~ pp. 42-43; M. Horam, *Social and Cultural Life of Nagas* pp. 24-26.

65. J. Roy, *op. cit.*, p. 38; L. Ibongobal Singh, *Introduction to Manipur*, p. 32.

66. This fact was established by Hundung Awlunga, A. S. wungnaoya Zirnik and his associate, A. S. Akhui Zimik during the field work of the researcher at Hundung village in October 1993.

67. This information is collected from Pareihanba Klong, a documentary collected and compiled by Narakari and Ngangoi Leiphaba, Imphal, 1993.

2

THE EARLY VILLAGE STATE OF THE TANGKHULS

Man is a social being, and so, he wants to live in the society where there is mutual love and co-operation. He has the desire to contribute his energy and skill for the upliftment of the society. Because, the welfare and happiness of the society is the welfare and happiness of the individual as he is a part of the society. However, unlike the other social animals, whose lives are guided by instinct and emotion, man has the power to hink and reason through which he can know what is right and good, and what is wrong and evil both for himself and the society as a whole. Moreover, he has the power to share and communicate his desire, ideas and skills to other fellow human being through dialogue and conversation. This makes man distinct and superior to animals. Comparing the distinction between man and animals, Cantor says, "Animals may form societies, but only man, with his superior mental equipment developed civilization."[1] Again, in animals, there is lack of dialogue and conversation between one another, as much as it is found in man.

However, human desire, interest and skill are different from individual to individual; and therefore, from community to community. No two individuals have the same mind and interest. Again, they have different physical and mental powers and capacities. All these inequalities in man create social and individual crisis. When this crisis is let go unchecked, it leads to quarrel, bloodshed and murder. War is a form of human crisis at the highest level. In order to avoid social disharmony and chaos, the need of a social order arises so that there exist harmony and unity, and peaceful co- existence in the society. Here all the individuals have to bow down and sacrify their private interests for the welfare and benefit of the mass.

In order to implement the social norms, men form several social organizations, and these different organizations are interlinked and co-ordinate with each other. They all work for the betterment and progress of the society. The state is the highest social organization of men. In this regard, Samuel Stumpf wrote: "it is evident that the State is a creature of nature, and that man is by nature a political animal."[2] The state tops on all organizations of the society with the highest authority and power to execute its functions of administration for the internal peace, harmony, security and progress; and also to exercise its power outside the state for peaceful and diplomatic relationship and coexistence with other states. According to Cantor, the efforts for successful agricultural enterprise led to the formation of strong and centralized governments in ancient near East.[3] Cantor regarded them as the first government and earliest literate and civilized communities.

The state has an area of land whether big or small, a population occupying the territory over which it has its absolute sovereign right and power. It is not subjected to any power and authority both internal and external. From time immemorial, every Tangkhul village was an independent village-state called Khawung pronounced as Kfa. It had its territory and population—big or small and weak or strong. As a village state, it had independent social, economic, political and religious concerns of its own; and independent external policy, free from the interference of other powers from outside. Regarding the early village-state of the Tangkhuls, Dr. Horam is of the view:[4]

> Whether or not, the village was always a social, political and religious unit, the fact remains that, it was an important unit. Among all the Naga tribes, in the days before Christianity came to the Naga Hills, every village was not only a religious unit but also politically and economically a distinct unit. The village is an independent unit in the tribe.

Regarding the state religious policy, the principle of 'Kujus religio ejus religio' is not applicable in the religious policy of the Tangkhul village state. The intensity and degree of faith, worship, rituals and sacrifices of an individual is for the person concern. No authority, even the Awunga of the village could impose his authority on a person though he was his subject. However, interestingly, the whole subjects of the village state was effected by the village taboos in matters of food, religious functionaries, ceremonies and religious festive observances. Though the Tangkhul village-state was not absolu'ely a theocratic state, but on the grounds given above, it had its own religious policy binding on all citizens of the state.

In the field of economy, each village had its own independent policy which its main economic concern was for the subsistence of the whole village. In early days, as at present, agriculture was the mainstay of the Tangkhul Naga economy. It was, however, subordinated by domestication of animals, and handicrafts like pottery, 'basketry, blacksmith, weaving and trade and commerce. The Tangkhuls, being an agrarian society, where both jhumming and terraced cultivation is practised, the Awunga, with the help of Hangwa (Councillors) regulated the rotation of agricultural land. Here, the entire village was under one economic policy of the Khawung. But the other side of the economic activities in the village was of the individual concern to some extent. For instance, every individual, family and Organization have the right to pursue for their economic development in which the village had no right to interfere except where the enterprise affects the society or village state otherwise. Thus in early Tangkhul village state, there existed a mixed economy-community control system and private individual system.

Politically, the early village state of the Tangkhuls had independent administrative policy for the peace, security and order of the whole village. It executed its power for the welfare and development of the entire village community. Again, it was responsible for the diplomatic relation with other village for peaceful co-existence; and to defend the village from the invasion of hostile and enemy villages around it. Whatever policy the Khawung formulated for both internal and external was final and binding; and no power outside had a say or interfere on the independent policy there. It made war and concluded peace. What a Tangkhul village state had agreed or decided a matter, it was immediately in force within the defined territory of the village state; violation of which followed with consequences of heavy penalties from the village state.

Formation of Tangkhul Village State

From remote past, Tangkhul villages were independent of each other. There were around 168 villages of the Tangkhuls in present Ukhrul District of which, Ukhrul, Hungbum, Tuinem, Chingjaroy and Nungbi were the biggest villages. Big villages are mostly found in northern and western Tangkhul areas whereas, eastern and southern Tangkhul villages are not big enough, even to the existence of 5 houses in a village. However, this did not affect the independence of small villages under any circumstances. The state of independence continued till very recently. No power was above their Khawung, but since they all came from the same origin, there was a "Tangkhul consciousness" that despite inter-village feuds, it kept the community together. This state of affairs continued till recently.

The formation of early Tangkhul village states is still obscure due to paucity of written records. Although the Tangkhuls possessed a good number of legends, traditions and folklore, which explain the proto-history of the tribe, they are silent in the area of their village state formation. However, it is a fact that there existed Tangkhul village states. The tradition of the Tangkhuls and their village state formation during their migratory stage, from the Chindwin Valley till their settlement at Samsok, tells of the formation of village under certain leaders. The same case may be well applied in the village formation of the Tangkhuls of their present habitation. Some modern Tangkhul writers like R. R. Shimray and Horam have given some information with regard to the formation of early Tangkhul villages.[5]

Regarding the formation of Tangkhul Khas, the general factors are most likely unapplicable in it. Because, in a Tangkhul village, the Awunga is not the sole owner of the village land. It belongs to the entire village community, every family having its own cultivable land as much as the Awunga. Thus, he does not have absolute control or power to dictate over the village land, and there was no land-tax as such. Therefore, the control over the economy and surplus products, which led to the formation of state as explained by R. Thapar,[6] cannot be the factor for the formation of the Tangkhul village state either. Here the author is of the opinion that the need of social order political stability and aggrandizement were the most important factors for the formation of Tangkhul village state. With the increase of population, the society required a certain set-up standard to maintain peace, order and harmony in the society; and every individual had to pay due obeisance to the set social standard. Again, because of the inter- village feuds which led to intervillage war in early days, the leadership of a strong ruler was required to establish a strong and stable village state so that he might protect it from the attack and destruction of enemy villages.

Further, when we discuss the necessity of having a strong leader or chief in the establishment of a village state, it is interesting to note that, from the context of the Tangkhul villages, anybody, strong, powerful, wealthy, courageous and skill in war cannot be the Awunga of the village. Though a leadership or chieftainship could be vested on anybody who had the quality and efficiency of the post, but to be an Awunga of a village, he required the nomination of the people and the divine sanction. Short of any of these, no one could claim to be an Awunga and no subject people could accept him to be their Awunga. This subject will be discussed in the chapter of 'Political and Judicial Organisation'.

In Tangkhul social life, when there is a village, there is a village state; and when there is a village state, there is an Awunga. It is the life of the Tangkhuls. A village cannot exist without an Awunga and the post of Awunga is inalienable in the formation and existence of a Tangkhul village. According to Tangkhul Customary Law, "Tangkhul Shiyan-Yanza"[7]

> Haklala teolala leiret akha leilaga lam khangava, Awunga khalei kala Mipha kahlei ramsom Chili kha hora.
>
> [Whether big or small, a territory with its defined boundary, having Awunga and population in the settled area will be called a village.]

From the above mentioned customary law of the Tangkhuls, it is clear that the Awunga is an important feature and component in the establishment of a Tangkhul village without which no village could be formed and exist. In normal case, the one who led a group of people and settled down at a place became the Awunga of the newly formed village and the others naturally became his subjects. But if a number of clans followed him, the heads of the clans formed the councillors and the council is called HANGVA. The Awunga and Hangva carried out the administration of the Khawung. According to Shimray,[8] Shokvao, Ukhrul, Shiroi-Kashung and Longpi were the first Tangkhul villages from where they dispersed to different parts of Tangkhul areas. Longpi was another important place of distribution from where western Tangkhul villages like Ngainga, Shongran, Phadang etc. formed. But no doubt, Phungcham and Hungbum (Hundung) were another early villages of dispersal. Today, the clans of these villages are found, mostly in northern and western Tangkhuls who are the descendants or mutators of those villages mentioned above.

In early days, both the Meiteis of the plains and the Nagas of the hills especially the Tangkhuls, Marings, Khoibus, Kabuis, Zemeis, Liangmeis etc. carried the same names of clans. Some prominent clans are Ghuman, Looang, Ningthauja, Angom, Khaba-Nganba etc.[9] However, though people of different tribes professed to belong to a particular clan given above, the name they used for the clan is different from tribe to tribe. Again, among the Tangkhuls also, though they belong to the same clan, the name of the clan they use is different from localities to localities. For instance, the researcher belongs to Ghuman clan of the Meitei name. But in his locality, the clan is called by the name Shuingtuidang, whereas, in the nearby locality it is again called Duidang; Ningthouja is called Jajo, and so on. However, mention of the names of some Tangkhul clans may be made such as: Zimik, Luikham, Horam, Jajo, Shingtuidang, Kashung, Longleng etc. But they cannot be necessarily called the leading clans of the Tangkhuls.

In early days, when the Tangkhuls were moving from place to place in order to find suitable place for settlement, they moved under a certain leader. However, it must be taken into consideration that they must be consisted of two or more clans since the Tangkhuls are absolutely exogamous by nature. Because, in those days, marriage from other village was not very convenient due to intervillage feuds. Therefore, there were clan chiefs along with the group-chief. When they formed a village, ultimately, the leader of the group took the office of the Awunga and the clan chiefs formed the councillors of the Hangva. In case of two or more leaders of equal rank, the one who lighted or made fire first became the Awunga and the others remained as members of Hangva.

They carried out the functions of administration of the village state together. Since then, the post of Awunga becomes hereditary, and by no means, it could be challenged under any circumstances.

There is no records, oral or written, of revolution or rebellion of the village against the government and amdinistration of the Awunga and Hangva in a Tangkhul village so far. It is because, the Awunga was the maker of the law called Mayonrin on the basis of democracy. Further, the Awunga had to exercise his power sanctioned by the law. Again, most of the laws of the Tangkhuls derived from tradition, custom, culture and religious principles that there was no room for the Awunga to be despotic and rule against the will and interest of the subject people. However, there are cases that some group or groups of people broke away from the parent village and set up a new village of their own, perhaps, on the ground of over population or so. They are called the new village of the old one. But in some other cases, they became altogether a new set-up village, different from the parent village. However, in both cases, when a new village was established, it became complete independent of the parent village. The relationship between the two was a matter of diplomatic relation of the villages concerned. They had their own Awunga and Hangva which carried out the administration of their newly established village state.

However, love and affection between the parent village and the "colony" did not permit complete severance immediately. Further, until or unless the "colony" village becomes strong enough to stand on its own feet and able to defend the attack of enemy villages, the "colony" village remained under the protege of the parent village. Visit and exchange of gifts continued.[10] This practice continued for generations without a breach in some cases.

Those who established the village together were the equal citizens and members of the village because there is no class division of the society. Further, slavery system is not prevalent in the Tangkhul society. Any immigrant, even from the hostile village also, after fulfilling the terms and conditions can become a member of the village in which he joined. For that, he has to offer a feast to the village community, and then the Awunga declares him as a citizen of the village formerly. The equal share and responsibility of the village rest on him and his family since then.

But wherever a person may stay, lapse of time and distance of land cannot change the clan and blood relation of a person. Therefore, marriage of a person with a member of the same clan, though they appear from far different villages is culturally prohibited. Further, according to Tangkhul custom, members of the clan, whether they live in a parent village or "colony" village, have to offer the meat portion of the game they kill to the clan elder, failure of which is a crime to the principle of the clan geneology. Thus cordial relationship is always maintained among the members of the clan living elsewhere within and outside Tangkhul territory.

The date of the establishment of the Tangkhul village states cannot be ascertained due to absence of written history. However, it can rightly be stated that, the states must have been formed when they occupied the range of Zibyu Taung immediately after the separation of the first son of Jingpo and his nephew Lengdo from the camp of Phungchaung. Again, when the descendants of the first son of Jingpo shifted their settlement from the Chindwin river valley and occupied the mountain range of Patkoi, the formation of these village states had been already in full shape; and the post of Awunga was held by Kabo-Khari (out of this patriarch emerged a clan under his name) and he ruled over the twin-village of Hongkha- Muja. The antiquity of the Tangkhuls and their organised settled life had been mentioned in the Chronicles of Manipur; and Hodson, the chief authority of the Naga tribes of Manipur remarked .[11]

> The Chronicles of Manipur make it abundantly clear that the Tangkhuls existed as an organised tribe in the occupation of much the same area as at present, at a period, coeval with the establishment of the Meitei hegemony in the valley, by the defeat of the Moirang tribesmen in A.D. 1431.

> In another book, he wrote:[12] From the records of Manipur we gather some important facts regarding the antiquity of the Tangkhuls. One of the earliest raids mentioned in the Chronicles of Manipur is dated 1435, and is said to have been the work of Tangkhuls who then, as on subsequent occasions, availed themselves of the opportunity afforded them by the temporary absence of the forces of Manipur on what the local historian calls a march of conquest in the direction of Thaungdut, to make a raid on the valley. Frequent mention is made of the Tangkhuls in this connection with attack on Manipuri settlements on the edge of the valley ... but it is quite clear that these tribes especially the Tangkhuls were settled in the areas they now occupy at an early date, when the Meiteis, now their masters were yet wild and untouched by the finer arts of life.

However, the date mentioned above cannot be taken as the date when the Tangkhuls formed their village states. Very much earlier than this period, when the Shans of Burma crossed over Naga inhabited area into Assam, the Nagas had been well organised and offered stiff resistance to Shan emigrants in 13th century A.D. This Shan exodus could be either by the invasion of the Mongols under Khublei Khan, General of Gengiz Khan in 1263 A.D. He dealt severely with the Shans and Burmans that they were scattered in different directions. Or the Shan exodus could be by the invasion of Anawrata, king of Burma (1010 A.D. to 1052) which also led to the dispersal of the Shans.

The presence of the Shans in Upper Chindwin District may be explained. When the Shans attacked Samsok Kingdom, and subdued the latter, the Tangkhuls were subjected to Shan principality. They adopted Shan culture and embraced Buddhism. In those days, the Tangkhuls had well established their state at Samsok. After the invasion of Samsok and establishment of a Shan principality, the Burmese again attacked the Shan principality of Samsok. The first Burmese attack of Upper Chindwin ever recorded was as early as 416 A.D. When the rulers were subdued, the Burmese king appointed a governor with the title 'Sawbwa.'[13] Since then, the Burmese were called 'Sowba' by the Tangkhuls and this name is still in existence. From the above mentioned events and date, it can safely be concluded that the formation of the Tangkhul village states had been as early as the first millennium B.C. This period was some centuries after the dispersal of Tibeto- Burmans of China as mentioned earlier.

Polity of Tangkhul Village State

In the polity of the Nagas, the village was a social, economic, religious and political independent unit rather than the tribe. Though the Naga villages were bound together by certain cultural and blood ties within the tribe, each village was independence, free from the dominance and interference of other village of the tribe. It may be compared with the Polis, ancient city state of the Greeks. In the territory of Greece, although the people belonged, to the same Greek nationality, every city or polis was an independent city state, and its ruler was made by the popular choice of the people on the principle of direct democracy. Here all the citizens assembled and chose a person to be their leader or ruler who could give them peace and security, and also the one who had the skill and power to lead them in time of war. Every adult had the right to exercise his franchise, but women, children and slaves were debarred from voting.[14] The city states made war one against another for supremacy which caused untold misery to the people until Alexander the Great subdued them all and brought about a unified kingdom under him. This was the end of polis-state and the beginning of a united kingdom of the city states of the Greeks. In many respects, the Tangkhul village state polity has much similarity with the city state of ancient Greece a self-contained social economic, religious and political unit. It was neither a city in the beginning in the true sense of the term. Therefore Cantor described the nature of Polis.[15]

> The centre of the Polis in the earliest days was not even a town, let alone what we call a city. It was merely a settlement of houses of the farmers who worked the land in the surrounding area.

So also the presence and practice of democracy similar to each other to a great extent. Indeed, the word 'Democracy' is very much modern to the people of the world; so also to the Nagas. In the same way, the work of democracy is recent political exercise. However, the democratic principles and activities had been exercised by the Tangkhuls since time immemorial. But unlike the Greeks who elected their leader by majority votes, the Tangkhul village Awunga is nominated, elected and approved by divine sanction. Since then, it has become hereditary. It can neither be disputed nor purchased or sold. Interestingly, the distinct characteristic of the Tangkhul Khawung is that, despite the hereditary nature of the post of Awunga, he cannot become despotic. The Principles of democracy is carried out in its perfect form. Because the right and powers of the Awunga derive from the customary laws within which he exercises his power. He is also assisted by the chiefs of the clans residing in the village. They are known as Wungnaos (discussed in detail at Chapter V) who automatically become Councillors. Where they assisted in the administration of the Awunga, they stood as check and balance to the possible despotic character of the Awunga. The council of the Awunga and Wungnaos and some elected members is called HANGVA. It is the highest institution of the Tangkhul village state. It also acts as the supreme court of the village state. The success of these Tangkhul institutions rests in the maintenance of the principles of democracy both in spirit and letter. It can neither be violated nor overridden at any circumstances.

As the post of Awunga and Wungnaos or clan chiefs are hereditary by nature, it cannot be disputed nor purchased or sold. But on certain condition, they can be transferred to the next eldest males of the family or clan. The Awunga and Wungnaos, being the highest court of the village, any issue or problem which the Hangva cannot solve, is decided by the Awunga and Wungnaos which is final and binding. In such case, the Hangva also cannot question the authority and verdict made by them under any circumstances. Its formation is all the same as the council of ministers at the village state level. They hardly sit together apart from the Hangva except in extreme serious and important cases; and their sitting is highly revered and feared by the people.

Normally, the Awunga and Wungnaos constitute the Awunga-in-Council or Hangva, because, it is represented by all the chiefs or Wungnaos of the clans of the village. But in certain cases, more representatives are taken from bigger clans. Men of skill in war, high calibre and understanding, eloquent in speech, good orators and influential people are taken into the membership of the Hangva. But they cannot sit in the "cabinet" council of the Awunga. Except the posts of Awunga and Wungnaos, the membership of the rest in the Hangva is either temporary or for life. It is purely conditional depending on the situation or the service rendered by a member.

Riyan/Unwritten Constitution

History has shown that communities which do not have the written word have preserved their history through oral tradition. The Tangkhuls do not possess any written record or book of their law. They have unwritten customary laws and usages which is handed down by their ancestors from generation to generation through oral memory. One of the traditions related to the constitution of the Tangkhuls is called RIYAN. The customary laws, usages and conventions of the Tangkhuls had been well-tried and tested by thieir ancestors. When they were proved acceptable and practicable in the lives of the Tangkhuls, they became Riyan. There are certain, rules and regulations introduced by the Hangva, and sometimes, by the general assembly for the convenience of day to day administration of the village. But they are introduced in conformity with the customary laws and usages, which are, however, subjected to change and modification in conformity with the changing situation.

However, any rule or principle discussed and agreed upon cannot be adopted as a law and incorporated in the customary laws merely because it has been agreed upon and accepted by the community to be their laws. Rather, the divine sanction has to be sought by passing through several tests and omens, and performance of religious rites and worships. Because, it was a must in a society where supersitition is strongly prevalent. Then the rules discussed about is adopted as Customary Law. In this sense, the Tangkhul customary laws can be called Divine Laws where the sanction of gods was a must. Further, it is to say that, when an individual, regardless of his person, whether the Awunga, Wungnao, Hangva members or a citizen of the village. violation of customary law incurred the anger and displeasure of the gods. The consequence is the divine punishment, not only to the breaker of the law, but to the entire population of the village in the form of famine caused by draught, flood, hailstorm, disease on both men and domestic animals and suffering from defeat in war. In secular law, naturally the one who breaks it will be awarded with punishment whereas, all the others are free from being penalised. However, this is not the case with the Tangkhul village state and its customary laws. The offence of one person against the law brings down the wraith of gods to the entire village population. Heavy fines in the form of confiscation of domestic animals are usually practised on the law-breaker, and the Awunga and the village priest (SHARA) perform ritual by killing animals, mostly chicken and sacrifice it to appease the wrath of the evil spirit. Any kind of the breach of law ignorantly or consciously involves the same amount of punishment of gods. Therefore, it is the bounden duty of every citizen that he/she is well versed in customary laws.

Awunga and the State

Awunga is an integral component of the Tangkhul village state. No Tangkhul Naga state ever existed without the Awunga and it can neither exist short of Awunga. Again, no Tangkhul village could exist without Awunga in the life of the Tangkhuls. As such, the role of Awunga is wide and extensive. There is no area in the life of the Tangkhuls where the Awunga has no role in it. Therefore, the life and activities of the Tangkhuls revolve round the post of Awunga. Regarding the state and Awunga, Horam explained:[16]

> A Tangkhul Naga village is a politically organised association. Villages are generally ruled by headmen who are vested with a great deal of authority. . . . The village chief is called 'Awunga' 'a tittle equivalent to the English word king'.

The post of Awunga being hereditary, it is permanent and the Awungaship continues in the family by the succession of the eldest male according to the principle of primogeniture. Therefore, a Tangkhul village state may be likened to a monarchical form of state. Election for the post of the Awunga is out of palce in Tangkhul polity. Further, no form of government other than this type of government will be accepted by the people since the Awunga is the only competent person to serve the village deity and perform rites and sacrifices to him.

A mention may be made which tells of a story relating to the point given above. In the remote pass, in a village called Ningthi, the Awunga failed to produce a male issue. Therefore, the Awungaship passed to the nearest male of the clan. The same fate occurred in the house of the new Awunga. Therefore, out of fear, he resigned the post. But no one dared to take the post seeing the successive bareness in the house of Awunga. The post remained vacant for days that during those days of vacancy, the village diety was left uncared. Because, there was no Awunga to serve him and perform sacrifices. As a result, the displeased spirit brought death and sickness on the people, and so they complained to the clan and family of the Awunga to fill-up the post immediately. The situation was saved only when a new Awunga was nominated from the nearest family and he offered sacrifice to the village deity and propitiated him.[17]

Again, the Awunga has extensive religious powers and functions. Though he is not the village priest, yet the important religious rites, ceremonies and sacrifices are to be performed by the Awunga. He also inaugurates the village festivals and other village social activities. In such functions, he represents the entire village community and propitiates the spirits. Sometimes, though the village priest has to perform religious rites and sacrifices, it required the presence or sanction of the Awunga. Therefore, the religious rights and duties of the Awunga is an alienable from the post of the Awunga without which no ceremony is complete and valid. When we discuss the religious function of the Awunga, the divine sanction on customary laws and the sanction of god on the ordination of the Awunga, we find the presence of theocratic feature in the polity of the Tangkhul village state.

Qualification of Awunga

The post of Awunga is the most important and holy in the establishment of a Tangkhul village. Its nature and extensive role in the village state make it worth-desired. Therefore, it is important to discuss the evolution of the post of Awunga. It did not appear all of a sudden. It did not come upon anybody by chance. Several factors were involved, in the formation of the post of Awunga and a person who would be the Awunga has to pass through several tests, rituals and omens. At last, he requires the sanction of gods to be the Awunga.

In normal case, according to Shiyan-Yanza,[19] the one who led the group when searching for settlement ultimately became the Awunga of the established village. The post is then permanent and hereditary in the family. Therefore, his eldest son has the right, to succeed the father when the situation so demanded either by the death of the Awunga or his inability to discharge his duty due to sickness or old age, and so on. But when two or more leaders of equal rank moved together, the one who first lighted fire at the place became the Awunga, and the other leaders will be councillors. The whole members of the community were equal citizens of the village. Then, by cusotm, the chieftainship of the Awunga cannot be challenged.

Further, the Awunga is required to obtain the divine sanction. In order to prove it, he passed through several tests and observations of omens. First, he sowed the paddy seeds, and if they germinated well, then he passed through the second test. In this, he sowed the bean seeds, but especially the peeled ginger.[20] When the second test proved positive, the third and last test was conducted with a living animal, usually a cock. They observed the sound of the cock crowing whether its tone sounded well or not. Sometime, the cock was strangled to dead and observed the position of the legs when it died. If the right leg slightly crossed on top of the left, it proved well. Then it is taken that gods favoured his assumption of the office of Awunga. Otherwise the proposed Awungaship was dropped. This method of test and observation of omens are used also in the case of dispute for the post.

The one who proved all the tests success became the Awunga, and he was the first to sow and the first to pluck the corn. He leads in all important village festivals and functions both religious and secular. He enjoys certain rights and privileges. He wears a special kind of cloths which are not entitled to common pepole. In all social and religious functions, he occupies the most prominent seat and receives the first and the best serve of food and drink. The Awunga gets a portion of the game killed in the hunt. Every household has to pay some amount of its products—rice, paddy, peas, seasmum etc. as a kind of his privilege and reward for Awungaship.

Further, the would-be Awunga of a Tangkhul village is bound by the principles of marriage, food and drink habits. He must be free from the act of incest. A person who marries a bastard or whose marriage is against the customary law cannot be an Awunga. In short, the marriage of the Awunga should be above reproach. Again, although the Tangkhuls eat almost all kinds of meats, and though there is no strict classification of animals called clean and unclean as is prevalent among many communities, certain animals are termed as unclean to Awunga. He should abstain from eating meats of animals such as dogs, cats, wild cats, bear, tiger, flying squirrels etc. In this regard, there may be some variations from village to village. But, it is the fact that clean food habit and sanctity of life has to be observed and maintained by the Awunga since he represents the entire village community. He should appear clean physically, morally, and even spiritually before the people and their gods. To be precise, the Awunga should not take meats of the class of tiger, eagle and creepers.

Some clans are under certain meat taboos whether the animal is regarded clean or unclean. For example, in early days, no Tangkhul took the flesh of goats saying that the one who partook mutton became fork-tongued. Again, among the Tangkhuls, some particular clans cannot take beef of buffalo, which is a taboo to them. In such cases, both the common people and the Awunga who belong to the tribe should abstain from such meat.

Hangva (Village State Council)

Hangva is an important powerful institution of the Tangkhul village state. All the powers of making MAYONRIN (Laws) is vested on it. It makes laws in conformity with customs and traditions. Even, the power of the Awunga derives from it. The Mayonrin made by the Hangva is executed by the Hangva. It declares war and concludes peace. It has the judicial power as well. Its seating is naturally held in the house of the Awunga as assembly hall and court. This will be discussed in detail in the chapter of Political Organisation (Chatper V).

Regarding the membership of the Hangva, normally, the Awunga and Wungnaos of the clans form the Hangva. But when the population of the village grew big, or if the population of certain clans is considerably big, more members are invited from those clans. Then the household heads nominated the representatives of their clans which is approved by the Awunga and the Hangva. In early days, no one contested for the prestigious post of Hangva, and hardly any member was elected. Usuallly they offered the privilege in honour of the other as a token of mutual respect and recognition. However, the clan elders, judging the ability and efficiency of a person nominated the most capable person to represent the clan. Female membership was never allowed. Illigitimate sons are debarred from this post. A slave who had been liberated could take part in it.[21]

The Awunga conducts the Hangva meetings which is usually held in the house of the Awunga. Although the Hangva represents the entire village population, it has a leaning of modern council of ministers than the general assembly. Because, at times of greater importance, there are general assemblies of the whole village where all the grown up male adults take part in deliberation and free discussions are held. Here we find the existence of a 'form of direct democracy where the majority interest prevails. General assemblies are held or called when there are matters of great importance like war, to chalk out war strategies, village defence construction, public house constructions such as the Longshim (Bachelor's Chamber), Ngalalong (Ladies dormitories) etc. However, the Awunga and Hangva lead the general assemblies and the Awunga declares the decision made by the assembly in the House.

Although we cannot say the definite date of the formation of the Tangkhul village states, it is interesting and important to note that it existed from early times. Though small it may be it stands as an independent state and formulates its independent policies. It has never been subjected to any greater powers. In this connection, Verrier Elwin remarks,[22] concerning the Naga tribes of Manipur:

> This singular race of people, says Lieutenant Pemberton, extending north western extremity of Kachar to the frontiers of Chittagong, from their poverty and peculiar situation have escaped the sufferings inflicted by a powerful enemy on the more wealthy occupiers of the plains below them. . . . Various attempts, in the days of their prosperity and power, were made by the rajas of Manipur, Kachar, and Tipperah, to reduce these savages to a state of vassalege, but uniformly without success - they steadily refused to acknowledge allegiance to either power, and policy restrained the two first from using coersive measures, where success was, at least, doubtful, and failure would effectively have closed against them the only direct communication between their respective countries.

Despite the presence of a well organised Manipuri forces, which at time was a threat to the power of Burmese emperor in Upper Burma, the various Tangkhul village states were never put to subjection. There were several occasions of raids and counter-raids between the Meiteis and the Tangkhuls. But the party which came with well preparation and made surprise attack got the upper hand and exploited the other. Thus the Meitei Raja failed to put the Tangkhuls to subjection under him. Therefore, Alexander MacKenzie made a lengthy and elaborate remark about the nature of the raids conducted by the Meiteis against the Nagas:[23]

> . . . while Manipur, whose only system of control consisted in raids as savage as those of the Nagas themselves, did occupy Semkhor for a time and harass the Nagas in a

desultory way, the only effect of which was to bring down the hillmen upon our villages in force as soon as the Manipuris had withdrawn. Captain Jenkins, now Commissioner of Assam, who knew something of the real position of Manipur in these hills, urged upon Government the impropriety of encouraging that state in its career of aggression against the Nagas. Its troops got no pay, and had to live on the plunder of the villages to occupy. The only effect of Manipuri occupation had been to exasperate the tribes. The Government was not prepared itself to take over the Naga country and still inclined to regard the Manipuris as the defacto masters of the hills.

The state of warfare between the Meiteis and Nagas continued till the advent of the British in Manipur. After the Treaty of Yandabo 1826, the British officials in Manipur became the virtual administrators of the princely state of Manipur, and the control of the hill areas fell under the British within no time. James Johnstone along with the British, troops and Manipuri contingent made extensive tour throughout Mao and Tangkhul country.[24] There was no armed resistance offered by the Nagas, but seeing the power of the British who were the greatest world colonial power of the time in whose empire where there was no sunset, the Tangkhuls came to accept the administration of a Political agent for the hill areas of the state of Manipur. But British officials realised the importance and necessity of continuing the internal administration of the Tangkhul villages. They did not interfere in the administration of the Awunga and Hangva according to customary laws of the people except when the laws had conflict with modern advanced setup rules.

NOTES & REFERENCES

1. N.F. Cantor, Western Civilization: Its Genesis and Destiny, p. 19.
2. Samuel Enoch Stumpf, Socrates to Sarte, A History of Philosophy, p. 101.

3. N. F. Cantor, *op. cit.,* pp. 33, 41.
4. M. Horam, *Naga Polity,* p. 61.
5. M. Horam, *op. cit.,* p. 55. R. R. Shimray, *Origin and Culture of Nagas,* p. 43.
6. Romila Thapar, in the Essay "Preliminaries" of the book, *From Lineage to State,* pp. 8-12.
7. The "Tangkhul Shiyan-Yanza" (Customary Law) had been approved by the TANGKHUL LONG, the highest social organisation of the Tangkhuls which is the guardian of the Tangkhul customary laws. It has its jurisdiction over all Tangkhuls villages in Manipur.
8. R. R. Shimray, *op. cit.,* pp. 31, 32.
9. T. C. Hodson, *The Meiteis,* p. 73.
10. M. Horam, *op.cit.,* pp. 55, 56.
11. T. C. Hodson, The Meiteis, p. 74.
12. T. C. Hodson, The Naga Tribes of Manipur, p. II.
13. G.E.R. Grant Brown, ICS, *Burma Gazetteer,* Upper Chindwin District, Vol. A, pp. 9-10.
14. Norman F. Cantor, *op. cit.,* pp. 99, 100.
15. *Ibid.,* p. 88.
16. M. Horam, *Social and Cultural Life of the Nagas,* p. 76.
17. The story was narrated to the researcher by his father Hongvaileng Shimray, from the oral chronicles of Ningthi village Awunga, and he was the Awunga of the said village. This event occurred, some ten generations ago, in the village mentioned above.
18. M. Horam, *Naga Polity,* p. 81.
19. Shiyan-Yanza is the customary law of the Tangkhuls prepared by the Tangkhul Long, the highest social organisation of the tribe.
20. When the Tangkhuls observed omen by planting ginger, they removed the skin and uttered the name of god invoking his presence to be the witness and give His right judgement. They believed that if God really favours the Awungaship of a person, even the peeled ginger will grow, and if not, it will rot.

21. Actually, there is no slavery in Tangkhul society. The pride of the clan does not permit slavery even at the extreme misfortune of a person or family. But in case, a person is captured in war he remains as a captive till he has been redeemed by the family or clan. If they failed to redeem him, some one, usually the captor adopts him and in course of time, he becomes a fr e-man in the village. If he wants to return to his original village, he is permitted.

22. Verriel Elwin, *The Nagas of Nineteenth Century*, p. 42.

23. Al~ander MacKenzie, The North-East Frontier of Bengal, p. 103.

24. James Johnstone, *Manipur and the Naga Hills*. Johnstone conducted several tours over the Tangkhul country as far as Somra Tract which is beyond Manipur frontier, surveyed the land himself and applied law of justice and punished the culprit. These terms were made before 1891, after which he became Political Agent, Manipur.

3

ECONOMY

The early Tangkhul village state was economically self-sufficient.[1] The use of the term 'self-sufficiency' in the context of the Tangkhul Naga economy seeks to explain that most of the needs of the numerous villages was produced in the village itself. There was no division of labour as in other Indian villages—for in Naga villages, men had their own preoccupation and women theirs. Agriculture played the most important role in the economy of the Tangkhuls. It was, and continues to be, the mainstay of the Tangkhul economy subordinated by handicrafts, weaving, pottery, domestication of animals and trade.[2] Although Tangkhul villages were self-sufficient and usually did not produce surplus, some villages as will be mentioned later were involved in particular professions and trade, which catered not only to the village producing items like pottery, iron implements etc. But this encouraged bartering of locally produced items beyond. They also manufactured salt from salt-wells located in northern and eastern Tangkhul villages. Regarding Tangkhul village economy, R. R. Shimray remarked:[3]

> The village states are self-sufficient and independent units. Each village owned independently cultivated land, salt lake, domestic animals etc. and maintained sufficiency in rice and vegetables. They lived simple, self-contained and happy life.

Both terrace and jhum cultivation is practised by the Tangkhuls. Rice is the staple food of the Tangkhuls; but other crops like maize, millet, and job's tears are also grown. Vegetables and fruits are grown along with rice. Domestic animal rearing serve both for diet and value of exchanges, and therefore, possession of cattles was regarded as great value. Purchase of fields, feast of merit, giving to the parents of the bride in form of bride-price[4] and other high economic ventures were counted and measured by the number cattle heads. It was next to landed properties in terms of wealth in Tangkhul society.

Though the Tangkhuls did not establish industries as such, handicrafts and small manufacturing units like basketry, pottery, blacksmithy, weaving and manufacture of salt had been well developed in all the Tangkhul villages, which need not necessarily have been traded. Trade and commerce on only certain items was carried out with the neighbouring Tangkhul villages, other Naga tribes, Meiteis and Burmese.

The Tangkhuls being an agrarian society, the Awunga and Hangva exercised extensive power in controlling the agriculture and cultivation of the village land. Though wet rice cultivation is permanent and scanty, the owner having absolute right over it, the use of water channel and water system were regulated by the village administrative authority, if there arise any dispute among individuals. In the case of jhumming cultivation, the rotation of shifting cultivation rests absolutely on the decision of the Awunga and Hangva. The owner of the plot of the land cultivates it when it falls in the rotation of cultivation. But most of all, the cultivation of the whole village is affected by the village taboo[5] (Genna) where the Awunga has the absolute rights and powers to perform the rite of the taboo. When he performs the rituals and offers sacrifices to God and invokes His blessing for good harvest of the year, then only the cultivation of the village for the year begins. Here, Hodson gave a befitting remark:[6]

> The village is an economic unit, so that all the rituals observed, for the cultivation of the staple rice, necessitates the expenditure of communal energy in the form of village gennas.

Here, we can see the dominant power of the Awunga in Tangkhul economy. After the performance of genna by the Awunga, mass cultivations follow. The Tangkhul economic activities are discussed under the following heads.

Landholding System and Cultivation

The Nagas, particularly, the Tangkhuls, have a distinct form of landholding system different from the Samas, Kukis and Mizos. Whereas the former have a socialistic pattern of landholding system, in the case of the latter, the chief is the absolute owner of the whole village land. When the Tangkhuls established a village, every family had the right to procure its own plots of land for cultivation and making house. So also the Awunga of the village. Sometimes, there are clan-lands separated for the use of the clan. Then the rest of the village land was declared as public land by the Awunga-in-Council. This public land is reserved for the purpose of collecting housing materials, firewood, grazing ground and other purposes of general public interest. The new immigrants in the village got their portion of cultivation from public land. According to this landholding system, the Tangkhul village Awunga was not the owner of the village land. As such, there had been no land tax paid to the Awunga. But a certain amount of products were sent to the Awunga as his portion for being the chief and ruler of the village. Beyond the limit of the land of the chief, he does not have any right or authority on the field of his subject people. The principle of equal sharing was well maintained among the early settlers although this rule could not be applied to the later immigrants of the village. However, their case was taken care of by the clan into which they attached.

Cultivation

Every year, cultivation begins after the celebration of LUIRA PHANIT, the New Year Festival of the Tangkhuls. The Awunga opens and inaugurates the festival. First, he proclaims the days of festival a few days ahead to enable the people to make festive preparations. When the festival day comes, he performs rites and sacrifices and offers prayers to God for peace, prosperity, good health of the people and bumper harvest for the year. The festive activities are discussed in Chapter on "The Social Life of the Tangkhuls." The cultivation of the year then starts when the Awunga performs the symbolic sowing of seeds.

Wet cultivation is permanent and scanty, and therefore, the owner of the field starts working right away. But for shifting cultivation, the Awunga and his council with the help of old people of the village, take decision to where cultivation of the year falls. Because, for shifting cultivation, the field is kept fallow for years—ten to fifteen years period. The field is cultivated again, which the village elders keep in memory better than the younger people.

Wet or Terrace Cultivation

The Tangkhul cultivation pattern is rather simple and primitive. The agricultural implements consist of spade, hoe, dao, axe and sickle. However, they attained high standard of agricultural fields which, perhaps, the best of its kind. Here Sir James Johnstone rightly remarked of the Tangkhul terraced cultivation:[7]

> We passed many skillfully constructed water courses and much terrace cultivations, indeed, the Somra villages have the finest system of irrigation I have ever seen, and the long parallel line of water courses on a hillside present a most remarkable appearance.

In course of time, efficient terrace cultivation spread even to the neighbouring tribes of the Tangkhuls, especially to the Maos and Angamis. Quoting from *Imperial Gazetteer of India* (Vol. XVIII), Shimray wrote:[8]

> The Tangkhul Nagas who live in the hill east of the valley, grow transplanted rice. The sides of the hills are cut out into succession of terraces, built up with 'stone retaining walls, over which the water from the hill streams is distributed through small irrigation channels. It is from this tribe that the Angami Nagas are said to have learned the art of terracing the hills sides.

Hodson also carried the same argument that the Angamis adopted the efficient terrace system of cultivation from the Tangkhuls.[9] Indeed, there are cases where big mounds of earth are removed and reduced into terrace fields. Available water from streamlets and rivers, far and near are collected and brought to the field. Fair water distribution is regulated by the Awunga and Hangva especially when dispute arises; and overflowing water of the upper-field is made available to those who cultivate below. Stone boulders are used as retaining walls of the terrace field; and they are constructed in such a way that they withstand rain and flood for ages. Therefore, Hodson convincingly remarked: [10]

> The Tangkhuls have earned, and very deservedly, a reputation as earth workers . . . such as trenches to drain wet fields or embankments for protection against floods. They are well able to protect themselves against the rapacity of the Manipuri and measure up their work and take out rates in a style which many a Civil Engineer would approve and appreciate.

Immediately after Luira Phanit, the ground of terrace field was tilled and prepared for transplantation, waiting for the monsoon to come. But as for jhuming, the forest trees are first felled down and exposed in the sun for two to three months till they are completely dry. When they are properly dry and burnt well, it enhanced the fertility of the ground and helps bring good harvest. No doubt, the

Tangkhuls feed themselves by the strength of their hard labour without using scientific technology of cultivation.

But according to superstitious belief of the Tangkhuls, and by virtue of the position, powers and functions of the Awunga, and for good crops and bumper harvest, he is the first to sow, to plant and to harvest. First, he performs 'rituals and sacrifices (animals) and offers them to the village deity with prayers for the prosperity of the village for the year. Then he sowed ceremonial seedling. This was followed by the entire village community, because, it is a taboo for the villagers to sow before the inaugural seedling was first performed by the Awunga. This is both for jhum and terrace cultivation. Along with it, sowing of vegetables and other crops are also started.

Weeding is done two times a year—one, in the months of June/July when paddy grows ten to twelve inches; and second weeding is done in the months of August-September when the plants are about to bear fruit. However, the early-harvest which is grown earlier is harvested in the month of September, whereas, the later harvest begins in the middle of October. Harvesting completes by the end of November or early December. The close of agricultural year is marked by the celebration of Thisham Phanit, a farewell festival to the dead souls of those died in the year.

Though the Tangkhuls practise both jhum and terrace cultivation, these practices are not evenly distributed all over the Tangkhul inhabited areas. Terrace cultivation is practised more in western and northern Tangkhul villages whereas jhum cultivation is mostly carried out in eastern and southern Tangkhul. The reason is not far to seek. The first factor is that, in western and northern Tangkhul, the villages are big and there is not enough land for rotation of shifting cultivation. The land is kept fallow for a period of fifteen to twenty years, less than which, the harvest is usually poor. In western and northern Tangkhul where the villages are big and cultivable land is small, they have to return to the fallow land within a short period. In such cases, more human labour investment is required for a good harvest. Hence, they resorted to terrace cultivation more than the shifting cultivation.

But in eastern and southern Tankhul, the villages are small, and there is less population in the villages. Besides this, the villages are scattered in far distant places and there is no shortage of land for cultivation. The availability of enough land and longer period of fallowing land helps bringing good harvest. Therefore, they do not bother much to turn to permanent and wet cultivation. As a matter of fact, under the above-mentioned conditions, wide and extensive cultivations are done, in southern and eastern Tangkhul and the yield is always larger than northern and western Tangkhul villages.

Secondly, water system plays a very important role in the agriculture of the Tangkhuls. It determines agricultural pattern of the Tangkhuls. Without good water system, terrace cultivation cannot be carried out. A lowland and plain surface is another factor for the success of wet cultivation. These conditions are somehow available in western and northern Tangkhul rather than in eastern and southern Tangkhul. Extensive wet cultivations are carried wherever there are possibilities. In certain villages of eastern and southern Tangkhul, terrace cultivation is far more extensive than jhum cultivation, and in certain other villages, both jhum and terrace cultivations are practised on equal basis. Some villages are fully dependent on jhumming only. Irrespective of the pattern of cultivations, they usually enjoy good harvest every year. There is no problem of sustenance; consequently, begging is not in existence in the Tangkhul society. Even though there may be failure of crops due to calamity, the people could survive somehow or other, because, they had adopted the method of self-existence and survival. This further made the Tangkhul economy a self-sufficient economy.

Before the harvest of the year begins, the Awunga has to offer sacrifices to God and make invocation prayers for bumper harvest for the entire village-community. The same example is followed by every household, and mass harvest begins. It starts by the middle of October of the year and closes by late November or early December. But according to forefather, in olden days,[11] the harvest continued till the months of February and March of today where they carried their paddy home when tender shoots of oak trees appeared to sprout. Therefore, the Tangkhul Luira-Phanit which is the New Year Festival is held in February/March. In those days, people followed the Lunar calendar by observing the size of the moon.

Other important crops grown in Tangkhul are maize, job's tear, millet and a kind of very soft and sticklyrice. The latter three are used both for cooking and brewing rice-beer. The Tangkhuls enjoy the tender corn, but when it becomes dry, they use it for feeding pigs and chicken. Vegetables such as beans, peas, pulse, yam, tarro, potato, tomato, pumpkin, cucumber etc. are grown in plenty. They are used both for human and animal consumption. Extensive cotton cultivation was carried out for making beautiful Tangkhul clothes of various designs. According to T.C. Hodson[12] "the only crop which is frown for the purpose of export, or trade, is cotton." Actually, the Tangkhuls exported cotton to the Burmese and Meiteis of the valley. In early days, the Tangkhuls had surplus agricultural products, and regardless of social status and bearing people could perform feasts of merit, in which wealthy men fed the entire village population for days, even weeks without measure. Rice, meat and country-wine were served to all alike; and the widows and orphans and poor people found their satisfaction and quenched their thirst.

According to landholding system of the Tangkhuls, there was no land tax as such. The whole village land belonged to general public where every household acquired its own fields of cultivation. But by virtue of office of the Awunga, every household had to pay a certain amount of paddy and crops to their chief. Again, during the time of settlement, usually the clan-chiefs including the Awunga divided the village land in area-wise; and they were the nominal owners over the portion of land allotted to them apart from the declared public land. Since they were not the absolute owners of the land, the general public had every right to acquire their individual fields. In such cases, they paid tax to the land owner out of their private. In a certain case, a great warrior who brought about great victory in war, or sacrificed his life for the defence of the village was apportioned an area of land from where he was entitled to collect tax. But whatever the case might be, oppression of the people by land owner never occurred in Tangkhuls society. Whether a person harvested much or less, the tax was always nominal —only one basket of paddy or less from the people.

Both men and women work in the field. Even a child starts working at his tender age, that when he grew into age, he could survive by being alone. But in early days, because of constant inter-village war, all abled men engaged themselves in the defence of the village, and so women and children alone worked in the field. But during normal situation, they all had to work together except in hunting, house construction, felling trees for making houses, pillars and other manly activities where womanfolks could not take part. There is no humble job for the Tangkhuls. Every kind of job is honourable to them because, they uphold the principle of the dignity of labour, and labour is nothing of imposition but the necessity of life. Here it may be noted that even the Awunga worked in the field. Therefore, a girl who can work hard is the much sought after in marriage market. The same applies to men.

The monotony and hard labour of the Tangkhuls is compensated by the Tangkhul technique of working together of boys and girls of the same age-group. This is known as YARTHOT. Youngsters of the same age of the village (in case of small village) or Tang (a block of the village in case of- bigger village) work together in their fields by rotation, and they continue the rotation of work till the field of each member is done. This is explained by a Tangkhul scholar:[13]

> Yarthot (Age-Group) was for the youngfolks. Their main objective was to exchange labour during the cultivation time. . . . The strongest and the weakest had the same privilege in all respects relating to social enterprises.

In Yarthot where boys and girls of same age work together in rotation, the family where the term of Yarthot falls has to provide lunch in the field with dainty food items. The joy and happiness of boys and girls meeting together and work makes them so much spirited that they do not feel tired of labour. Despite a member being sick, or meeting some misfortune as such he/she cannot join the Yarthot for a day or two, the chain of labour cannot be broken. It continues as it is, and even at the absence of their member, the group works in his/her field out of love and team spirit. Group labour leads some boys and girls to marriage. It is an opportunity of choosing one's life partner.

Sometimes, exchange of labour and competition between two different groups is also done. Here the two second best—one boy and one girl are chosen from their group and sent them to the other group to compete with them in the field. The same thing is also done from the other group and sent them to the first group for the exchange of labour and competition. However, the best two, a boy and a girl are always retained in their respective group in order to meet the competition of the two coming from the other group. In this way, the skill of labour of a boy or a girl is exhibited, which is highly honoured in this agrarian society. It is one of the best criteria of a youngster in marriage market where such a person is highly demanded. No doubt, hard worker is respected as a man of great quality in agrarian societies since it is the mainstay of their life.

In group working, the work is accompanied with a harmonious-singing and producing a harmonious tone of ho-ho. There are different songs of work depending on the nature of the work. For example, there are different songs for tilling the ground, songs of transplantation, harvest etc. Hard labour is sometimes interfered by good humour of jokes with a hearty laugh. Therefore, there is a relief in the midst of toil, laughter in sweats. Singing as they work and healthy joke of laughter minimises the fatigue. Sometimes teasing and insults to competitors make them to land in hot exchange of words - and quarrel which later become another form of joke again. Such is the technique and instrument of Tangkhul labour and thus, the team work is highly desired and coveted. This helps the development and progress of Tangkhul economy. Those who cannot participate in Yarthot feel very much insulted and humbled. The people really long for it.

There is no Yarthot of married men because they involve in village war and defence. But it is not totally absent in their society. They really practised it when there was no danger of war. However, married women have their own working group known as Parei-Yar meaning the working group of wives. They also work in turn in their respective fields. But it is to say that, Yarthot is not only for the grown up people. Children of tender age who can handle agricultural implements also form their Yarthot as early as seven to eight years of age. It is like schooling of children today in our present society.

Technology of Implements

Agricultural implements of the Tangkhuls are rather primitive and unspecialized. Despite the scientific and technological development of modern age, there is no change in their implements except the use of animals for ploughing the fields. Thus, the method of agriculture and cultivation remains simple and unmodified. But they put their, hard labour in agriculture. The agricultural implements which they widely use are hoes, spades, daos, axes and sickles. Spades and hoes of bigger size are used for terrace cultivation whereas, daos, axes, hoes of small size are used for clearing the jungle for shifting cultivation, and hoes are meant for sowing paddy seeds and weeding. Sickle is used in second weeding of jhum cultivation and for the harvest of both terrace and jhum cultivations. In early days, people were not aware of chemical fertilizer and they depended only on natural fertility of the soil. Good harvest was, therefore, mainly at the mercy of natural soil and favourable monsoon of the year. The field are watched constantly against animals, birds, rats and other insects and pests of the crops.

The Tangkhuls, when they were at Samsok, used to import iron from Taunghai, a market at the Chindwin river port where the Burmese sold in large quantity. Later on, when they settled down at present Tangkhul area, they imported iron both from the Meiteis of Imphal valley and Burma. The village blacksmith made all agricultural implements, war weapons, hunting and fishing instruments. But most of the village-folks had the skill of making their own implements, that their dependence on village blacksmith was very much insignificant despite the presence of some skilled workers in iron works.

Other Crops

Chilly cultivation is a minor, but inalienable crop of the Tangkhuls. It is beyond doubt and argument that, they consumed considerable amount of chilly. Ginger, onion, pumpkin, cucumber, tobacco and other vegetables are grown both in the field and homestead. According to Hodson, potato was grown only by the Tangkhuls among the Naga tribes of Manipur. Further, he stated that wild tea and rubber were also grown or found in the hill countryside of Manipur.[14] However, tea is grown by the Nagas of Manipur, though it is done in a very limited way for domestic consumption only. According to Grant Brown, one British writer:[15]

> Tea is grown in the Kowya, Maungkan, Tazon, Maingwe, Tamanthi and some other village tracts, all on the Chindwin above Homalin. The wild plant is not found, and it is

probable that the cultivation was introduced by the Nagas from Manipur.

These are the subordinate agricultural products of the Tangkhuls which helped their economic development for self-sufficiency. They have both wild and domestic bamboos which is used in making houses, basketry and weaving mats. Domestic bamboos are bigger and better in quality that they are grown for various purposes. No wonder, almost all their domestic materials, like making traps, war weapons, pikes for village fencing against the approach of the enemies are all made of bamboos. Collection of firewood and housing materials are taken from both public land and private lands.

Horticulture

In the past, the Tangkhuls did not practise horticulture as such. However, sporadic fruit plantations were there at places where they were convenient to grow. Except from animals, they did not require fencing or watching for fear of thieves and robbers. They were left uncare of for the whole season waiting for the fruits in its own time except some irregular visit to see the condition of the plants and their fruits. Some are planted at homestead.

However, with modern education and development of road and communication, and better transport facilities, emphasis is given in growing fruits and other cash crops for local consumption as well as commercial purposes. With proper guidance and capital, Nagas, with the promise of the land, one day may become one of the biggest fruit producers and exporters in the region.

Horticulture of banana, orange, lemon, plum, pears, and coffee plantations are coming up fast. All these are private and individual enterprise, and due to lack of state subsidy, the venture cannot be more successful. Again, due to absence of market facilities, the products cannot bring much return.

Domestication of Animals

The Tangkhuls are fond of meat as other Naga tribes are; and they eat almost all kinds of meats. Therefore, in order to meet the demand of meat, they domesticate animals as much as they can. However, domestication of animals was selective in early days. Rearing goats and eating mutton was prohibited, because, according to their belief, by eating its flesh, a person became forked tongue. Therefore, rearing goats is a recent practice. The domestic animals the Tangkhuls keep today, and before are cows, bulls, buffaloes, mithuns, pigs, dogs, cats and chicken. It has been in practice since time immemorial. According to the Tangkhul custom, during the time of migration in search of suitable place for (settlement) they used to take a crowing cock for omen, and they believed that when it crows with a tone of high and low voice, the place is regarded to be good for their settlement. Peace, prosperity, increase of population and victory in war are insued for them. When the Tangkhuls were moving in the Chindwin Valley and Samsok, they moved along with pigs, and they acted as the main agent of searching water.

Though rearing animals serves to supplement their diet, it is also used for commercial purposes. No doubt, their daily meals cannot be enjoyable without the taste of meat. But there is no regular butcher for daily supply of meat. Therefore, every family has to rear their own livestocks. This made them ready availability of meat. Again, entertaining a guest without meat is disgraceful and meat should be made available for the guest who may come unexpectedly—whether friend or a stranger. Further during the festivals, meat and rice beer were the most important food items without which a festival was not worth the name. All kinds of festivals are favoured by killing a number of bulls, buffaloes, pigs etc. where dogs and chicken are not usually counted. The strength of a Feast of Merit offered by rich man is measured by the number of cattles killed. Moreover, in the marriage of the Tangkhuls, the family of the groom has to pay the so called bride price to the parents of the girl in terms of cattle heads. Hence animal husbandry plays an important role in the economy of the Tangkhuls, and this serves the commercial purposes of the people. Purchase of field is also measured in terms of cattle and iron pieces. Therefore, cattles are used as a unit of value before the emergence of money economy.

All kinds of criminal punishments were also measured in terms of cattle heads due to absence of money economy in early days. The breach of the law, those who failed to turn up in the village social work, common labour and other social activities were also punished and fined in the form of livestock, either a cow or buffalo, or pig depending on the nature of the case. Indeed, a cattle was regarded as the highest unit-value of the movable properties. Apart from possessing landed properties like terrace fields, jhum-land, forest land etc., the possession of cattles was counted as riches and wealth. In this way, a person earns social prestige by the strength of cattle-wealth he had; and those people who possessed a good number of animals could perform Feast of Merit in the village.

However, taking milk was averse to the Tangkhuls in the past as in many other tribal societies of the region. They never took milk, and no cattle was milked. Taking fresh milk is a matter of recent occurrence. This was another feature of the Tangkhuls and Nagas in rearing cattles.

Hunting, fishing and trapping formed another source of meat supply to the Tangkhuls. A village which has vast forest land and big rivers was more favourable for hunting and fishing. These two games are carried out during favourable seasons only. Group hunting and fishing are more or less games of enjoyment than hankering for meat. Whether group hunting and fishing or individual enterprise, or whatever the case it may be, the Awunga and Wungnaos had their portions from the hunted games. There are also portions of meat for the Hangva that when a good amount of such meats are collected, the councillors had their feast when the Hangva was in session. But hunting and fishing are limited within the territory of the village. If the game happens to escape into the territory of a neighbouring village, a portion of the game should go to the said village. Hunting is exclusively the game of men whereas fishing can be done both by men and women. Children who can participate may join it.

Since the Nagas lived a simple and rustic life, their needs were limited to basic necessities only, and the resources to meet those needs were readily available, and they are within the reach of the people. Labour is honoured and respected, while laziness and dependency on others was counted as a reproach and burden to the society. So by nature and life-style of the people, every Naga was supposed to be able to live by himself.

Industry

In early days, there was no industry of modern technology in Tangkhul area. Even today modern industrialization is yet to this society in a larger way. However, they have developed small scale industries and cottage of their own from remote past. Some of their industries attained high efficiency, and their products are of superb quality. We may discuss them under the following heads.

Blacksmith

The Tangkhuls, being basically an agrarian society they had a reasonably developed blacksmith industry from early days, because their life and occupation was involved in the production of agricultural implements and war weapons. They also neede of necessary implements for making houses and household materials. The use of iron by the Tangkhuls can be as old as the introduction of agriculture. These requirements were made by villag : blacksmiths from the iron imported from Burma and the Meiteis of the valley. Though there were some skilled workers in iron, almost all menfolk of the village had the art of making their requirements. Due to lack of sophisticated equipments and tools, the instruments and materials they produced are yet to improve. Appreciating this skill, Hodson notes:[16] "They display no mean skill in minor manufactures, but their tools are yet unspecialized." The articles they made were daos, axes, hoes, spades, sickles, spears, arrow-heads, chisels etc. With these simple and limited tools, the Tangkhuls could meet the necessities of their lives.

Handicrafts

In Tangkhul, natural resources viz., wood, bamboo, cane and other forest products are bountifully available, and due to easy accessibility to material resources, they have rich culture in handicrafts such as wood-carving, basketry, mat weaving and other domestic articles. Wooden drums for storing water, rice, rice-beer; wooden box for keeping cloths and other valuable things are made by themselves in large number. Giant pounding tables of four feet by ten feet were made of a huge wood logs and carried home from far distant forest. Some of these have lasted for a century. The Tangkhul attained excellency in making wooden plates of various sizes and designs. The woodcrafts so much perfect that the only improvement they need is painting and colouring. Certain wooden dishes of extraordinary size used for giving bath to children can contain a few children. Since there were no industrial manufactured goods available to the Tangkhuls, most of the domestic articles for their daily use were made of wood and bamboo.

Basketry and mat weaving are another important handicraft of the Tangkhuls, and varieties of bamboos and canes helped them produce baskets of different sizes and designs to suit their purposes of daily use. They made baskets of extraordinary size of 20 to 25 feet circumference and 5 to 6 feet high with narrow neck and lid for storing paddy either in the dwelling house or in the granaries. Baskets for keeping cloths, containers, carrier and mats are all made of bamboos. But articles of this kind made of canes are of high quality which are mostly made by the .eastern Tangkhul Nagas. They make morah, a seating article and Liphan, a dining table of bamboo and cane. These articles are more popular today. Bamboo and cane mats are used for wall as well as for seating. Bamboos are used for carrying water, drinking vessel and container.

Apart from basketry and mat weaving, bamboo materials are used for housing. The walls of dwelling houses, granaries etc. are all made of bamboo and wood (planks). The use of bamboo in Naga society is next to wood only. No house could be made without bamboo ropes and slits for thatching the roof and tying things together, and so on.

Bamboo and cane are used for making ornaments and decorations like head-gears, helmets, legging, and other festive decorations. Cooking in a utensil of bamboo tube has a high quality taste, which is still very popular in Burma. During hunting and journey, people use to cook in bamboo tubes. Due to availability of vast forest land, wood and bamboos are readily acquired by the people, especially by the eastern Tangkhuls; and they are more skillful in these professions. Hodson has remarked: "The skill and ingenuity with which they make baskets, collars, gaiters, armlets, headbands of plaited cane are very notable."[17]

Pottery

Pottery is an important asset of human civilization. Whether earthen pot, utensil, or whatever the case may be, without cooking food, no human culture and civilization can progress and develop. The art of pottery had been developed in Tangkhul since remote past, although no definite date can be ascertained regarding the origin of it. However, it is beyond doubt and argument that Tangkhul pottery is one of the oldest industries of the people which is still continuing and improving.

Almost all the villages of the Tangkhuls had pottery. But Hodson, the chief authority of the Naga tribes of Manipur remarked:[18] "Three clans of Hundung and the village of Nunbi make earthen pots from beds of clay close to their villages." He continued further:

> They make vessels of all sizes. These vessels are devoid of any but simplest ornamentation, but are, nevertheless, strong and well-suited to the requirements of the purchasers and command a large sale over the whole of Tangkhul country.

The method of making jars, pots and vessels is very simple and primitive. From early days till today, no improvement of technology has been developed so far. They do not use wheel and other advance tools for making pots. They simply collect two kinds of earth materials—one is clay and the other is a kind of pottery stone. Both the clay and stone are ground to powder, mixed together; and applying water, moulded the earth with hands into any form and size they required. Finally, they are tempered in a furnace outside the village. The pot is then ready for use.

The Tangkhuls make not only cooking pots and vessels, but they also make jars the size of some of which is very big. The height varies from 3 to 4 feet high. Today, the people of Longbi (Nungbi) village have made pressure cooker of earthen ware. They make vase, container and decorative vessels.

During the field study of the author, he contacted several potters at Longbi village, the only surviving village of potters. The other villages have lost this art as manufactured utensils are readily available today. Among them, the skill of Machihan Sasa, son of Kuishum Sasa of Longbi village, Ukhrul District in Manipur State is worth-mentioning. He is considered one of the best potters in India. He bagged several awards both at state and national level. At one time, he got the best national award in pottery in all India pottery competition. In 1987, he got the State Award of Manipur in pottery. On 26th January 1991, he got one gold medal, a cash award of Rs. 10,000/- and one red woollen shawl (a shawl of honour) for his excellence in the field of earthenware. Again on Manipur State Day (February 3, 1991), he got both State and National Awards from Manipur and the Central Government of India. In one pottery competition at all India level held in the State of Haryana in 1992, he got the best award—one Gold plate and Medal because of his excellence and perfection in pottery. Appreciating the skill, excellence and achievements of Machihan Sasa, the Office of the Development Commissioner, Handicrafts, and Office of the Development Commissioner, Handlooms, Ministry of Textiles, Government of India certified him and recorded: "Sri Machihan Sasa receives the National Award for excellence in Hamphai Pottery", National Award for Master Craft persons and Master Weavers, 1988. The technique of making earthen vessels remains unchanged till today. The people have not sought to improve their skill and neither the governmental agencies have been successful to have a change in pottery making of the Tangkhuls.

Weaving

Weaving is another important industry of the Tangkhuls. They make varieties of cloths, shawls, loin cloths for both men and women, cloth fit for the use of Awunga, married men and women, youngsters-boys and girls. The most important Tangkhul cloth are Leirum, Haora, Thangan, Changkhom, Yangrei etc. They are speckled with white, black, red and green colours. Single colour cloths are also made by the Tangkhuls. No machine—made cloths and textiles have been able to match the fineness and quality of the Tangkhul cloth. Their age-old handloom has therefore, been retained even today, although, it is rather painstaking and time consuming process to produce even a single cloth. This is because, the designs and fashions of their cloth bear the identity and culture of the people and its popularity increases with the awareness of national and communal identities in the world today. Again, no fashion of cloth and textiles, however, costly they may be, can replace the ceremonial cloth of the Awunga and those who perform feast of merit and heroes of war. This makes the Tangkhuls and other Naga tribes to retain their traditional method of making tribal cloth.

Some European writers have different pictures with regard to the cloth manufacture of the Tangkhuls. According to James Johnstone:[19]

> Four villages, in the Tangkhul country, apparently monopolised the bulk of the cloth manufactures, and different tribal patterns were made to suit the purchase. Some of these cloths are very handsome and strong, and calculated to wear for a long time.

However, Hodson, on the other hand, had a different assessment and wrote:[20]

> Six Tangkhul villages, Ukhrul, Toloi, Naimu, Sandang, Tuinem, Phadang are specially engaged in the industry of cloth weaving. They obtained the raw cotton from the Manipuri women in the Sena Keithel or Royal Bazaar, the main centre of commerce of the state.

Yet it is a fact that, almost all the villages of Tangkhul grew cotton in large quantity that they even exported cotton to Burma since early days. The Meiteis purchased cotton from hill people including the Tangkhuls. As such, Tangkhul villages made cloth for their use. Efficiency and skill of making cloths may be different from village to village, and no doubt, the cloths made in western Tangkhul are more popular and demanded than others because of quality. Northern Tangkhuls were a little behind the others. However, today, they manufacture cloths in the same footing as other Tangkhuls.

Weaving is exclusively the occupation of women in Naga society; and so, it is a taboo for men to weave cloth, even to touch the weaving materials, especially in the days when a person is observing taboo for a venture like war, hunting etc. Weaving, being an indoor business, can be carried out throughout the year. However, cloth manufacture is preferably done in the intervals of field works, e.g., immediately after ploughing the terrace-field and clearing the forest of jhum on one hand, and before the advent of transplantation and sowing seeds on the other. During the break of field work, women are very busy collecting firewood and making cloths. So also, they make cloth during the interval of first weeding and second weeding. But intensive weaving is carried out immediately after the harvest where women folks are very busy making, beautiful cloths for their families for the coming Luira-Phanit. In this festival, many festive activities like beauty contest and virginity test of the unmarried girls are held. Usually girls start learning the technique of making cloths from four-five years of age, and when they attain teen-age, they are well versed in weaving cloths and can manage themselves to meet their needs, and support their parents, brothers and sisters. They make cloths for commercial purposes and the money they earn from weaving are used to buy things of luxury and comfort.

Different kinds of barks of jungle trees were used for the purpose of dyeing cloths, and this was practised before manufactured dyeing materials were available in the market. The Tangkhuls dyed cloths in black, blue, red and orange. Mixed dyeing materials produce different colour again. It has been practised by the Tangkhuls from remote past.

Of the various types and patterns of Tangkhul cloths,[21] Changkhom is meant for women, and unmarried boys and girls. Hoara is made for the use of menfolks and for those unmarried males who have attained well-grown up stage. Thangan is worn by clan chiefs and village elders as a sign of honour and position. Wearing Luirum is assigned to old and aged people in the village. It is also a sign of honour of the aged ones in the village. However, this cloth is mostly purchased from the Meiteis of Imphal. The village Awunga and those who offer feast of merit are entitled to wear a special type of cloths printed with different patterns. This type of cloths is not allowed to be used by common people as it carries the mark of honour and status of the wearer. They are specially decorated for this purpose. Womenfolks wear loin-cloths as their skirt covering their lower body reaching down the knees, but not a ove the knees as a token of modesty and respect to man. However, making it lower is commendable.

Whatever different types and fashions of Tangkhul cloths may be, they have a pattern of design known as aphor which is distinctly different from all kinds of Naga cloths. This pattern is used by the Tangkhuls only; and therefore, it bears the identity of the Tangkhul tribe. The Aphor is designed at the edge of border of the cloth where "The stripes of the decorative border are pointed like the pattern on a backgammon board, and when these cloths are new and in good condition, they are very handsome."[22] Hodson described it "as trade marks, possibly as 'luck' marks, and therefore possessing a magical value, and as ornmanets, their presence adding to the price."[23] No doubt, the quality and designs of tangkhul cloths remain unbeaten that he described them in the following way:[24]

> It is hardly necessary to say that this process is slow and labourious and Manipuri competition is beginning to be felt. Manchester goods find no market here because no attempt is made to study and understand native requirements, customs and desires.

Indeed, the beauty of Tangkhul cloths was rich that even Verrier Elwin remarked.[25] "Their women make cloths superior to any of other tribes excepting the Murrings."

Even though there are several invasions of foreign cloths of different fashions, designs and purposes in modern era, but the beauty and utility of Tangkhul cloths stands undiminished. Rather, because of social, political, economic and literary intercourses over the world, the popularity of Tangkhul cloths increases; and people are now, realising the importance of their cloths even at the merging and changing situation they live in today. In early days, cloths were made of cotton yarns of both countrymade and imported from outside. However, now-a-days, they are made of wool only. The use of cotton in this respect is very insignificant.

Salt Manufacture

Salt manufacture was not a wide-spread activity in Tangkhul country. However, there were several salt-wells from the brines of which they manufactured salt. Although salt making is not an easy job for the people due to lack of modern salt making technology, people's demand for country salt is very high. It is used not only for daily normal consumption, but the locally manufactured salt is used in medicine as well. Despite the inflow of modern drugs and other chemical products, the use of salt-powder and salt liquid as medicine is still continuing in the countryside. This makes the country-salt popular and in demand.

The important salt-brines were located at Marem, Namrei, Chatlao, Maremphung in northern Tangkhul; Kongkan and Sanam in eastern Tangkhul and at some places in southern Tangkhul near Imphal valley which had been controlled by Meitei Raja. In western Tangkhul, an important spring is found in a river bed between Ngari and Thiva villages (now in Senapati District). There are still some salt springs which have not been explored.

Salt from those places was supplied not only to different Tangkhul villages, but even to the people living beyond the frontier of Tangkhuls. At times, the Meitei Raja tried to monopolise the salt manufacture of some Tangkhul villages.

But they failed in securing it due to strong resistance of the Tangkhuls. Hodson commented about the salt manufacture of Tangkhul and its supply to different Naga tribes in early days. He wrote:[26]

> The salt thus manufactured is full of impurities but meets with a ready sale among the hill people, so that the salt wells are a meeting place for all sorts of traders, men from Naga Hills, from Khonoma and Jotsoma, and from the Somra villages.

The salt wells of Kongkan and Sanam were located at the Burma border, and so the Burmese also came and manufactured salt from those wells. Today, because of the international law which is strictly imposed, crossing the border is prohibited. But the neighbouring villagers still continue to come across the border and make salt for their own consumption. The Awunga of the respective salt-wells have the right to control over the salt manufacture of their wells. There are cases when the Awunga collected nominal tax when neighbouring villagers come to make salt. Some amount of salt had to be shared to the Awunga concerned. But the tax was paid in the form of cloth, chicken, paddy etc. The Awunga also had the right to impose tax on salt manufactured by his own villagers.

It is no wonder that the Tangkhul got sufficient salt supply from those salt brines. That there was surplus salt is evident that people from beyond their frontier purchased the commodity from the Tangkhuls. According to Lima Imchen,"[27] the Aos also got their salt supply from the Tangkhuls. Further, he said that the salt supply of the Tangkhuls crossed even the frontier of Ao country.

Trade and Commerce

A Tangkhul village was basically a self-sufficient unit. A village could exist by itself from its own economic resources and products. But all Tangkhul villages did not produce the same goods and commodities. One village may be rich in certain goods and commodities but poor in other areas which were found abundantly in other villages. Hence the need of exchange of goods arose. It led to the exchange of goods and services among them. This could be achieved through trade and commerce, and therefore, inter-village trade and commerce had been in practice among the Tangkhul villages since very early days. This strengthened the economy of the people and improved their living condition. Sometimes inter-village trade and commercial contact helped establishment of diplomatic relationship and war alliances; and thus small and weak villages found secure from the threat of bigger and hostile villages. For instance, at a time, the eastern Tangkhul fell under the threat of the Meitei Raja. There the village of Ningthi and other neighbouring villages made alliance with Khangkhui village and its neighbours which were bigger and therefore, stronger. The latter agreed to help the former in the war; and in return they contributed their agricultural products like chilly, ginger, sesamum etc. They also arranged great feast by killing animals where they feasted together with merriment; and strengthened their diplomatic and trade relationship.

There was, and still is continuing, a village fair called LEINGAPHA in Tangkhul hills—where buying and selling and exchange of goods was carried out. The dates and seasons may be different from village to village. However, different dates of holding village fair from village to village serve the people the opportunity to participate in buying and selling at other villages, where there was no such fair of their own. Naturally, the Awunga fixed the date of the village fair weeks ahead allowing the people to prepare for it so that when the actual day came, there might be a good sale and buying in the village. All kinds of-'economic goods and items, available in the villages such as foodstuffs, cloths, handicraft products, beads, meat, live animals etc. were sold and bought in the village market.

Other villagers were also welcome in the Leingapha. According to traditions and stories, narrated by our forefathers,"[28] the first known fair held was at Hongkha-Muja, a twin village at Ango-Ching (Patkoi-Range) as mentioned in Chapter I, after the Tangkhul shifted from Zibyu Taung and Chindwin Valley under the leadership of Kabo-Khari and Chaphang-Hong. All sorts of articles were brought from different directions and surrounding villages and made the Leingapha a grand fair. This was held every year. Selling and buying continued for days, even weeks; and along with it, there was merry-making with songs, dances and sports competition. Similar Leingapha, was held at Samsok kingdom where the fairs were more elaborate. According to tradition, it lasted for a month where hectic competitions in sports, virgin-dance, song competition etc. were conducted.

The Leingapha of the Tangkhuls continued even after their settlement at present area without diminishing its importance and merry-making. Indeed, it can be held several times in a year according to convenience. But the biggest of its kind, and the most convenient season in a year is in January-February of the year along with the celebration of Luira-Phanit which is the New Year Festival of the Tangkhuls. Perhaps the Samsok fair was held in this season that the Virgin-Dance was performed along with it. The Virgin-Dance is usually held along with Luira-Phanit in the months mentioned above.

Today, we can see changes in keeping the date and season. Hundung village, for some unexplained reasons holds the fair in the month of October. In early days, Paoyi village was a big centre of Leingapha of the northern Tangkhuls. In this fair, people of surrounding villages of Tangkhul, some of them are in Senapati District, participated and carried on selling, buying and athletic competitions. According to R. R. Shinıray,[29] some 300 years ago, on one of the Luira-Phanit festivals of Paoyi village, as nature of the feast, the athletes challenged one another in wrestling, spear throwing and other sport activities. In one episode, Kapang of Ngari village challenged Luivao, chief of Longpi village publicly. But because of his giant figure and his fame in war, Luivao could not accept the challenge. However, in order to save the face and prestige of the chief, Maringthei, a bossom friend of the chief took the challenge. He was a man of excellent health and sturdy physique, but not a match of the huge size of Kapang. To the surprise of spectators, the giant was down in wrestling competition, and lost the game. Hundung village was the place for the fair of the surrounding area called Kathur-Mashang. But the biggest fairs were held at Hangkha-Muja and Samsok palace in eastern and southern Tangkhul. At a Virgin-Dance competition held at Samsok palace, Langtung Zangengla was declared the most beautiful girl of the time.

Before the advent of money, the medium of exchange was barter system, goods exchanged for other goods. So in commercial business of the Tangkhuls, one commodity was exchanged for another. Cattle was regarded as the highest unit value of movable goods and property. Therefore, cattle was used for exchange of costly things. Bride-price was discussed and determined in terms of cattle heads. So also the feast of merit is measured in terms of cattles killed. Money economy came into being in Tangkhul country with the establishment of the British colonial control over the region. Even in those days, the flow of money in Tangkhul was meagre.

Tax

Despite a small circulation of money economy, the Tangkhuls when they came under indirect British administration were to pay a house tax of Rs. 3/- per house.[30]

This was collected first by the Meitei Lambu and later by the village headman, and in this case, by the Awunga and deposited to the office of the Manipur Maharaja. The Awunga was usually given a commission for this collection.

The hill tribes did not pay any land revenue. According to Shakespear,[31] who was Political Agent and Superintendent of the British in Manipur, the house tax of Rs. 3/- was not high as the hill people could easily earn this amount and more from forest products.

Trade and commerce was not confined to among the Tangkhuls only. They were also involved in inter-tribal trade and commerce with the neighbouring states as well. In the earliest period, the Burmese were the biggest trade partners of the Tangkhuls, particularly, the eastern Tangkhul Nagas through Samsok, and the northern Tangkhuls through Somra tract. They established trade relationship with the Zawbas (Avas and Shans) and Kachins of northern Burma. In the north, the Maos, Angamis and other Naga tribes had close trade relations with the Tangkhuls which was further strengthened by salt manufactured in northern Tangkhul. In the west, they had trade partnership with the Meiteis, Mayangs and the Kacharis of Kachar and Silchar. But the forefathers said that, the trading venture in Kachar and Silchar was not much encouraging due to climatic condition as the climate of Kachar and Silchar was not salubrious for the hillmen. They often suffered from malaria and typhoid while in the Surma valley.

The ancient Tangkhuls, including those who are living in Naga Hills of Burma had intensive trade relations with the Shans and Avas (Burmans). The Tangkhuls, being largely an agrarian society, imported iron pieces for making agricultural implements and tools. But their supply consisted of agricultural products and precious stones etc. A large amount of precious stones and gold was found in Tangkhul areas of Burma, particularly in the region of Chindwin river Valley and its tributaries. Regarding the trade of the

Tangkhuls with Burma, Grant Brown, an authority of Upper Chindwin District remarked: [32]

> There are practically no other exports by way of the river, but salt, iron, cotton, piece-goods, and other articles are supplied to the Chins and Nagas along the border. . . . The Chins and Nagas supply bee wax, maize-leave, mats etc. in exchange of articles mentioned above as supplied to them.

Again, on another occasion, Brown recorded:[33]

> Gold dust is found in the Chindwin and other streams which flow into it from the east, but appears to be most plentiful in the Uyu river and its tributaries; in fact, some of the inland villages in the Maingkaing township have had a gold currency from time immemorial. . . . The chief exports of the district are teak and rice . . . and also a large proportion of other timber, bamboo and canes, and other forest products.

The export of the Tangkhuls to the Meiteis were mostly agricultural products like, cotton, maize, potato, peas, sesamum, soybean, ginger, chilly etc. In return, they imported iron pieces and the local manufactured goods of the Meiteis for making Tangkhul cloths. Iron goods, salt, Manipuri handloom cloths were also brought from the Meiteis of Imphal. Supply of logs, timber and wood to Imphal valley is a matter of recent development, though in early days, the Meiteis imported it from the Tangkhuls in lesser amount. Cooking utensils and other household articles were later imported from the Meiteis, from Silchar, and from Burma.

Agriculture, small scale industries, Lingapha and trade and commerce of the Tangkhuls stand as the assets of the Tangkhul economy. Grant writes: "The wants of the people are extremely few and are largely supplied at home."[34] Division of labour was not needed, and indeed, there was no such division of labour since every Tangkhul was familiar to all kinds of livelihood. No doubt, there were some skilled workers in certain areas like carpentry, blacksmith, basketry etc., whose skills were used for the village and its economy. Exchange of goods and services is, was and continues to be an important element in the economic life of the Tangkhuls.

NOTES & REFERENCES

1. A. R. Desai, *Social Background of Indian Nationalism*, pp. 7-13, has been applied with some changes to suit the Tangkhul Naga situation.
2. Trade did not constitute a very important aspect of Tangkhul Naga economy. It was used to supplement certain deficiency and requirements. Trade did not necessarily touch on all Tangkhul Naga villages.
3. R. R. Shimray, *Origin and Culture of Nagas*, p. 46.
4. Actually, there is no dowry system or bride price in Tangkhul marriage. Some cattles are given to the parents of the girl as gifts. This point is well explained in the Section of 'Marriage' in Chapter IV.
5. The word Genna comes from Angami word 'Kanyu' meaning Taboo, forbidden—forbidden to speak, to touch or to do—by custom and religion. But in Naga society, the term 'taboo' is also used in sanctification of a day or days, set aside and observe it in order to perform religious rites, ceremonies and sacrifices to propitiate the spirits; or on account of death, calamities etc. which occurred in the village. In those days, any form of labour is strictly prohibited. But most writers w ongly interpreted Genna that even joyful festivals are also termed as Genna.
6. T. C. Hodson, *The Naga Tribes of Manipur*, p. 166.
7. James Johnstone, *Manipur and the Naga Hills*, p. 231.
8. R. R. Shimray, cited in his book, *Origin and Culture of the Nagas*, p. 159.
9. T. C. Hodson, *op. cit.*, p. 54.
10. *Ibid.*, p. 4 9.
11. In early days, the Tangkhul forefathers did not have the calendar system of today. They had their Lunar calendar. In those day, when they carried paddy home, it is said that the oak trees had

already sprouted tender shoots. By other way of speech, they said that they walked on dry leaves of the oak. The new and tender shoots sprout in the month of March usually.

12. T. C. Hodson, *The Naga Tribes of Manipur,* p. 55.
13. Y. K. Shimray, *An Interpretation to Tribal Language and Culture of Manipur,* p. 10 .
14. T. C. Hodson, *op. cit.,* p. 56.
15. G.E.R. Grant Brown, *Burma Gazetteer,* Upper Chindwin District, p. 37.
16. T. C. Hodson, *Naga Tribes of Manipur,* p. 39.
17. *Ibid.,* p. 50.
18. *Ibid.,* pp. 47, 48.
19. James Johnstone, *op. cit.,* p. 184.
20. T. C. Hodson, *op. cit.,* p. 45. Of these six villages the proper names of two need clarification: Naimu-Ngainga, Sandang-Somdal.
21. R. R. Shimray, *op.cit.,* pp. 212-217.
22. T. C. Hodson, *op. cit.,* p. 47.
23. *Ibid.,* p. 46.
24. *Ibid.,* p. 46.
25. Verrier Elwin, *The Nagas of Nineteenth Century,* p. 490.
26. T. C. Hodson, *op. cit.,* p. 48.
27. An interview with Lima Imchen. Lecturer in Sociology, NEHU, Shillong, 4th September, 1994. Also see J. H. Hutton, The Angami Nagas, p. 70.
28. According to oral tradition, when the fair was held at Hongkha-Muja, the people of Ningthi village, beat the Log-Drum, the sound of which could be heard as far as Hongkha-Muja, located a hundred miles away.
29. R.R. Shimray, *op. cit.,* p. 86.
30. Manipur State Archives, *Manipur State Administrative Report* of Lieut. Col. H. St. P. Maxwell, Pol. Agent in Manipur and Superintendent of the State (1891-1895).

31. Manipur State Archives, *Administrative Report of Manipur* by J. Shakespear, Political Agent and Superintendent, (1904-05).

32. G.E.R. Grant Brown, *op. cit.*, p. 42.

33. *Ibid.*, p. 41.

34. *Ibid.*, p. 41.

4

SOCIAL SETTING

The Tangkhuls are one of the major tribes of the Nagas and they live a well organised social life under the leadership of the village chief called Awunga. Many writers have branded the Naga people as nasty, brutish, ravage, uncivilized, naked and head-hunters.[1] By expressing such opinions, they have ignored the inborn qualities of the Nagas-their love, honesty, sincerity, bravery and love of independence without interference from outside. In this connection, M. Horam. remarks:[2]

> There are elaborate moral codes in a tribal society. The outsiders, the so-called civilized man—very often arrive at the hasty conclusion that the tribes live a life of unbridled licence and youthful corruption. In their approach, they commit two errors; one of method and one of fact. Their method of approach is wrong, for they import their own ideas and standard into tribal culture and judge their culture by theirs. They are also wrong in point of view. Tribal life regulated by exact and far reaching unwritten laws which are strictly obeyed.

However, those who go deeper into the social life of the Nagas cannot but agree that, they are a people, well-organised, simple, happy, honest to one another, ready to admit his own fault when one has wronged a person; but never a coward, rather ready to sacrifice his life for the society whose social structure is based on the principles of traditional and customary laws, well-tried and preserved for generations. This type of life is hardly found among the so-called civilized peoples of the world. This is further elaborated by J. P. Mills, who wrote:[3]

> Agriculture is the sole means of livelihood and all wealth is in grain and cattle.... Every girl marries as a matter of course. Prostitution is unknown. . . . There is no destitute, orphan and aged people are looked after by their clans. . . . Grain and cattle are values not to be hoarded, but to be distributed in the ceremonial feast which entitles the giver to wear certain coveted ornaments. . . . On the whole, the life of the Naga is completely better than that of a western city dweller.

Regarding the life the Nagas were living, Grant Brown remarked:[4]

> The Nagas are described by a Deputy Commissioner of the Naga Hills. . . . As a people, they are neither insolen nor cringing, and if they think they are wronged by any order, they will say so plainly. It is the qualities of frankness, cheerfulness, hospitality, and obedience which have endeared them to all those officers who have been stationed among them long enough to obtain a knowledge of them and their ways.

The Tangkhuls have an open society. They have a practice whereby other village members and even other tribes are accepted into a village with full membership rights. This may be done by fulfilling an oath of allegiance followed by an offering to the Awunga. This in consequence meant that acculturation of the new members to the village culture and custom was the requirement. By definition, this also means that villagers could leave a village and settle down in other villages. Tangkhul Naga village is, therefore, were not exactly a form of close society as has been the belief for so long.

The Tangkhul Naga society, however, was not a classless society nor was the society egalitarian. This has been an over simplification of Naga society in general. Tangkhul society particularly shows an inequal relationship on the basis of political and administrative power between the Awunga and villagers. The inequal relationship extends to the members of the Hangva and for those Tangkhuls who during their lifetime have had one or more feast of merit. The Awunga and the village functionaries noted above enjoyed greater political, economic and social benefits than the ordinary villagers. By virtue of their position, the Awunga and his associates also enjoyed greater prestige and status within the village over the villagers. As a result of this, the traditional village society is seen as stratified society, characterised by unequai social relations.

The position of Wungnao and members of the Hangva can be discerned, as a duplication of the Awunga' s position although in a de-escalated sense of a pyramidical structure. Writers such as Hodson, Shimray and Horam whose works have been the basis of this study have given a setting seeks to give a simple account of what is attempted above.

Tangkhul society, being an open society, there is no segregation of sexes (except in the Longshim and Ngal along). Both men and women, boys and girls and old and young, live together, work together and eat together with an open mind. Men and women are placed at equal setting without fear of being harassed by the stronger sex to the weaker. In this regard, Sardeshpande made an elaborate comment on the Patkoi Nagas which is applicable to all Nagas:[5]

> Above all, it is a proud society where family members, clansman and villager are cared for by the family, clan and village as a matter of human obligation and tribal cohesive pride. Orphans, destitute and sick, old and helpless members are not thrown at nature' s mercy....

He continued further:[6]

> There is no discrimination between one man and another.... There is due respect, regard and awe for elder, and the brave and the rich; but no cringing or fear that one seen among the downtrodden in the Hindu society. Man and woman in the society have considerable liberty, equality and regard among each other. Fear of the male sexual covetousness towards female . . . are all conspicuous by their near total absence. . . . Women roam freely and even singly in the field, jungle, village street even after dark without any apprehension of male mischief.

In Naga society, women, being weaker sex, are tenderly and affectionately taken care of. Only on biological grounds and culture, Tangkhul women are not allowed to go to war, hunting and 'howling.[7] However, enough liberty was given to woman that they could freely take part in all social and festive activities like dancing, singing, playing games etc. Yet, the sexes are expected to maintain strict standard of discipline and decency; and it is a matter of fact and moral standard that a boy is not to touch a girl before marriage.

In Tangkhul social life, there is a strong force of mutual love and respect which is the asset of social equality, and equality in the society brings about peace, harmony and progress. To achieve all these demands strict adherence to customary laws and a well-organised society under the leadership of the Awunga who is the custodian of the customary laws and religious practices. Indeed, by custom and tradition, a Tangkhul cannot address his elder by name. Doing so is regarded as a social offence. This had made the Tangkhul society of a village state happy, compact and secure. Therefore, B.C. Nag writes and Shimray refers to him:[8]

> We talk of welfare state, of social security and the like, but there is a society in which they have been in practice long before most of the progressive countries of the west got any such ideas.

There is some distinction on account of wealth, birth and sex, or even by virtue of the ol ice a person occupies.

However, the same custom and tradition binds the entire community of the village including the Awunga. Therefore, the Awunga cannot rule over the subject people with despotic and discretionary power except by the sanction of the customary laws. Again, since a Tangkhul village is a social, political, economic and religious unit, the spirit of belonging and possessiveness of a person to the society prevails among the people, that they care one for another. So they cherish the idea that the welfare of one is for the whole group and the ignorance of one will affect the interest and benefit of the whole group.

Family

The family is the oldest institution of man, and the formation of a family is as old as the beginning of human life. However, the establishment of family is neither by human knowledge nor his skill. Rather, it was effected by human instinct which urges man to constitute a family of their own, with love and care. Family is the basic unit in the social organisation of the Tangkhuls. Its composition is different from tribe to tribe in Naga society. Normally, the Nagas do not have joint family system, and therefore, single family system has been the norm of Naga family life. However, joint family system was not completely absent among the Nagas in ealry days though it is no longer prevalent now. For instance, the Maring Nagas and Rongmei Nagas of Manipur had joint family system where the oldest man, usually, the father exercised his power as the head over his sons-married or unmarried-daughters and the grand-children born to his married sons. This is one exceptional case in the family system of the Nagas.

Among the Tangkhuls, there are slight variations in the composition of families. Among the western and northern Tangkhul Nagas, a family consists of married couples -- husband and wife, and their children. Sometime, other relatives are also found living together with them. In these two Tangkhul groups, the parents,brothers and sisters of the married son hardly live together with him and his family. The moment the eldest son marries, either the family members vacate the house in favour of him and his wife, or immediately, the married couple establish a new house of their own; which Horam describes "as the sense of independence is very strong among the Tangkhuls."[9] However, the spirit of togetherness and belonging which binds the family members to live together is found lacking among them than the eastern and southern Tangkhul Nagas.

Among the eastern and southern Tangkhul Nagas, a family consists of husband and wife and their unmarried children. If the husband happens to be the eldest son of the family, by any means, he cannot leave the house. He has to live with his wife along with his parents, brothers and sisters. The responsibilities of maintaining the house; taking care of the parents and the unmarried members of family rests on him. Even though the girls leave the house soon after their marriage, the eldest son has to host the married couples of his brothers till he establishes new houses for his married brothers. Then only, they will leave the family. However, he has to look after his parents whether they are old, weak or otherwise. If he shirks his responsibility, he is frowned upon by the village community; and soon he has to appear before the elders of his clan to discipline him and to reform his manners and take the responsibilities as the eldest son of the house. This aspect of family life will be taken up in more detail under the discussion on Inheritance.

Nature of Family

Unlike the Garos and Khasi-Jaintias who are matrilineal, the Tangkhuls, indeed, all the Nagas, are strictly patriarchal by nature. The father is the head of the family, and as such, he has rights and duties which other members of the family cannot perform. Being the head of the family, he has to maintain the house in order, provide the family needs, protect it and take care of the welfare of the house. The social recognition of a man is measured by his capacity and efficiency in the maintenance of his family. The head of the Tangkhul family is also its family priest[10] and thus he performs religious rites, ceremonies and worship in front of the family alter. He represents the family in clan meetings, even in the general assemblies of the households of the village. He is responsible for the marriage of his sons and daughters; and for the construction of the houses of his married sons. But, in this, the members of the clan, and in small villages, the members of the whole village, have to come forward in aid of him. In that case, he has to provide food and drinks to the villagers assisting in the construction.

The whole members of the household have to make obeisance to the head of the house, disobedient children are disciplined; sometimes beaten[11] but the relationship between parents and children is quite healthy. Mutual love and respect guide the day to day life of the Tangkhuls both in the house and outside. Sometimes, disobedient and delinquent youths are brought before the elders of the clan and were publicly admonished. If they remained stubborn, punishments were meted by the Awunga and Hangva according to the customary law of the village.

Status of Women and Their Role

The status of women is by no means inferior to that of men in Naga society; so also in their role and contribution they make in the social life of the Nagas. Both men and women are placed at an equal footing. From the practical point of view, there are certain rights and duties of women which they alone can perform; and in such areas, men are not supposed to involve there. This was based on sex or biological point of view. Later, this had the sanction of custom and religious belief. Being regarded as the weaker sex, women are loved, tenderly taken care of, not to make them feel that they are the weaker sex.

Under such care and affection, women are given a considerable amount of freedom. They have the freedom of moving about whether in groups or single without the least fear of harassment. They can go to the field alone and always expect the aid and protection of men in time of trouble which a man is by duty-bound. They have the right and freedom to take part in festive activities and games and sports of the village. Indeed, good houswives and daughters are the pride and enviable ornament of the family they belong to. Therefore, Haimendorf remarked and Horam quotes him:[12]

> Many women in more civilized parts of India may well envy the women of the Naga Hills, their high status and their free and happy life; and if you measure the cultural level of a people by the social position and personal freedom of its women, you will think twice before looking down on the Nagas as 'savage'.

On women falls the duties of domestic activities and cultivation. They work in the fields from the sowing of seeds till the harvest is over. In early days, because of inter-village feuds when menfolk would engage in warfare and village defence, most of cultivation was done by women only. At home, the entire domestic and household affairs were, and continue to be, exclusively taken care of by women. Naturally, a child is more closer to the mother as she is the first teacher in the house. She is usually the first to get up early in the morning for all those works and then goes to the field. In the evening, again, she takes care of all the household works; and she is the last to retire to bed. Family management lies in the hands of the mother, and good harvest and prosperity of the family rests on her. Indeed, whenever, there is shortage of foodgrain, before the harvest comes, it is regarded as the poor management of the housewife and she is accused of this misfortune.

Weaving is solely the work of women. As such, the mother has a great responsibility in imparting the knowledge of making cloths to her daughters. In Naga society, a girl of three or four years starts to pick up the art of weaving, first from her mother; and when they attain adolescence, the girls exchange their skill of making cloth and embroidery with one another. When a household is poorly clad, the fault is with the womenfolk of the house. When the family wears festive finery, the credit goes to the mother and daughters of the family.

The role of women during war is still greater. In days past, when there were wars and fight between villages, woman acted as messengers of peace, and as a matter of fact, they were peace-makers which averted war and loss of lives of many. Sometimes, such messengers of peace were mistaken for spies, and so the role of a messanger was never safe and secure. When a girl of one of the warring villages married with a boy of the other warring village, she was called Pukreila, an emissary, and to peace between the two enemy villages. She could move to and from for this mission free from danger of war and molestation. But as a sign of peace, she had to hold a branch of green leaves.[13] As a matter of fact, wise and prudent Pukreila, as peace maker, often averted many a bloody war which no man could achieve in early Tangkhul life.

Restrictions on Women

As much as women are tenderly and affectionately taken care of, she is under certain social bindings and restrictions. Unlike the women of the west, a woman in the life of the Tangkhuls is always to be humble and submissive to man without reservation. She should be adorned with modesty and chastity, preserving morality, always ready to listen than to speak. Further, the Tangkhuls, being a patriarchal society, women should be under the control of men. Such moral laws demanded and fashioned Tangkhul women that their morality is above reproach. Prostitution was unknown in the history of the Tangkhuls.

Every year, during Luiraphanit, the New Year festival of the Tangkhuls, they hold a dance called LAAKH-

ANGANUI. It is also called "Virgin Dance" and modern Tangkhul writers have called it 'Beauty Contest" of the Tangkhuls.[14] In this "Virgin Dance", all unmarried girls have to take part to prove their virginity. Refusal to participate in this dance would question the morality and virginity of the girl. This dance, therefore, demanded the Tangkhul girls to maintain a rigid and absolute moral life. The dance was performed in the open air for public view as they were the judges of the "Beauty Contest". The proportion of a girl's body, mostly the developed bossom in proportion with her body is taken into consideration as a criterion of the contest.

Apart from modesty and high moral character required of a woman as a token of submission, there are certain customs and taboos binding on women. These are: (a) a woman cannot inherit the landed property of the house except movable articles, (b) a woman cannot wear certain types of cloths which are mainly made for men, e.g., Haora, Luirim, Thangan etc., (c) a woman cannot sit crosslegged, (d) women cannot loosen their hair before the Awunga and the village elders. Further, there are certain taboos which prohibited women from doing certain things. For example, (a) women cannot go for hunting, (b) they cannot go to war, and even to touch war materials was a taboo to women. Again, when people are victorious in war, or catch wild games in hunting, it is natural for the Tangkhuls to howl as a sign of victory. But it is absolutely prohibited for their women.

However, despite some restrictions on women as mentioned above, their status is .by no means lower than men. All the important matters of a house are discussed with them and their ideas are well accommodated in decision making. Indeed, mutual love and respect make a healthy relation between men and women. The principle of give and take is always respected and upheld in Tangkhul society by both sexes. The modesty and humble submission of women to menfolk is rather the reciprocal act of women in response to the loving care of men on them.

Clan

A Tangkhul family in time past, lived in the land of the clan called TANG,[15] of the village. Several families of blood relation form a clan called SHANG. The origin of a clan can be traced back to a single family from where numerous families in the male line emerged to form into a clan. Therefore, the name of a clan is generally taken from the name of the patriarch from whom all those families multiplied, which later the name became surname of the descendants of the patriarch and identity of the particular clan. Since then, it stands as it is for all generations to come. Sometimes, though the clansmen scattered and spread to different villages and countries, the name of the clan remains unchanged as the identity of a person in which clan he belongs to. In this although people lost their contact due to geographical isolation and lapse of time, through the identity of the clan, they carefully avoided endogagmous marriage within the clan.

In Naga society, a clan is strictly exogamous. Marriage within the clan is, therefore, prohibited by custom and religion of the Nagas, since it is the formation of families of paternal line of the same ancestor. Naturally, the founder of the clan becomes the head of it, and by the law of primogeniture, the eldest surviving son succeeds the father. If there is no male issue, the headship goes to the eldest surviving brother. After him, it goes to his eldest surviving son. Failure to find surviving son, it goes to the next surviving brother and so on. Therefore, the people of a clan are called SHANGNAO which means clansmen. In Tangkhul, the name of a person; and attachment of people is effected by the name of the clan rather than by the name of a person.

Function of the Clan

The powers and functions of the clan are numerous and important. It is the most important administrative unit in the village of the Nagas, in general, and the Tangkhuls in particular. As a matter of fact, it is neither the family, nor the village that controls the life of the people. Rather, it is the clan. The Awunga and his Hangva can handle the matters of individuals, families, clans and inter-clans only when these institutions concerned cannot solve them.

In a family, the father or the eldest male is the head and ruler of the house, and he is reponsible to solve the household problems and issues. However, if the clan deems it fit to intervene in a mismanaged family, it has the right and power to override the authority of the head of the family. Therefore, the head of the house and members of the family cannot act independently apart from the interest of the clan.

In matters of inheritance and division of properties of a family, the head of the house alone cannot do it without the consent of the clan especially in the case of landed properties. If the head of a family does it by himself, it should be within the norm of the clan. Otherwise, the clan treats it null and void and a new arrangement is immediately carried out again.

The marriage of a clansman, his separation from the family and construction of house after marriage of a son are arranged by the clan. A person cannot marry against the advice and .interest of the clan. For the coherence and unity of the clan, it has to see that the house of a clansman is collectively done and allow the married people to settle down under the protection of the clan. The widows and orphans are taken care of by the clan so that no one should remain destitute. In early days, due to inter-village war, when a clansman fell in the hands of the enemy, it has the bounden right and duty of the clan to take revenge of it. In the same way, no one is free from the membership of the clan and his responsibility towards the welfare of the clan is equally great as much as his household responsibilities. There are cases where a clan has its own taboo, although, it does not involve the whole village. For example, a certain clan is prohibited from taking beef or buffalos meat which is not a taboo for other clan of the same village.

In the past, inter-clan fortifications were erected due to inter-clan and inter-village feuds. Sometimes, one clan made war against another at the scale of inter- village war causing blood-shed and loss of lives. It was particularly found among the Angami Nagas. However, in Tangkhul villages, there was no inter-clan feuds which led to bloodshed and inter-clan war within the village. Though they had their own clan fortifications, it was for the safety and security of the clan against the attack of hostile villages. Because, the social cohesion, common love of the village and by the presence of village festivals had melted away, not only the personal grudge, but even the spirit of clanism and inter-clan quarrels, and rivalries. In fact, the Awunga and Hangva cannot allow the subject people of different clans of the village to fight against each other.

All kinds of clan business are carried out by the clan under the leadership of the clan-chief. This office is hereditary. The clan chief is the permanent representative of the clan in the Hangva of the village. When he sits with the Awunga, he is called Wungnao. The cases which the Awunga-in-Council cannot decide or solve are decided by the arbitration of Wungraos whose decisions are final and binding. However, this does not mean that the Wungnao is above the Awunga. Even in the sitting of the Wungnaos, the Awunga is the Ex-Officio Chairman of the sitting. Therefore, the role of the clan chief is great and important both in the clan and village administration. He is respected for the prestigious post he holds in the village.

Village

It has been mentioned earlier, that, in the social organisation of the Tangkhuls, several families of blood-relations formed a clan, and several clans made a village. Naturally, a Tangkhul village was, and is, composed of several clans because of the exogamous nature of marriage. In early days, due to inter-village feuds, the villages were isolated one from another; and therefore, marriage outside one's own village was positively inconvenient that one was better to take a bribe within his village. This was an important condition for the establishment of a village by several clans.

Most of the Naga villages were perched on top of the hills or on spurs of the hillocks; and therefore, free access was difficult. This was mainly for military strategy which also gave a commanding view around it. The villages were well protected and guarded by several defence lines of spikes, bars, stone boulders, even by cliffs of natural defence. Again, they were under constant vigil of the village defence force day in and day out against the invasion of enemy villages. But whatever the defence measure of a village may be, availability of water is very essential. As the villages are established on top of hills, the water source from nearby point is another important criterion. The isolation of Naga villages ultimately enhanced the independence of Naga village.

Usually, Tangkhul villages are large and they live in well demarcated village land instead of scattering in different hamlets. This involved several factors. In the past, the Tangkhuls were mainly agrarian people that by nature of shifting cultivation, they had to live at a particular place so that the village land might be brought under the rotation of the jhum cultivation which this process would be disturbed if they lived in scattered hamlets. Secondly, the establishment of a strong village force required a big settlement of the people. Further, the social spirit of the Tangkhuls is so strong that life is nor worth-living to them without social activities which can be had in a big society only - not in a small hamlets.

Whether big or small, the first settlers of each village demarcated out enough land for cultivation of the villagers.

The first settlers divided the village land among themselves thereby advancing the right of ownership. In this way of distribution of land, clan lands are parcelled out for the support and utilisation of the clan; and in the same manner, public land was also carved out to support the future immigrants of the village. The leader of the first settlers who ultimately became the Awunga also got the same amount of land for the support of his family. It was not necessary that he should take a larger plot than the people who followed him. Further, he was not the absolute owner of the village land either.

Unlike the Kukis, a Naga village is permanent. The attachment of a Naga for his village is so strong that no price is too costly for him to defend the hearth and graveyard of his ancestors. This is explained by R. R. Shimray:[16]

> From the cradle to the grave, a Naga identifies with his village. Hard life or any grave dangers will not affect in the least the love and pride that a Naga has for his village. He will always subscribe his interest and welfare to that of his, village and strive for the good of the village. It was considered as sacred duty that all the young people should defend the village.

Elwin also wrote:[17]

> As the Nagas are not a migratory people like the other hillmen around them, their villages are stationary and unchanging.

It is, therefore, a matter of fact that a village site chosen and occupied by the ancestors remains unchanged. So strong is the attachment for the village that Nagas who may reside outside their village usually want to be buried in the village of their origin. Instances of these are that A.Z. Phizo, President of Naga National Council and his colleague Z. Ramyo who died in London and Colorado respectively, the bodies of both have been taken home and buried in Nagaland.

The site of the village settlement is divided into blocks called Tang, as mentioned above, according to the number of the clans; and each clan occupied one Tang. However, at the advent and spread of Christianity, the converts were expelled from the original village site, and so they formed a new village site called 'Christian Compound'. There the converted Christians of different clans lived together as a big Christian family, and different Tangs on the basis of clan was no longer respected. This was the beginning of the Tangkhul experience of different clansmen living together despite the existence of their original Tangs. Christianity brought about a great change in the settlement pattern of the Tangkhuls.

Laws of Inheritance

Laws of inheritance relate to acquiring property whether movable or immovable, titles to an office in the event of one's death or withdrawal from the office. Whereas, there are certain amount of liberalities in the laws of inheritance with regard to the cases mentioned above in which the principle of hereditary is not applicable, they are rigorously enforced in matters related to hereditary properties, titles, office etc. The important inhreitance in this respect are, the office of the village chief, titles and properties. Regarding properties, Horam wrote[18] "Property consists of lands, houses, movable articles, money, ornaments and debts. The sons or male heirs inherit all property including debts." However, among the Nagas, the laws of inheritance vary from tribe to tribe. For most of the Nagas, the eldest son inherits the house and greater portion of the landed properties. Some other Nagas, like the Angamis, allot the house to the youngest son. But in all other cases, the eldest son gets the largest share, and the rest is divided among the sons either equally or in precedence of the sons, the elder acquiring more than the younger. Hodson informs that, among the Kabuis, the youngest got larger share than those of other sons.[19]

But whatever variations in the laws of inheritance among the different Naga tribes may be, there is one peculiar characteristic which is the same to all the Naga tribes. Unlike the Khasis, only male issues can inherit the property. The widows and daughters can get some portion of the properties as gifts out of love of parents and family; but never in the forms of landed properties. In some extreme cases, among the eastern Maos, parents give a plot of terraced rice field to the daughter at her marriage for a period of time in order to settle her in married life. However, after the expiry of the period, the property (field) ultimately goes back to the house of their parents. But by nature, the Nagas share the movable properties, not only to male issues, but even to the daughters and sisters at the time of their marriage. The marriage of a girl is honoured by the amount of properties she gets from her parents.

Among the Tangkhuls there are some variations in the laws of inheritance. The people of western and northern Tangkhuls have similarities with that of the Maos, Angamis, Eastern Angamis and Aos. The system of inheritance is the same among the eastern and southern Tangkhul Nagas. They follow the principle of primogeniture for inheritance of properties whether landed or movable. This rule is also observed by the Shans, Kachins and Burmese of Myanmar.[20] The similar laws of inheritance of northern and western Tangkhul Nagas with their neighbouring tribes may be because of the geographical and physical closeness between them that mixed culture emerged in these neighbourhoods. Therefore, among those Tangkhul Nagas, the parental house and two-thirds or the greater portion of the parental property go to the eldest son, and the rest is divided among the remaining sons. When the eldest son marries, the house and property mentioned above are immediately vacated by the parents and other family members of the house in favour of him. This process continues till all the sons are married. At last, the aged parents reside with the eldest son or with any one of the sons whom they favoured most.[21]

Although, the sons are separated after marriage and live in separate houses, the lot of the marriage of the daughters or sisters are jointly borne by the sons or brothers together with their parents. Again, though the daughters are not entitled for inheritance of the family properties, enough and necessary articles are provided in order to establish her married life. This is a custom among the Tangkhuls. Even at the death of the father, the widow-mother is properly looked after by the sons and daughters. Enough substances, including fields for cultivation during her life time are provided to her. When she remarries all these should be left behind to the heir. However, she is also well provided as much as they do to their daughters or sisters. Again, she can carry whatever articles she had procured along with her.

Among the eastern and southern Tangkhul Nagas, the principle of primogeniture is strictly enforced, and there is no compromise against the rule whatsoever. All properties of the father, movable, immovable, office and title if any, absolutely belong to the eldest son; and no other sons and daughters has any right of inheritance; and possession of the family properties procured in the name of the family go to the family except individual articles for their own. 'Immediately after the death of his father, and to some extent after his marriage, the whole burden and responsibility of the family rest on him being the heir; and so also inheritance of landed properties, articles, office and title. Further, he has the right and duty to look after the parents, brothers and sisters for their well-being which is a religious and sacred duty of the eldest son. Unlike the western and northern Tangkhul Nagas, the eldest son of eastern and southern Tangkhuls has to live together with the parents, brothers and sisters till their marriage and separation from the house. Otherwise, the fmaily cannot separate; and the parents cannot be deserted under any circumstances. As by custom, the parents should live with the eldest son till their death.

The eldest son, being the heir, inherits not only the properties of the father; but also the responsibility of the father to look after the family. He has to arrange the marriage of his brothers and sisters. When his brother marries, he will make the house of his married brother and settle him in the new house, and provide all necessities required for the establishment of a new life since inheritance cannot be divided. Until he constructs a house for his married brother, the latter and his wife have to stay with him in his house. After their separation it is the duty of the heir to provide land for cultivation to younger brother; and. the younger brother, in return, has to bring the head of the game hunted to the house of the elder brother as a bounden duty and homage to the elder brother.

Again, it is the responsibility of the eldest son to look after the aged parents since he takes over the management of the family properties; and under no circumstances, the parents should be sent out from the house to live by themselves. If the son or daughter-in-law neglects the parents, the judgement of the clan falls on the couple, and they are sternly warned by the clan elders that the aged parents be properly looked after. The remarriage of the widow-mother and the marriage of the sisters are also arranged by the eldest son and he sends them away with enough articles and presents as they cannot claim property of the house. Some more well-to-do people share valuable articles including cattles to their daughters and sisters as presents at their marriage. In this regard, the system of inheritance of the eastern and southern Tangkhul Nagas is all the same as those of Kachins, Shans and Burmese of Myanmar[22] The Nagas now in Myanmar also follow the principle of primogeniture. The eldest claims the whole property of his father, and the younger brothers are liberally provided at the time of their marriage and separation from the house.

In the event of the death of the eldest son, the next eldest surviving son becomes the heir and succeeds to the properties of the father. This process of inheritance goes on to the youngest son. If a man dies without male issue, his wife and daughters can share movable articles, even valuable properties like cattles; but never the landed properties, house and title. In such cases, the property goes to the surviving brother of the deceased or to any of the nearest kin. The same rule is applicable to the office and title of the deceased. Hereditary in Naga society is solely on the male line - never in the female line. In this connection, J. H. Hutton wrote:[23] "Only male can permanently inherit real property and the males of one generation share alike."

Marriage

The Nagas consider marriage as a sacred institution given by God for the procreation of human kind and to occupy the earth and thereby fulfill the mission of God. To the Nagas, to remain single is a reproach. The institution of marriage is as old as human kind and it is the beginning of the formation of human society by establishing a family which is the basic social unit. There are generally two types of marriages. One is 'arranged marriage' and the other, 'love marriage'. 'Arranged Marriage' is found among many Indian communities where the marriage of a boy and a girl is arranged by both parents even though the couple have not known each other. In some cases, they do not see each other till they marry. 'Love marriage' on the other hand, is the marriage effected out of the mutual love of a boy and a girl. Such marriage is either with or without consent of both the parents. However, in the marriage of the Tangkhuls, both patterns go together. When a boy and a girl love each other and are willing to marry, they must secure the consent and approval of their respective parents. In the same way, when both the parents of a particular boy and girl want them to get married, they must seek and secure the love of the boy and girl for marriage. There after they enter into marriage negotiation and engagement. In due course, the marriages are a happy blend of tradition and affection. It may be mentioned here that this has made the institution of marriage strong among the Tangkhuls. Consequently, divorce is rare.

In Tangkhul society, marriage is necessary for social cognizance, and a bachelor person cannot be a member of the village council, or hold any important and responsible office. Though a man separates from his family and establishes his own house, it cannot be called a household until he marries. Shimray has elaborated this by writing:[24] "It was a Naga concept that one must get married, because, he or she cannot have a place in society without having a family."

The Tangkhuls, like any other Nagas, are exogamous by nature, and so marriage within the clan is a taboo, and thus it is forbidden by the law of exogamy. Marriage against customary law like incest, consanguineous marriage etc. are met with expulsion from the village. Such a crime is so serious that it cannot be erased, and their children have the stigma of illegal marriage of their parents. Cross-cousin marriage is also forbidden by the customary law of the Tangkhuls. The family line from where the mother comes is regarded as the base and foundation of the Tangkhul marriage. A person has, therefore, to marry the daughter of his mother's brother, and in early days, under no circumstances, such marriage could be denied by any party. If either party failed to fulfill this term, and broke the cord of traditional marriage line, heavy fine was imposed on the defaulter. 'In this way the cord of marriage was maintained for generations. It is only a matter of recent occurrence that this rule is not strictly observed with the advent of Christianity and modern ways of life.

Monogamy is the standard of marriage in Tangkhul society which is the manifestation of strict standard of moral principle of the people. In this regard, Bimal J. Dev and Dilip Lahiri remarks[25] "Monogamy is universally prevalent among the Tangkhuls. The principle of clan exogamy was deeply entrenched among them so much so that any violation led excommunication from the village. Cross cousin marriage with mother's brother's daughter is allowed but not vice versa." Polygamy is frawned by the society, and it is regarded as a reproach to peaceful existence of the family atmosphere even though polygamy is not completely absent from the Tangkhul society. Before the advent of Christianity in Tangkhul region, there were a few cases of polygamy among some village chiefs and rich people. But their lives could never be so happy and peaceful, as that of the families of single wife and husband. Apart from the principle of moral standard and family factor, polygamy is decried due to the heavy expenditure incurred in the marriage of a person. Polyandry is never mentioned in the lips of the Tangkhuls. Child marriage or infant marriage is absolutely unknown among the Nagas.

There is no dowry system in the marriage of the Tangkhuls wihich is prevalent among the Mizos, Kukis, Semas, Konyaks and some other Naga tribes. Again, there is no bride price as such. Unfortunately, some writers misconstrue the articles or money given to the family of the bride by the family of the groom as bride-price. The fact is: "Who will sell his daughter at a price whether it is much or less?" True, there is a demand of a few cattle heads, dao, spear, iron etc. by the parents of the girl from the family of the boy just to compensate the loss of service by the departure of the girl from the family by her marriage. Sometimes, out of extreme necessity, the girl may remain in the house of her parents even after her marriage in order to bear the burden or misfortune of her parents.

High moral standard is honoured and virginity before marriage is strictly maintained in Tangkhul society. Outsiders always form erroneous notion about the open social life of the Nagas where there is no segregation of sexes. It is the ethical culture of the Tangkhuls that a woman can move freely whether in the light or darkness without the least fear of sexual abuse or any form of harm. Such is the moral and ethical standard of the Nagas that Haimendorf remarked, "prostitution is unknown"[26] and R. Brown observed, "Venereal diseases appeared unknown,"[27] and a Naga authority makes it clear, [28] "For so broad-minded a people the codes of behaviour are very strict, and traditionailly a boy is not supposed to touch a girl before marriage." By the observance of the "Virgin Dance', social work of the age-group called Yarthot where a girl had to work bare body from the waist above, Ngala-Long and other social activities demanded a girl to remain virgin and chaste. Adultery and fornication are mostly the cases which lead to divorce; and in such cases, the seducer is liable to be killed and the woman is never taken back by the husband of the molested woman.

When the love affairs of a boy and a girl comes to the notice of their parents, usually the parents of the boy take the initiative for marriage contract—negotiation, engagement and marriage ceremony. But first, they have to find a go-between usually an elderly woman who is able to win over the hearts of the girl and her parents. When the mission is over and positive, then engagement and marriage of the boy and the girl are carried out by both parents and clansmen. They fix the amount of articles and number of cattle to be given to the parents of the girl. Soon after, marriage takes place. If the boy happens to be the eldest son, he will occupy the parental house. But for the younger brothers, they have to make new houses and settle them down there when they also marry. This is the beginning of a new life of the couple.

By custom and culture of the Tangkhuls, the couple cannot divorce whatsoever hardship may come in their lives. The mutual understanding and agreement of the couple for divorce does not arise either. But under dire consequences like adultery on either party and borrenness of the woman, the case of divorce is sanctioned by the Hangva and the society accepts it.[29] Widow remarriage is sanctioned by the custom of the Tangkhuls either to the brother of the deceased or any other provided the marriage is based on the principle of exogamy.

Marriage of the Awunga

Normally, the principle of exogamy in the marriage of the Tangkhuls is applicable to all including the Awunga. All forms of marriage, whether among common people or the Awunga should be guided by those principles, rules and practices of customs, culture and traditions of the people. However, for status and honour and prestige of the Awunga, it has been the tradition of the Tangkhuls that the bride of the Awunga should be the daughter of another Awunga or a girl of high birth or equal status. He should not marry a widow, an orphan girl or a girl of low estate; and under no circumstances, the Awunga should marry a bastard or a girl of illegitimate birth. Consanquineous marriage and incest leads to the forfeiture of the office of the Awunga. In short, the marriage of the Awunga should be above reproach since he is the model of the life of the people as their head and the mediator between the people and their God.

Naturally, the marriage of the Awunga is celebrated in a grand manner. A good number of cattles and pigs are killed. Rice, meat and rice-beer are served to the people lavishly. According to Tangkhul culture, shortage of foodstuff in such a ceremony brings ill-luck or misfortune in the family.

The Awunga had to appear in his finery with the distinct clothes entitled to him. The people revere and grace the marriage of the Awunga; and they find their satisfaction at the lavish serve of food and drinks. It is the usual custom of the Tangkhuls that the bride is escorted by the villagers, particularly by the clansmen to the house of the groom; and the groom and his family members come out to receive the bride. In this occasion, the father of the groom utters blessing for happy and long life of the couple for their peace, prosperity and successful life with many issues. The feast lasts for days according to the substance of the Awunga.

However, these days the sanctity of the institution of marriage has been polluted by the invasion of western culture. Boys and girls get married without love and approval of their parents. The result is constant marriage and divorce. This is one evil that has crept into Tangkhul society. Marriages have to get the approval of the Awunga and Hangva. Otherwise, the new family cannot be recognised as a household in the village and their children are termed as illegal citizens. The recognition of the household by the Awunga and Hangva is a must as a family so that it may get its own share in the labour and portion of games killed by the villages.

Tangkhul Festivals

The Tangkhuls, being an agrarian society, most of the Tangkhul festivals have their origin in agriculture. Some festival like THI SHAM is closely related to their religion of animism. Others such as YARRA are neither agricultural nor religious in character. It is purely a social festival celebrated by unmarried young people of age-group of boys and girls. The American Baptist missionaries which brought Christianity to these hills had a wrong and apathetic attitude towards the Naga festivals since they were celebrated by the Nagas before the coming of Christianity. Therefore, all festivals of the Nagas were regarded by them and their followers as paganism; and ignorant new converted Christians developed the same attitude toward their fellow Nagas and their festivals. Thus celebration of the Naga traditional festivals are frowned upon by the Christian missionaries and their followers. This led to the social, cultural and economic degeneration of the Nagas. Because, when Naga festivals are affected, there is a corresponding effect on agriculture and economy of the Nagas since their festivals have a close link with agriculture.[30]

Festivals are celebrated by the entire village community together with eating, drinking, singing, dancing and sports items without which no festival is complete and worth the name. There seems to be a magical power of healing touch to the wounds of individuals, families and clans of the village and all the grudges are melted away at the instance of festive activities. All the Tangkhul village festivals are celebrated at the behest of the Awunga who announces the dates and seasons of the festivals by observing the lunar calendar; and he has important role to play in their festivals. He has to perform rites, sacrifices, and offer prayers and inaugurates the festivals. Some important Tangkhul festivals are discussed below.

Luira Phanit

Luira Phanit is the New Year Festival of the Tangkhuls. It is also known as the festival of sowing seeds, or festival to begin cultivation of the year. Hence this festival marks the beginning of the year. In order of precedence, it is the most prominent festival celebrated in the full moon of February-March of the year. It lasts for about ten to fifteen days. There are slight variations in details of observing and celebrating the festival according to the nature of locality. But the general principle of the festival is all the same. Since it is the biggest festival of the Tangkhuls, in a year, preparations of food, drink and clothings are made in advance; and it would not be an exaggeration to say that the whole year is spent in preparing to make Luira Phanit a grand celebration.

The village Awunga fixes the date and period of the festival where the village crier announces it to the entire community. On the first day, animals, generally pigs and cattles are killed; but before the Awunga tests the festive meat and blesses the people, it is a taboo for the villagers to eat. The village gate is closed for the first few days against the entering of outsiders, and so also the villagers are prohibited to leave the village in those days. These first few days are observed 'as solemn days where no work was to be done. But feasting, singing and dancing are carried out through day and night. This relieves the people of their monotony of daily routine work of the year. Men and women, young and old enjoy the mirth of the feast alike -

not only eating, drinking and singing alone, but with the best attire and jewellery.

At the end of the first few days of solemn period, the Awunga and his wife go to the field with a chicken and perform cermeonial rite, offer prayers for the protection of the crops and bumper harvest of the year. The blood of the chicken is sprinkled on a clean handful of paddy seeds and sprayed on a prepared ground as a symbolic sowing. Thus the sowing season is inaugurated, and this occasion is followed by the common people. If anybody violates the rule and sows ahead of the Awunga, the harvest is usually very poor and the whole village might face famine. Therefore, heavy punishment is meted to the encroacher of the law. The festival continues after the ceremonial sowing of seed.

By the middle of the festival, the relatives and outsiders are invited and welcome to the village and they are lavishly entertained. Another important occasion of the festival is the LEINGAPHA which is the village fair where all the available goods for disposal are brought out. Seliing and buying continues throughout the day. Before the advent of money economy, selling and buying was conducted through barter system. Thus, the shortage of one commodity is supplied by the surplus of another.

The festive occasion is graced by all items of Tangkhul games and sports. Singing and dancing competition of boys and girls, mixed competition, tug-of-war, wrestling, long jump, high jump, javelin throw are held. There are games exclusively for boys and girls, for, no Tangkhul festival can be celebrated without feast, game and sport and merry making. The most important festive event of Luira Phanit is the Tangkhul Laa Khanganui where all unmarried girls after attaining puberty have to participate wearing their short skirt, armlets, bangles, necklace and head-dresses. The most important part of the dress is huge beads of necklace of several rows called Kongsang which is the lone cover of the bosom of the girl. In order to expose the body, a girl is permitted to wear the beautifully coloured embroidered short-skirt and her jewellery for judgement who is the most beautiful girl. This pageant will again be discussed in. the section on Tangkhul games and sports. Then, the girls in single file moved into the open air surrounded by the spectators where the general public judge the 'Beauty Contest' of the village girls. This is the most exciting and fascinating event of the Tangkhul festive activities. The dance is soft and slow in uniform movement of hands and legs rocking the body gracefully according to the tune of their songs.

At the end of Luira Phanit, the relatives are invited, friends are sent off with presents. It is natural among the Tangkhuls that when married sisters visit their brothers at such an occasion, at their departure for home, they are richly provided with the presents especially in terms of meat. The festival being over, people prepare for cultivation. It may be noted that according to the nature of terrace and shifting cultivation, there is a slight variation of its season. The people of eastern and southern Tangkhul Nagas follow the season of jhumming cultivation and its festival seasons.

Yarra Phanit is the 'Youth Festival' of the Tangkhuls. It is not connected with religion and cultivation of the village. It is purely a social festival of boys and girls of the village. They celebrate it during the off season of cultivation. The festival is celebrated by different age groups of both sexes. Before, cultivation starts and normally after tilling the ground in the terrace-field and cutting the jungle for jhumming, young people of different age groups celebrated this festival, sometime in April-May. It lasts for three-four days; even for a week. Eating, drinking, .singing and sharing of joy and happiness of the youngsters is the character of this festival, free from the interference of parents, family worries and personal cares. If any boy or girl had married earlier than Yarra, they are also invited or sent a good portion of meat as a token of love to a member of their age group. Teenage boys and girls rarely miss this festival.

Mangkhap

This is a village festival celebrated at the end of June or the beginning of July when'ardous work of sowing seed of shifting cultivation and transplantation of rice seed of shifting cultivation and transplantation of rice in the terraced fields is over. It lasts for three-four days and people spend time with much relief after the hard labour in the field. They spend time in feasting and singing. In some Tangkhul villages, the festival is celebrated by burning lamps or torch of pine resin, the trees, which are found in its natural state in this hill country.

Dharshat Phanit

Dharshat is the harvest festival of the Tangkhuls. It is a village festival involving taboos. First, the village Awunga has to go to the field one day ahead of the people and bring a basketful of paddy and performs rites and ceremonies, and offers prayers for the rich harvest of the whole village. On the next day, the villagers are allowed to pluck the ear of the paddy, and they also perform the same rites and offer prayer to their respective household deities so that there might be enough food throughout the year. The day is observed with solemn prayer where no form of work is done.

Chumphut Phanit

After the harvest is over, Chumphut Phanit is celebrated. It is a new rice eating festival preformed by women or housewives since they are responsible for the management of the barn. It involves two taboos to be strictly observed. For the first two nights, the male members have to stay outside the village gate lest they happen to see the performances of their women at night. According to custom and belief, if they see their housewives performing the Chumphut ceremony, ill-luck comes to the house and there will be shortage of grain for the house before the next harvest comes.

The village ponds are cleaned - old water ot the pond is thoroughly drained, and new rice is cooked with the fresh water. In this, a virgin of the village whose character is above reproach has to draw the water first, then she is followed by other women. During the festive days working at home and outside is strictly prohibited. It lasts for three to four days. Blowing bugles is allowed till Thisham Phanit festival. When they test the new rice for the first time, they say *Rice is bitter, rice is bitter,* lest the evil spirit feels jealous of the new and sweet rice; and the barn will be exhausted for it is believed the spirit will not enter where there is bitter rice.

Thisham Phanit

Thisham Phanit is another important festival of the Tangkhuls. This festivals comes next to Luira Phanit in order of precedence of the Tangkhul festivals. The celebration of the festival marks the end of the Tangkhul year which is held sometime in December-January. This festival is expulsion of the dead from the village - Kathi means death; Kasham, expulsion. According to their belief, the soul of the dead remains in the hosue before he goes to KAZEIRAM,[31] the 'land of death'; and has its rightful place in the house enjoying food and drinks of the family until he is sent off with a ceremony performed on Thisham festival with a special arrangement of food items, cloths and other articles for his journey to, and daily use at, Kazeiram where Kokto, king of the dead rules.

The festival lasts for about ten days. As a matter of fact, the festival is meant for the families where death occurred in the year and the festival is celebrated in order to send off the spirit of the dead. However, the entire village community celebrates it together and observes the festive taboos and merry-makings. Animals are killed by the families of the dead and prepare other articles for the dead. They engage the service of the village priest,. not the Awunga in this case and the Shara propitiates both Kakto and the soul of the dead by singing, dancing and chanting. First, he pleads the Kokto to receive the soul of the dead and not to bring death in the house any more, and then he asks the soul of the dead to depart in peace with the gifts made by the family for his journey and for the use in the land of dead. The priest, or in some case, a person who acts as the dead one, donnes the cloths and articles of the dead and throw outside the village gate, never to be picked up again and bid farewell to the departed soul.

On the last day of the festival, the relatives of the dead' take a procession at night, singing, dancing, howling war cry and march outside the village gate and bid farewell to the departed soul. Some of them stay awake throughout the night. It is said that they can see the departed souls moving towards the east on the way to Kazeiram. The celebration of Thisham festival marks the close of the year.

The advent of Christianity brought in by the American Baptist Missionaries had an adverse effect on the Tangkhul festivals.[32] Whether they are related to agriculture or their traditional religion happened to be the centres of attack by the Christians, and the importance of festivals in Tangkhul life was frowned. However, with the recent development of education, and progress of modern civilization, the importance of Tangkhul festivals has been revived again. Songs and dance with strong cultural elements have become the main items of communal functions today.

GAMES AND SPORTS

The Nagas love sports. We may trace the origin of many of their games of the early days of the Tangkhuls. Some of them included both arduous games like high jump, long jump, javelin throw, tug-of-war, boat race etc., and less arduous sports such as singing, dancing, beauty contests etc. Some games were and are exclusively for men or women; and some others are both for men and women. A Tangkhul authority has written, "It is said that the games and sports of Samsok Kingdom went on from full moon to full moon, according to legend."[33] Most of the verile games are extinct today but some others are still in practice. The winners of the competitors were awarded with five-six years old buffalo, mithun, bull, boar etc. in order of merit; and Kongsang (beads of precious stone) Zeithing (iron stick), silver beads etc. were awarded to women athletes and competitors of dance and songs. Some important Tangkhul traditional games and sports are discussed below.

Mahar Kapai (High Jump)

High jump is one of the most ancient games of the Tangkhuls which is still in practice. This game is for men only and it demands much courage and strength. There are three main types of high jump of the Tangkhuls. In the first and the most simple form of high jump, a small bar is placed on the branches of two poles where the competitors jump over the bar. The level of the bar is raised higher and higher. The one who can jump highest wins the first prize.

The second form of high jumps is to jump over the flame of a fire holding a spear as pole-vault. It is such a dangerous game that the Awunga warns the young competitors in advance that if any death occurs, the case cannot be taken to the court. This game is meant only for energetic and able bodied youth. The third type of high jump is equally dangerous as the second form of high jump. In this game, young athletes have to jump over a number of spears fixed on the ground. If a young man fails in the attempt and is pierced by the spears and dies, there is no case, for it is a game where the competitors participate at their own risk. For those who could perform the fearful games, their fame is well spoken of and their strength and physical achievements were respected by the people.

Long Jump

Long jump is held in two ways; one is a simple far jumping on a prepared ground. But the other way of long jump is quite dangerous again. Live charcoal is spread over an area of three to nine yards long and six yards wide. It demands much strength and courage. All these dangerous games were played in Samsok Palace in the early days. Today such games are not played.

Catching Animal Barehanded

Another verile game worth to be mentioned is to catch animal with barehand and kill it. This game was played by energetic young men. Here the stalled pigs of four-five years are let loose in the open ground and selected young men are sent to catch and kill the animal with their own hands. A more verile game than this is to let loose a middle aged bull in open ground or jungle and the selected young people chase it and pull down to the ground. Even today, among the Maram Nagas, young people compete to kill mithuns and buffaloes by hitting it with their elbows. These are quite dangerous games, but those who could perform such games are admired by the people for their extraordinary body strength.

Boating

Boat race was once practised at Samsok kingdom, but due to non-availability of big rivers, it is no more practised in present Tangkhul occupied area today. However, in early days it was an important game and performed at the junction of the Chindwin and Nampan rivers called Dilong.

Wrestling

Wrestling is an important game of the Tangkhuls as with other Naga tribes. It is an important game as much as it is a man-to-man fight without any weapon. This game is played in most of the festivals, between married and unmarried men, one Tang and another Tang. But the most exciting wrestling was held in the marriage festivities where the wrestlers of the bride challenged the wrestlers of the groom. In early days good wrestlers were admired by the people and their names of fame have survived for generations.

Tug-of-War

Tug-of-war, which is the rope-pulling game of the is known as *Thingneira Khangakhun*. The distinct characteristic of this game is that it is a common game of both men and women, including children. Further, religious belief is connected with the Tangkhul rope-pulling for good harvest and prosperity of the people. In this, they pull the rope as if they are pulling a big amount of bumper harvest and wealth of the people. Here, all the able persons, young and old have to take part. When they play the game as a social game, various groups take part - married men versus unmarried men, so also the woman folks; and one clan versus another clan. The rope used in this game is a wild creeper or a big long cane selected from the jungle. Before the game starts, the Awunga or the village priest chants over before the rope was used for the game.

Polo

It is populatly spoken that the game, polo, started from Manipur, and it is called Kang-jei by the Meiteis. Even today, people of this state are famous for thi game. It is said that polo has been played in Manipur since 1606.[34] According to T.C. Hodson, polo was introduced in Manipur during the reign of Khagemba, circa 1600.[35] However, Elwin recorded:[36]

> As to polo - a game which had been mentioned by Dr. Watt. This was a game equally well known to the Baltis and Ladakhis of the north-west Himalayas and was, Capt. Temple understood, very like the form adopted by the Manipuris.

The Tangkhul call this game Hongkhara Khagareo. Special kind of cane called Hongkhara is curved as the walking-stick specially made for the game. According to the ancestors, this game had been practised by the Tangkhuls at Samsok before it was introduced in Imphal valley. Therefore, it is assumed that the Meiteis adopted it from the Tangkhuls of Samsok when the former attacked and conquered it. However, the Tangkhuls do not play polo these days.

A few other games of minor importance are top, Saotheila, (seeds of sword bean), hide-and-seek, lungkhotla (knuckles bone) etc. These games are mostly meant for women and children. Grownup men hardly play these games. Spring season is the best time for these games. But most of the Tangkhul festives, marriage and games fall in this season of the year.

Music and Dance

Singing and dancing are the important features of all festivals of the Tangkhuls. Indeed, there is no life of the Tangkhuls where there is no music and dance. As for the Tangkhuls, they sing while they work, carry heavy loads or as they walk. When they sit together and make merriment, the gathering is seasoned with music. Music and dance competitions are for all Tangkhuls—'men, women, boys and girls, young and old. This is held in age-group wise, Tang wise, married versus unmarried etc. The first prize usually goes to the aged and elderly group since they are well-versed in traditional songs and different arts of dance. But war dance is exclusively for men while women are spectators around the field. People dance with war weapons such as daos, spears, and shields with formidable war dresses, howling, shouting and crying ho-ho for several hours.

Laa Khanganui

Laa Khanganui is exclusively for maidens. All unmarried girls who have attained puberty must take part in it without exception. As it is the dance of maidens, it is also called the "Virgin Dance." However, it is more than a dance. The true meaning of Laa Khanganui is song or music competition. But it is not a mere music competition either. It is the occasion held in such a way where the most beautiful girl of the village is selected among the virgins every year. In order to know who is the most beautiful girl, the competitors are allowed to wear a well-designed and embroidered traditional short skirt exposing the calves and the upper portion of the body from the waist. Their heads are deocrated with headgears, the hands with armlets, bangles and Kong sang for the lone covering of their bosoms.

As per nature of the dance, the "Virgin Dance." of the Tangkhuls is the most colourful and grandeur show, the most awaited and exciting scene of festive events of the year. Any girl who refuses to join the dance without a convincing reason is suspected of being pregnant and heavy punishment is meted on her. The participants move into the ground thickly surrounded by the spectators. As they move in, they rock their bodies in uniform footsteps striking their bangles in their hands with the tune of the music. Slow movement of the body and dancing characterised their dance. Here the general public is the judge and the name of the most beautiful girl soon passes from the lips of all spectators.

A girl who had been defiled by a boy pretends to be a virgin and joins the dance, it may so happen that either she misses the uniform footstep and falls down on the ground or one of her ornaments falls off her body. From this, people judge that her morality is not above reproach. Heavy fine is imposed on such a girl by the village as well as by the Ngalalong (Ladies Dormitory) where she belongs to.[37] This makes Tangkhul girls to remain chaste and maintain high moral standard till they marry and live with their husbands.

It is said that, in the days gone-by, people of surrounding villages participated at the Laa Khanganui held at Samsok palace. At one time, Zangengla of Langtung village was selected as the most beautiful girl of the age. However, she was the daughter of, and brought up by, a widow that men of high social status did not marry her, but the story of her beauty still survives.

Maran Kasa

In early days, men of wealth and generous people used to serve food and drink to the village community. Here the poor people, widows and orphans including men of status enjoyed rice, meat and rice-beer to their content. Then people praised the man who offered so generously to them without expecting anything in return. This is called Maran Kasa in Tangkhul, which may be translated as Feast of Merit. After two-three times performances of Maran Kasa, the donor was entitled to wear a special type of embroidered cloth and erect Tarung[38] in front of his house or to raise house horn called Lenchangkui at the facade of the house.

In the early days, communal feeding by certain rich men was not to receive social recognition, prestige or any form of reward. It wa.s purely a social and philanthropic service that he shared his wealth to people generously. Therefore, Christoph von Furer Haimendorf wrote:[39]

> The wealth of the ambitious was employed to provide food an enjoyment for the less prosperous members of the community, for at Feast of Merit, there was meat, rice and rice-beer for every man, woman and children.

Again, regarding Maran Kasa, R.R. Shimray wrote:[40]

> The deeper philosophy involved is, however, the sense of generosity and the warm-heartedness towards the poor people who are fed on the occasion. It is, in essence, sharing of the wealth and fortune by the rich people with the community.

Feast of Merit is common to all Naga tribes with only slight variations. The one who intends to perform Maran should observe certain taboos which involve restraining conjugal relationship with his wife and perform some rites and divination with the village priest to see the omen and consult the spirit. When the result is positive, he makes public declaration of his intent. Preparation of meat, food and drink begins months ahead of the great day.

When the day of Maran comes, the selected tree for the post of Tarung is felled down and carved into its design. Then the able male population of the village drag it home with the noise of ho-ho cry filling the air. Supply of food and drink should be in plenty in the course of dragging. It may take days to bring the post home; sometimes, even weeks, for the post is often from a very large tree, and from far distant forest.

To erect the Tarung, a good number of cattles - buffaloes, cows, pigs and dogs were killed. But in eastern and also southern Tangkhul Nagas, this Maran called Zameng, the whole livestock of the household should be killed sparing none. The blood of animals sacrificed is smeared to the post and erected in front of the house of the donor. In this ceremony, the Awunga was invited and offered the prominent seat and served the best choice of meat and wine. The entire population of the village was also invited and the feast continued for days, even for weeks until all the domestic animals were killed and eaten. Then the whole village community blessed the one who performs the feast and offer prayers that they may enjoy happy and prosperous life.

However, with the advent of Christianity, performance of Maran Kasa was frowned upon by the Christian as they believed such act as paganism. The spirit of generosity and public feeding turned to individualism hoarding wealth for private gain and benefits. The rich culture of the Tangkhuls has, therefore, degenerated in this respect. Yet some generous Christians feed their church members during the Christmas season although it does not necessarily mean a Feast of Merit as before.

Longshim

Next to the institution of Awunga and his council called Hangva, the most important institution of Tangkhul village is Longhim. Long means association, group of people or collection of people; and Shim means house, club, or chamber. Every Tangkhul village had one Longshim or more, where unmarried boys and girls slept in their separate sleeping Longshims. So they can be called the 'Sleeping Chamber' of boys and girls. In English, modern writers use the term - *'Dormitory'*. Yet in local term, they called it Morung which is of Assamese Origin.[41] Longshim system is practised by all Naga tribes, Kukis, Mizos, Garos, Adis, Mishimis, Mikirs, Singphos and some other tribes of central India.[42]

Longshim plays a role not only of a sleeping chamber. It is the centre of the totality of the Tangkhul life - social, economic, political, military, cultural and religious activities. It is in Longshim that all boys and girls get useful lessons and trainings for the individual, family and community living that it can rightly be called social centre of the village where many kinds of training is imparted to young people worthy of the society. Yet life in Longshim is not full of fatigue and labour; rather, all activities in Longshim are blended with mirth and merriment. Therefore, it is an entertainment centre as well. Several writers give their observations with regard to the establishment and functions of Longshim. According to Jyotirmoy Roy:[43]

> They are the headquarters of village defence, recreation clubs and the centres of education, art and ceremonial functions. Young men are trained here in various arts and crafts, dance and music, morality, discipline as well as in the arts of offence and defence. Discipline is strictly enforced. All the young men in the village sleep there sending out batches of armed sentries to watch and guard the village.

According to Haimendorf:[44]

> The bachelors' hall is an institution much like the English public school. One may agree or argue with the principle

> giving boys a training in community spirit outside the individual family, but there can be no question that the Morung was one of the main pillars of the Aos' social order. The bachelors' hall was the social centre of the village, the age group of the Morung were the natural labour teams for every public work, and the rights and obligations of every member of the community were regulated by his place in the age group system.

But as a matter of fact, the members of public school are not entrusted with the responsibility and functions similar to those entrusted to the members of Longshim. The Longshim was under the authority of the Awunga and the Hangva. The Hangva regulated the rules of Longshim based on custom and the internal administration was left to the elders of the Longshim. This gave excellent training to youngsters for future village leadership. Violation of rule is awarded with punishment.

Discipline is the basis of all Longshim activities. Juniors are under strict disciplinary training. Discipline, obedience and good manners shaped the life of a member; and then courage, skill and efficiency temper it. After undergoing such a training, a boy is ready to discharge any form of duty and responsibilities of the village. Juniors are subject to rigorous training. They are supposed to run errands in obedience to their seniors, collect firewood, fetch water, and all sorts of tasks, big or small, easy or otherwise. To test their courage, they are also sent to the jungle in the dark of the night and ordered, to bring branch of certain trees situated at a distance. They have to carry out all these with prompt action. This is the probabitonary period of junior members. After the completion of three to five years, they are admitted to intermediate group with greater responsibilities.

The intermediate group has important functions of helping the weak and distressed of the village and assisting the seniors in the administration of the Longshim. Seniors should remain always alert to run the Longshim well. If anybody fails to fulfill the work assigned to him; appropriate action was taken. Disobedience was punished with the expulsion from Longshim for a period of time, and there was nothing more disgrace for a member than expulsion from membership of Longshiro. R. R. Shimray further explains that in the Longshim, family pride and personal arrogance had no place in the Morung. Rich or poor - everybody was equal in the membership of Morung in particular and society in general. [45]

As a training centre in the Longshim, young people had to learn all kinds of handicrafts prevalent in Tangkhul villages. Being a spacious house, village elders bring their unfinished works where young people learn wood carving, weaving mats, baskets etc. A spirit of keen competition and ambition to excel others helps them to learn fast and soon, they can excel in all forms of handicrafts. Education was imparted to young Tangkhuls through oral instruction in their Longshims. Teaching of Tangkhul history is imparted in the evening after meal and on festive days. First, the orator (a person who is well versed in history) narrates the story and then puts it into folklores, songs and poetry. Again, in early days, because of constant war among the Tangkhul villages, Longshim was the centre of military training and defence of the village. All sorts of war tactics like the use of dao, spear, bow and arrow, holding shield, offensive as well as defensive trainings were given to the members of the Longshim. The spirit of sacrifice was the utmost trait of the members for the protection of their village. People of different shades came and lived together in a Longshim so that it developed the spirit of team work; and this spirit plus the danger of war melted away personal and individual differences. Therefore, Longshim is no doubt, a place of understanding and reconciliation.

The Longshim also served as custodian of war trophy. All war trophies (human heads) collected in the inter-village feuds, which was the highest glory of the Nagas in early days were deposited in Longshim.[46] Religious functions and ceremonies of the village were also conducted, in Longshim. The village festivals and other social activities begin from Longshim. Therefore, Longshim is the centre of socio-religious activities of the village as well. Longshim is also regarded as a sacred place for which its sanctity was to be honoured. Entrance of women in Longshim is prohibited, otherwise, the village, it was believed, would not prosper in war, hunting, fishing etc.

Longshim fostered sports activities and produced good sportsmen. The young members were taught the art of singing, dancing, wrestling, spear-throwing etc. In the evening after meal, when all the members came together, they spent time in singing, dancing and merry-making. Here the young boys learnt folklores, singing and all sorts of dance. Without entertainment of mirth and merry-making, the meaning of Longshim is incomplete. At night, it is customary for youths of Longshim to pay romantic visit to the "Girls' Dormitory" called Ngalalong in groups. However, pre-marital sex is strictly controlled.

Membership

Membership of a Longshim is open, and a must to all unmarried boys who have attained puberty. But in order that a boy may learn the art of living and able to master the problem of living as early as possible, generally boys of ten to fifteen years of age were admitted into a Longshim. The membership continues till a member marries. In rare cases, according to the demand of the situation, a married member was required to continue his presence for a year or so. His conjugal relationship with his wife was restricted by his membership of Longshim.

The new entrants were required to undergo severe trials and ordeals for three to five years. This is the probation period at the end of which, they were promoted to full membership as intermediates. This group of people has to involve in important village responsibilities. The last and highest category of membership is the senior group who are required to be active members as well as leaders in all village affairs and business.

Ngalalong

While Longshim is the dormitory of young men, Ngalalong is that of young women. This institution is found among other Naga tribes as well. *Ngala* means maiden, and Long means group/association. Therefore, Ngalalong is the "Dormitory of Maidens" or "Ladies Dormitory". Haimendorf called it "The Girls' Club".[47] Some Naga tribes such as the Mao-Maram have a separate building for Ngalalong whereas the Angamis, Semas, Rengmas,, Lothas, Tangkhuls etc. do not provide separate quarters for it. In most cases, it is attached to the house of a clan head or a rich man who becomes the patron of it. The running of Ngalalong; admission, training and functions is all the same as Longshim. All unmarried girls who have attained puberty should take membership of Ngalalong and sleep there till marriage. J. P. Mills remarked:[48]

> It is as shameful for girls as it is for boys to sleep with their parents when they reaoh years of understanding. Corresponding to "morung" for boys, there are therefore, dormitories for girls . . . from the age of six or seven till they are married.

Ngalalong is also an autonomous institution for its internal administration under the regulation of the Village Council. Weaving, spinning, stitching and embroidery works are taught, and done at Ngalalong, by senior members since parents are naturally busy with household duties. Music and dancing are also taught at Ngalalong. Here, the girls are instructed to maintain strict moral standard not to pollute the sanctity of the house. The girls also learnt social behaviour, manners, obedience and politeness, most of all, how to behave towards the opposite sex. According to Tangkhul culture, girls should always be modest and humble before a boy. Thus, in Ngalalong, the character of a girl is moulded for future responsibilities of motherhood.

With the coming of Christianity to the Tangkhuls and other Naga tribes, the importance and values of the Longshim and Ngalalong have been wrongly assessed by Christian Missionaries. They did not appreciate the cultural and traditional instututions of the Tangkhuls, and consequently, these ideas also become accepted in the minds of the new converts. They sought to introduce western cultural values with Christianity. As a result, social and cultural degeneration of the Tangkhuls is evidenced. Therefore, Horam laments: "We see them that, it was the Longshim which fostered the Tangkhul art, craft, music and dance. The disappearance of the Longshim talled the death-knell of Tangkhul culture.[49] Crying out on the abandonment of the Morung, Haimendorf remarked, "Gone are the days, perhaps never to return."[50]

Log Drum

Log Drum is an important item of the Naga life. It is used in all forms of activities - in time of war and peace. Since Longshim is the centre of village activities, a log drum is stationed there. The occurrence of war, death, victory in war, advent of festivals and all important events of the village is signalled by beating the log drum varying in sound according to the nature of the occasion. Accordingly, people should be ready to respond to the sound whether for war, festival, sports, singing and dancing. In early days, when inter-village feuds were common, there was constant vigil, and the moment the march of the enemies against the village was spotted, they sounded it that people should take position in defence against the raid and attack of the enemy.

These drums were hewn out of single giant tree about fifty to sixty feet long and ten feet in diameter. The trunk is made hollow all along with a slit in its upper side. When it was beaten with drum sticks, it produces mighty sound reaching about hundred miles distance. In the remote past, at Ningthi village there was a giant log drum called Daorila (the name was given by the spirit) which when beaten the sound could be heard even at Hongkha-Muja, one of the earliest permanent residences of the Tangkhuls at Patkoi range, some one hundred miles away.

NOTES & REFERENCES

1. M. M. Clark, *A Corner in India*, pp. 15-17; Ursula Graham Bower, *Naga Path*, pp. 2-3; C. Haimendorf, *Naked Nagas;* pp. 73-74; T. C. Hodson, *Naga Tribes of Manipur*, p. 186.

2. M. Horam, *North East India, A Profile*, pp. 92-93.

3. J. P. Mills, *The Effects on the Naga Tribes of Assam*, of Their *Contact with Western Civilization*, pp. 71-72.

4. G.E.R. Grant Brown, *Burma Gazetteer*, Upper Chindwin District, p. 26.

5. S.C. Sardeshpande, *The Patkoi Nagas*, p. 125.

6. S. C. Sardeshpande, *Ibid.*, p. 163.

7. Howling is performed only by Tangkhul men to chase animal, in killing of wild animal (game), in war and in their dances.

8. Y.K. Shimray quotes B.C. Nag in K.B. Singh (ed.), *An Introduction to the Tribal Language and Culture of Manipur*, p. 29.

9. M. Horam, *Social and Cultural Life of Nagas*, p. 61.

10. By this, is meant that the head of the family was a priest in respect of the traditional religion of the Tangkhuls. This position has ceased with their conversion to Christianity.

11. According to Hodson, the Nagas hardly chastised and disciplined their children. He wrote, "Children are scolded but seldom chastised," *The Naga Tribes of Manipur*, p. 7. However, this had been the poor assessment and judgement of many outsiders that they always gave wrong notion of the actual social life of the Nagas which marred the true picture of the Nagas.

12. M. Horam, *op. cit.*, p. 62.

13. Y. K. Shimray, *op.cit.,* p. .20; R. R. Shmray, *Origin and Culture of Nagas,* p. 168.

14. Y. K. Shimray, *op.cit.,* pp. 13-14; R. R. Shimray, *op. cit.,* p. 145.

15. In early days, when a group of people settled at a place, and established a village, the settlement was divided into blocks called TANG. Each clan was allotted one TANG for the settlement of the clansmen where they made their houses there. Most writers call this Khel which is an Assamese word.

16. R. R. Shimray, *op. cit.,* p. 44.

17. Verrier Elwin, *The Nagas in Nineteenth Century,* p. 100.

18. M. Horam, *Social and Cultural Life of Nagas.* p. 84.

19. T.C. Hodson, *op. cit.,* p. 194.

20. E. R. Leach, *Political Systems of Highland Burma: A Study of Kachin Social Structure,* p. 213.

21. R. R. Shimray, *op.cit.,* p. 165.

22. E. R. Leach, *Political Systems of Highland Burma,* p.213. In this book, Leach presented the laws of inheritance of Kachins and Shans which was effected in preference of birth of the sons of a man.

23. J. H. Button, *The Angami Nagas,* p. 135.

24. R. R. Shimray, *op. cit.,* p. 170.

25. Bimal J. Dev and Dilip K. Lahiri, Manipur Culture and Politics, p. 13.

26. Christoph von Furer-Haimendorf, *Return to the Naked Nagas,* p.. 90.

27. Verrier Elwin, *The Nagas in Nineteenth Century,* p. 498.

28. M. Horam, *Social and Cultural Life of Nagas,* p. 59.

29. The Tangkhul marriage being both love and arranged marriage of the boy and the girl and their respective parents, there is hardly any room of idea for divorce. Therefore, Hodson comments - "Divorce is of rare occurrence among the Tangkhuls" —Naga Tribes of Manipur, p. 97; Bimal J. Dev and Dilip K. Lahiri, *Manipur Culture and Politics,* p. 13.

30. Christoph von Furer Haimendorf has made several references in this respect in his book. Naked Nagas. For references, see pp. 47, 50, 51, 174. Also P. Imchen. *Ancient Ao Naga Religion and Culture,* pp. 148, 159, 160, 161; M. Horam, *Naga Polity,* p. 133.

31. Kazeiram, according to Tangkhuls, is the land of the dead which lies in the heart of the earth. Therefore, it is an underground world where the soul of the dead lives as he lived on this earth doing the same cultivation and other activities.

32. M. Horam, *Naga Polity,* p. 33.

33. A. S. Vashi Shimray, "The Naga Kingdom," unpublished manuscript, no paging.

34. Sipra Sen, *Tribes and Castes of Manipur,* p. 32.

35. T. C. Hodson, *op. cit.,* p. 49.

36. Verrier Elwin, *op. cit.,* p. 472, Footnote.

37. The immoral girls were penalised by the community of Ngalalong for bringing bad name to the institution in the form of imposing fine, temporary expulsion from dormitory or is boycotted from Yarthot.

38. Tarung is a large woodpost erected in the form of totem.

39. Christoph Von Furer-Haimendorf, *op. cit.,* p. 47.

40. R. R. Shimray, op.cit., p. 113.

41. Though this institution is called differently, and Morung by the Tangkhul writers, it does not give the essence of the Tangkhul institution which has its own term 'Longshim'. It is preferred that the Tangkhul word for this institution be used in preference to the term referred above.

42. M. Horam, *Naga Polity,* p. 66.

43. Jyotirmoy Roy, History of Manipur, p. 195.

44. Christoph Von Furer Haimendorf, *op.cit.,* p. 47.

45. R. R. Shimray, *op.cit.,* p. 194.

46. In certain case, the war trophies were deposited in the house of the chief of the clan, whereas in certain other case, they were deposited in the house of Awunga.

47. Christoph Von Furer Haimendorf, *op.cit.,* p. 83.
48. J. P. Mills, *The Rengma Naga,* p. 52.
49. M. Horam, *Social and Cultural Life of Nagas,* p. 73.
50. Christoph Von Furer Haimendorf, *op. cit.,* p. 46

5

POLITICAL AND JUDICIAL ORGANISATION

The Tangkhuls, as we have seen are a major tribe of the Nagas, occupy a compact area of some protions of Sadar Hills District, eastern Senapati District, the whole of Ukhrul District and north-western parts of Burma (Myanmar). The formation of the early Tangkhul village states were based on the territorial divisions which by the division of village territory became village states. In early days, every Tangkhul village big or small was an independent state and exercised, its independent power. They also had independent judicial organisation, free from intervention of outside forces. Because, unlike the Kukis, the love of the Nagas for their village is so strong that, for them, it was, and is, everything life or death. An observation was made on the nature of Naga village by Elwin that they are not migratory people and their villages were stationary and unchanged.[1]

The Awunga

Every Naga village was, and is, ruled by a chief assisted by a Council of Elders. Some Naga tribes like the Aos, Lothas and Angamis have a republican form of government in which chieftainship is not permanent or herediatary, whereas some other tribes like the Konyaks, Maos, Rongmeis and Tangkhuls have a form of government akin to monarchical form of government, in which the post of chief is permanent and hereditary. Again, some monarchical village states are despotic as is found among the Konyaks and Semas, whereas, the monarchical government of the Tangkhuls is essentially democratic despite the hereditary post of the chief called Awunga. The polity of Tankhul village state is discussed below.

The Tangkhul village state was a type of monarchical state ruled by a chief called Awunga. Although the Tangkhuls do not exercise, the theory of the divine origin of the Tangkhul Awunga, yet they believed that the chief had divine sanction, "He is the accepted person of God to be the Awunga of the people", and therefore, his position cannot be challenged. The whole administration of the Khawung is carried upon his head. Yet for day-to-day execution of the government, he is assisted by a Council of Village Elders called Hangva. M. Alemchiba called it 'The Parliament of the Village'.[2] Horam has called it 'Council of Ministers.'[3] As a matter of fact, Hangva functions as Council of Ministers being the executive of the village state as well as parliament as its members represent the people of various clans of the village.

Along with the monarchical form of government, we find the presence of democracy in the village state of the Tangkhuls which made it a popular government. The word democracy is modern to the Nagas. However, the system of democracy has been in practice by the Tangkhuls from remote past. In the democratic system of Tangkhul Village State, only grown-up adult males can take part in the deliberation of the General Assembly of the village. The presence of Hangva and democratic principles check the virtual absolutism of the Awunga. Further, he has to exercise his power based on the customary laws that there is no room provided for his being autocratic. In this regard, J. Roy writes:[4]

> Hill-men have their indigenous tribal polity which varies from tribe to tribe. The variation ranges from despotic chieftaincy

> of the Thadous to the democratic village council of the Maos, from Semi-republic gerontocracy of the Kabuis to the limited chieftainship of the Tangkhuls... are strictly observed. In some cases, the democratic institutions work as a check on the autocracy of the chief.

Again, in the Riyan (Unwritten Constitution) of the Tangkhuls we find the presence of religious elements. The Riyan is based on social customs which is the foundation stone of the Tangkhul customary laws. Further, the Tangkhuls believed that, violation of customary law entails not only legal punishment, but the wrath of God and His ultimate punishment. From this point of view, the customary law has religious sanction. Apart from the secular function, the Awunga has religious powers and will be studied in the following chapter.

Function of the Awunga

The Awunga has a dual functions as the head of the Village State. These' are secular and religious. However, secular functions are fa more important and outnumber the religious functions. His former duties cannot be taken over by anybody as he alone is the ordained and consecrated Chief of the village. His religious responsibilities can be shared by the village priest.

The secular duties of the Awunga are manifold. In early days, due to constant warfare among the villages, the primary concern of the Awunga was for the peace, prosperity and defence of his subject people. Hence the erection of village gates.[5] There should be constant vigil by village defence force without lapse.

For the prosperity of the villagers, he parcels out cultivable land to the people in consultation with the village Councillors. He has to ensure that every family of the village gets sufficient land of cultivation for their sustenance for the entire year.

He summons the Village Council (Hangva) and presides over it, and in this, his house serves as the Assembly Hall of the village by custom of the Tangkhuls. When dispute or any case otherwise arises, here agin, the residence of the Awunga becomes the Village Court. Whereas every clan has its own court, the Court of Awunga-in-Council renders the Supreme Court of the village, because, there is no court of appeal above the Court of the Awunga-in-Council.

As the head of the village, all the visitors in the village should report to him about the nature and purpose of the visit; and it is the responsibility of the Awunga that no stranger is maltreated. If they do not have any place to reside, he has to take them in and feed them.

Regarding the religious functions of the Awunga, he has several religious rights and duties along with the village priest. Since he cares for the life and welfare of his subject people, he has to put himself under strict religious discipline and taboos. He has to observe food taboos restraining from meats of birds like the eagle and its kind, tiger and its kind, squirrel and' its kind, flying fox etc. He has to keep the village taboos and live a holy life above reproach.

All village festivals, social functions, religious functions and solemn days are to be opened with the performance of rites and sacrifices by the Awunga. When calamities like draught, hail storm, famine and epidemics visit the village, he offers sacrifieces and propitiates the village deity and invokes for the prosperity of the village. At times, the actual worship and sacrifices were performed by the village priest, yet the presence of the Awunga in religious ceremonies was important.

The Tangkhul Awunga enjoys certain rights and privileges. The Awunga is the head of the village and his office is permanent and hereditary. Therefore, he is the 'First Man' among the equals. In all functions, and gatherings, he deserves and occupies the best and prominent seat; and the best portion of wine and meat is served to him. He gets a portion of animals killed in the village and from all hunted games. In token of his service to the people as the chief, the villagers help him build and repair his house; and cultivate his field. He is entitled to get portion of the harvest from the villagers. As a matter of fact, the Awunga is honoured and revered as ordained Chief of God. It is a Tangkhul cultural trait that a man should not speak to the Awunga in his face.

The Hangva

In every village, there is a council of elders called the Hangva. It is the most important organ of the government machinery of the Tangkhul Village State. Hence, it is the most desired post of the village which the people aspire for. However, the membership in the Hangva is confined to the clan heads only. Sometimes, a big clan, according to its size, requires to represe it more members in the Hangva apart from the representation of the clan-head. Further, some influential persons whose representation in the Hangva will be found beneficial to the people are also taken into the membership of the Hangva. Therefore, the real Hangva is composed of the membership of the Awunga as head, clan heads and some selected or nominated members of the village. This carries the day-to-day administration of the government of the Village State. But under any circumstances, no unmarried person is eligible for the post of a Councillor, as marriage is a sign of maturity.

In early days, according to convention, custom and practices, contest and election system never occurred in Tangkhul polity how prestigious the post might be. Although two-three persons were nominated for one post, they used to withdraw in favour of their friends. In such cases, the elderly people chose one of them which the people would accept. It contributed strong and stable government of the Village State and there was no room for corruption when the state was run by efficient village statesmen.

Functions of the Hangva

Following the pattern of the functions of modern government, we can also divide the functions of the Hangva into three categories: (1) Executive, (2) Administrative, and (3) Judicial. These functions are discussed below in brief.

(1) *Executive Functions:* All the rules and regulations and decisions made in the Village Council or in the General Assembly of the village should be effectively implemented by the Councillors. The Hangva formulated policies for war, peace, economy, social activities etc., and they should be well-executed. Because, the life of the Tangkhuls was guided by superstitious belief that violation of any law brings down the wrath of gods and punished not only to the law breakers, but to the entire village community. Therefore, it is collective responsibility of the entire village community that all the laws and decisions are well-kept and do accordingly without exception. Those who violated the law were punished with fines according to convention and practices of the ancestors depending on the nature and conditions of the case.

(2) *Administrative Functions:* The administrative functions of the Village Council is rather important and prominent. Construction of village defence, village gate, village compound, water supply, footpath, inter-village footpath etc., are regularly carriedout by the village community at the decision and order of the Hangva. It was, and is, custom of the Tangkhuls that inter-village paths are cleared and maintained. Bridges are made across the streams. It decided portion of village land for cultivation, fixed the dates of cultivation, sowing seeds, village ceremonies, festivals etc., which the villagers had to follow. Village mass- hunting and mass-fishing are fixed and arranged by the Council and the return is celebrated with eating and drinking. In early days number of houses to be constructed was also fixed by the Council and it arranged supply of wood, and bamboos from the village land. The houses were built together by the villagers. The occupant would have to offer food and drink.

Village festivals and fairs were also held according to the dates fixed by the Hangva. When any death or accident occurred elsewhere among the villagers, it was the Council to arrange for transportation of the dead or the patient, and the needy people always get help from people under the good office of the Hangva. The poor, widows and orphans were not left at the mercy of misfortune. The Hangva ensured their care and sustenance.

(3) *Judicial Functions:* Judicial function is the most important function of the Village Council. The Awunga and the Councillors constitute the highest Court of Justice above which there is no other court of appeal. After hearing the matter from both parties, the arbitration of the Council is final and binding. All cases and disputes are settled by this Court. But first of all, the Court tries its best to solve the cases peacefully in the form of conciliation and compromise. However, when this measure cannot bring solution, the matter is settled according to customary laws. Before the case reached this court, clan elders usually tried to solve the matter as far as possible in a peaceful way so that the differences of the people may be narrowed down, and the case may not go to the Village Court. In Tangkhul society, to go to court of any form was regarded as an act of disgrace.

Council of Wungnao

Council of Wungnao is not a formal body in the true sense of the term. It does not have a clear definition of its functions. This body is constituted by the Awunga and the chiefs of the clans residing in the village; and they are the members of the Hangva as well. Therefore, they have no separate function of the Village State. However, any case or problem of any form, when neither the General Assembly nor the Village Council is in a position to solve the issue, the Awunga and the clan chiefs, a body which is called Wungnaos, set themselves aside and discuss the issue in question. The arbitration of the Council of Wungnaos is final and binding. No one can challenge the decision of the Wungnaos whatsoever. Therefore, the seating of the Wungnaos is greatly feared and highly revered.

Riyan — An Unwritten Constitution

From times immemorial, the Tangkhuls had their Village State and its government. It was an independent unit in all respects. This continued to exist intact for centuries and until recent times without much change. There was no formal constitution as such in the pattern of modern state. However they have an unwritten constitution known as RIYAN which is far more better and effective than many of the written constitution of today. This is testified by the fact that there has been no reaction against the established government of village authorities till date. The Naga customary laws have been well-tried and tasted for centuries that their forefathers found it good and effective in the administration of the Village State.

Culture, traditions, usages, customs and conventions serve as the foundation of Riyan with the religious sanction. Because, most of the tribal customs and laws were based on religious practices and faith that, they are divine by nature. Therefore, Tangkhul Village State can rightly be termed a theocratic state. In this, Horam writes: "In Naga Polity, generally speaking, laws fall into two broad categories: (a) Laws given by God, i.e., Divine Laws, (b) Man-made Laws, i.e. Secular Laws."[6] According to their belief, violation of traditions, customs and culture entailed divine wrath and punishment. Therefore, they are known as divine laws; and it was believed that divine laws were given by God through the priests, oracles and wise-men of early days. For example, marriage within the clan is violation of customary law, and in such a case, not only the one who violated the law or committed sin was subjected to divine wrath and punishment of God; but also the entire village community. However, secular laws are those made by wise-men and elders who are conversant in tradition and culture. For example, they made different laws on theft according to the nature of theft committed and the value of article stolen. Punishment on theft committed in a field is lighter than theft committed in a storehouse, and so on.[7] These are the secular laws made by wise-men of the village in early days.

All the constitutions and written laws are subject to amendment in conformity with the changing situation. But the unwritten constitution of the Tangkhuls (Riyan) is rigid; and there is hardly any room for alteration due to their belief in the presence of divine sanction. They are in the nature of a Standing Law. Based on Riyan, certain secular laws are framed for day to day administration of the village. They are known as Mayonrin. Again, Mayonrin is not flexible and all the laws are strictly enforced. In early days, breaking of the laws was heavily and drastically punished by the court of the Village Council. There lay the strength of the Riyan and it was the Riyan on which the Khawung was established. The people were ably governed, law and order was excellent, life was peaceful and secure, and prosperity was conditioned and guaranteed.

Tangkhul justice is cheap and effective and is made available to all high and low, rich and poor and all are equal before the eyes of law. Widows and orphans always get their protection and justice under the Village Court. Since judges are represented from each clan, justice is within the reach of every villager. Cases are settled on the principles of customary laws and religious principles; and therefore, there is no room for favouritism and respect of person. All kinds of quarrels, disputes and problems referred to Village Court are speedily settled by it.

Cases within the clan are handled by the clan Chief and elders as far as practicable. Interclan cases are also handled by the clans concerned in a peaceful way. When the differences of the two parties are too wide and a solution to the problem cannot be sought out, then only the case is referred to the Village Court. Whatever the case may be, judgements are quick and effective, and naturally, both the parties accept the verdict issued by the Village Court.

When any case is referred to the Awunga then immediately he arranges and summons the Hangva within a few days. He also summons parties involved in the case for hearing. The residence of the Awunga is the Village Court and he presides over it. First, he gives a brief account of the case and presents it to the Council. But before the deliberation, both the parties are given time to plead their part.

At first, the Court attempts to bring about a peaceful solution of the case in the form of compromise and conciliation. However, when two parties persist in their stands and cannot agree, then the jury, after deliberation, makes arbitrary verdict and the .decision is final and binding on both parties. There is no higher court of appeal above the court of Hangva.

Oath

Should one party or the other or both the parties do not agree to the arbitration of the court of Hangva, then oath is taken and the verdict goes in favour of the one who takes the oath. Sometimes two parties take oath, and in such case, a time limit is given within which if a party suffers death or misfortune, it is deemed to have sworn falsely. Indeed, it is the last resort of the village Court to decide cases of disputes and quarrels of any form. When this measure is taken, no party can deny the outcome. By any means, they have to accept it either in peace or in grudge.

All the Naga tribes honour and revere the swearing and oath-taking except the Semas. Swearing is a life and death question, not only to the one who swears, but the whole members of the family, clan, and even the co- villagers also. Therefore, the Nagas never take oath lightly, except in extreme serious cases when a man is convinced that he is right. The words of the oaths are framed in the most solemn way invoking heaven and earth to be the witnesses that the swearer is innocent. Or if he has taken oath falsely, uttering the name of Almighty God and solemnly declares that he be the most accursed on this earth, the result is sure to follow. H. H. Hutton remarked about oath taking of the Semas:[8]

> The Sema oath has not the value of the Angami oath, and as it is far less common among the Semas, for one party to be quite willing to accept the oath of the other, the oath is less resorted by Semas than by many other Naga tribes.

Of the Tangkhuls, Hodson wrote:[9]

> Among the Tangkhuls, there are many forms of oaths. . . . The weightiest oath is that which concludes with imprecation, "If I lie, may I and my family (or clansmen or co-villagers) descend into the earth and be seen no more."

Whatever form of swearing an oath may be, a person utters calling the name of Almighty God that if he swears falsely, God may punish him, and he be the most accursed on this earth. In some cases, oaths are taken in such a serious way that, even the lives of the family members and clansmen may be in danger of the false oath.

There are several forms of oath taking among the Tangkhuls. Sometimes, the earth of disputed area is taken into the mouth and swallowed. to testify that he is the owner of the land. In another oath a lump of the earth is dipped into water and drunk. Tiger's tooth is also used for oath-taking. The man who swears bites the tiger's tooth and imprecates that if he takes the oath falsely, the tiger may tear him into pieces in the way he bites the tiger's tooth. Sometimes, people call down thunder-to hit at them should they swear falsely. Whatever form of oath may be, the result is sure to come, some how, sooner or later. No one can escape the words he utters in the name of God. Therefore, before they resorted to swearing, the Village Court and parties concerned try to settle the cases.

Ordeals

Trial by ordeal is another means of deciding case. It is

in practice even today. It is the most simple way of deciding a case.

The result is instant and true to the letter that both parties, even the spectators also honour the outcome of the ordeal. There are different way of trial by ordeal of the Tangkhuls, of which one is, that both the parties are asked to bite burning charcoal and the one who is innocent or guiltless will escape the burn of charcoal unharmed. Sometimes, a fire is made and they are asked to .jump over the soaring flame. But the most prevalent trial by ordeal is to dive into a pond of water and the one who stays longer under the water is declared the winner of the case. This form of ordeal is used to decide cases concerning women.

The most awful ordeal of the Tangkhuls is to fight out justice by combat. However, they rarely resort to this method of ordeal to settle their issues. It was not the interest of the Village Court either since it involves bloodshed. Nevertheless, sometimes, the two contenders, out of ferocity and concern for the case which each believes to be the right, ask the Hangva to sanction combat to fight out justice when other means of solution was out of sight. Then the court makes two clubs or daos (swords) of equal size-length, breadth and weight. The weapons of the combat were kept in a safe custody for one or two days. After that when the Hangva took them out, it is found that the weapon of the one who was right was bigger or longer than the other, they would ask the other person to withdraw his stance since the instrument clearly testified the matter. Yet if he persisted for the combat, it was allowed by the court. The one who hits the opponent first was declared the winner and ultimately, the case was thus settled. Sometimes, it caused loss of life or even handicap for life.

Warfare

This section on warfare is incorporated in this chapter 'as it relates to the village states and their defence. War is one of the criteria which determines the existence and formation of a nation. To resort to war is as old as the existence humankind. Like other nations of the world, the Nagas also involved in several warfares, and they are known for their warlike character. Yet their life is not devoid of peace. Rather, their love for peace is greater than war; and once peace is established, they are more friendly, honest, hospitable, trustworthy, dependable and loyal to their, trust. An anthropologist has remarked:[10] "...the Nagas never faltered in their loyalty." According to Maj. Godwin Austen.[11]

> However warlike a people may be, their quarrels are not fundamental to their lives and unhappily the history books have little to tell of the real life of this enterprising, hard working and romantic people.

Further, Haimendorf wrote:[12]

> Popular opinion was inclined to imagine the Nagas as a fierce warlike people, continuously occupied with head-hunting, human sacrifice, and another exciting customs. But this picture drawn by journalists who spent perhaps a week in Naga Hills had very little in common with reality.

The question arises - why then did the Nagas collect heads? According to the nature of Naga war, how can the society know that a warrior kills the enemy without the head of enemy being produced by him? Therefore, collection of the enemy heads killed in the war was a must for a Naga warrior to testify his achievement of killing the enemy in war. In this regard, Hutton remarked:[13]

> What man or at least what Naga, who has killed his enemy does not want to boast about it? And unless he can show the body, where is the proof? .... If the slayer can produce the body of the slain, his statement is likely to be accepted as true, and since retrieving the body would be laborious, not to say often dangerous, proceeding the head is the natural part of it to bring back as

> testimony as it gives a definite assurance that the foe has been killed, not scatched. Most Britishers are headhunters at heart, and to a Naga, every sort of head is welcome.

History is full of incidences how soldiers collected the heads of fallen enemies, yet they are not called headhunters. This derogatory term has been applied to tribes such as the Nagas because they procured human heads fallen in war. This is the wrong approach of people to Naga war and they are wrongly branded as head hunters.

The Nagas, in general, and the Tangkhuls in particular, have refined laws and principles of war that guide their participation in warfare. In history, there are references where torture, rape and molestation of women and children are common. As for the Nagas, it is a ta)oo for a Naga warrior to touch a woman immediately before and after the war for a certain length of time, even for months, when he is observing divination except for chopping of heads. This shows high moral standard of the Tangkhul war. In this, R. R. Shimray wrote"[14]

> Since sex was taboo in war, Naga warriors never touch a woman when in a state of war except for chopping the head. That is why rape was unheard in Naga war history. Head- hunting was a cruel practice but physical torture or rape before actual killing are more appalling and beastly.

Summing up all these facts, Shimray concludes: "It is therefore erroneous to generalise that Naga war means head-hunting only. It would be more appropriate to call it a war rather than head-hunting."[15]

Cause of War

There are several theories and explanations with regard to the causes of Naga war, and all these theories are connected with the belief that possession of human head brings about fertility of women, soil, social prestige and happiness after death, the soul of the victim being the servant of the soul of victor who killed him, in the land of the dead called Kazeiram. But none of these theories holds true on the ground that no war can be fought and ever fought for the fertility of women, soil, or under any circumstances without legal cause. When there is a legal cause occasioned by the violation of the established inter-village state laws by one party, then justice must be fought out. Hence the inter-village war. By fraud, if a man of one village had taken the head of another village, this also led to the outbreak of war on the principle of "An eye for an eye, a tooth for a tooth." Sometimes, violation of inter-village boundaries, divorce of woman without reasonable cause, and the like draw the villages into war.

Types of War

The Tangkhuls are warlike people as well as peace loving society. They can be in any form as the situation demands. When war comes, no price is too costly for them for the defence of their village and the people. There are several types of war of the Tangkhuls of which some important ones are discussed below in brief. Whatever type of war it may be, several days preceding the war, a person should observe some taboos. First, he had to abstain from conjugal union with woman, and not to touch any thing pertaining to woman and keep food taboos. He performed rites and sacrifices, and consulted dreams and divinations. When he found positive response of the spirits, then only he could go for the war, equipped with dao, spear, shield, helmet etc. Only the eastern and southern Tangkhuls used bow and poisoned arrow.

Declared War

When a certain village violated the established law of the inter-village state and it effected the neighbouring village, then, the latter has every right to declare war upon the former. The declaration of war was sent to the enemy village through a war messenger[16] It is custom that he should be treated well. If the security of the messenger was in question, the declaration of war was sent through a neutral village. The two parties met either at the appointed battle field, or the aggressive party could make surprise attack to the enemy village using their tactics. Each Naga village had its own defence system surrounded by stone boulders, ditch and sharp-pointed bamboo spikes. The village gate was well secured with heavy solid beam. The gate and the whole village was under the constant vigil of the warriors.

The war may continue for days, months, years, even for generations. Agricultural seasons however, are always honoured so that there may be enough sustenance for the people. Peace could be initiated by either side and used the service of Pukreila, usually a woman married to a man of the enemy village. She is called "Ambassador of Peace", who cannot be harmed. She has to hold a branch of green leaves as a sign of peace. Peace could also be brought about by the intervention of a neutral village. When peace was established, there was exchange of food and di nk to signify that they were one and in peace. There was exchange of daos and spears to signify that war- weapons should not be used against each other.

Undeclared War

Undeclared war may be termed as "War of Revenge." It is rather individual, family or clan war against some other village. There were cases where the entire village was also drawn in it. In most cases, undeclared war was the result of divorce of a woman who had been sent back to her village without proper reason, or slaying a person by fraud in order to bring a head horne. Here the family of the deceased is always on the lookout to take the head of the enemy village as a revenge for the loss of its member. Sometime, it can be the continuation of the declared war when it protracted for a long time. Then-various means of war tactics came into operation. Sometime, they ambushed the enemy by the way of the field, and sometimes, adventurous people entered into the heart of the enemy village and escaped with several heads.

Single Combat

Another interesting warfare of the Tangkhuls was a "Single Combat System." In this type of war, the warriors of the two warring villages agreed upon to meet at an appointed place where both the villages chose the best warriors from each side as representatives of their respective villages so that they might fight the war, and that the entire villages might not suffer. In such type of warfare, the two challenging warriors equipped themselves with full armour and on one hand hold a shield and on the other a spear. They come forward with war-dance and war-cry and measured footsteps. They displayed their war tactics and met each other. Their action was either to displace the shield or the spear of opponent. Always the spear was pointed to the feet since the upper part of the body was covered with the shield. Each of them tried to step on the spear of the opponent and pressed it hard on the ground. Then immediately the one who was in a better position demanded his opponent to lay down his shield and surrender. The one who had surrendered should not be killed and his head could not be taken under any circumstances. The village of the one who gained the battle was declared winner of the war. Peace had to be concluded on certain terms and conditions. It may be of interest to write that, in the history of Tangkhul war, the dominant village hardly reduced the defeated village into vassalage.

Inter-Clan Warfare

Apart from inter-village war, we find inter-clan war within a village. This type of war was fought between two or more clans of the same village. It was prominent and typical among the Angamis and some other Naga tribes.[17] In this situation they raised inter-clan fortifications and the clan gates were closed at night. However, no Tangkhul

Awunga can allow a war of his subjects within the village under him. In some extreme cases, when an inter-clan hostility crossed the limit, they were allowed to challenge one another in the form of wrestling and other athletic competitions. Sometimes, wrestling was used as a form of war between two enemy villages in order to avoid bloodshed. In such case, a small village could defeat a big village through good sportsmanship of some good wrestlers.

War of Hostage

Sometimes, an aggrieved village waylaid to catch hold of a hostile villager, but never a woman, when the latter failed to fulfill their obligation. However, the captive should never be put to death but kept alive in their custody and sent message to the family or village concerned of the matter. When the obligations were duly fulfilled, the captive was set free. This kind of war is known as "War of Hostage," Kharingtuk in Tangkhul. If the capturing village could not give appropriate reason for the act, or if the captive village failed to redress the wrong after the release of the hostage, it could lead to open hostility and ultimately to a war.

Whatever type of war might be, the victorious party, coming back home with heads as war trophy, yelled and howled with war-cry as a sign of their victorious return. Then people at home came out with burning torch at the village gate and welcomed their war heroes. On the night of their return, they beat a Log-Drum of victory"[18] and spent the night singing and dancing with war weapons. Lavish food, drink and meat were served. Then the head was deposited at Longshim, whereas in some other tribes, the head was deposited in the house of the clan chief. "Women could not touch war meat nor could they participate in the war rites and ceremonies."[19] Those who killed the enemies and brought heads were entitled to wear a of shawl embroidered in a special way. This type of cloth could be worn by the Awunga, and those who performed Feast of

Merit. They then rose to social recognition. They had the privilege to decorate their dresses and war weapons with human hair. But surprisingly, those who killed women and children are more honourable than those who killed a warrior in the belief that, during those period of constant war, women and children were kept in the most secured places; and only those who were strong and courageous could penetrate through and take their-heads.

However, according to the rules of Tangkhul war, women and children should not be killed. Again, a woman of the attacking village who happened to live in the village under attack by virtue of her marriage, should be spared at any rate. In the war such a woman played the role of Pukreila as referred to earlier. Regarding the rules of Tangkhul war, Horam wrote:[20]

> Wars had their own rules. No pregnant women would be killed; no children could be killed; a woman belonging to the attacking village by virtue of marriage residing in the village under attack should not be killed.

Further, Y. K. Shimray wrote that the Tangkhul Nagas never killed an innocent person; for they believed it to be the most heinous and unpardonable crime.[21] According to Tangkhul custom, though a stray weapon or flying arrow happen to kill women and children, the corpse should be covered with a cloth and respect should be paid to the body.

Changed Situation

However, thanks to Christian missionaries, especially the American Baptists and the effects of British administration over the Naga inhabited areas, the Naga wars have come to an end and head-taking has become a thing of the past. The Nagas have learnt to live together in peace and head-hunting turned to "soul hunting". Slave trade and human sacrifice were stopped. Commenting on the changes brought about by Christianity, Horam writes:[22]

> The new religion proved beneficial in countless ways such as removal of superstitions, introduction of schools and hospitals, cleanliness, and a turning away from head-hunting and such other practices.

Former inter-village feuds, hostility, bloodshed, fear of spirit and superstition in the minds of the Nagas has been changed to mutual love and cooperation. The fear of God and worship to Supreme God set them free from the fear of their traditional spirits and superstition. Modern education that came along with the start of Christianity helped the Nagas to adjust into a new life style. The Nagas were no more isolated from the people around them and beyond.

Further, British control and administration over much of the hill areas of north east India helped in putting to an end inter-village and inter-tribal feuds. Even beyond the extension of British control over Naga inhabited areas, it has been the policy of the British that the Naga head-hunting and raids in British territory should be stopped.[23] For this, the British officers of Naga Hills District conducted punitive expedition of which the important one was against Pangsha.[24]

In 1881, the British took over the administration of some portion of Naga habitat. However, they did not directly rule over the Nagas. The village administration was left to the village chief and council of elders. But inter-village war was effectively controlled by the colonial power. The heinous act of chopping human heads, slave trade and human sacrifice was suppressed not only within the administered area, but even to free Naga territory beyond the British frontier by sending punitive expeditions as given above. Realising the strong arm of the British rule, independent Nagas of the free Naga territory invited the British officials to come and settle their village differences.

After Manipur war of 1891, when the British subdued the power of Manipur, the Government of India made Manipur kingdom subordinate to their rule. During the minority of Churachand Singh, who was made Raja of Manipur, the administration of the kingdom was entrusted to a Superintendent and a Political Agent. The Political Agent was also empowered to introduce any reforms which would be beneficial to the state with due regards to the customs and tradition.[25]

In 1908, when Raja Churachand Singh was coronated, a Dorbar was constituted, the Raja himself being the president of the Dorbar and one British I.C.S. Officer the Vice-President with six Manipuri members. In 1916, he vacated the post of President holding only supervisory control and the British I.C.S. Officer took over the post of President. The post of Vice-President was abolished.[26]

Immediately after the subordination of Manipur to the Government of British-India, their administrative power extended to the hill areas including the Tangkhul country. Administration of justice both in the plains and hills passed to the court manned by the British assisted by Manipuri staff to interpret the customary laws and traditions. At one stage Mr. Congrave, I.C.S., Vice-President of Dorbar of Manipur had the charge of revenue and finance, and was directly responsible for the administration of the hill tribes.[27] All original cases in which the hillmen are involved were tried by the Vice-President of the Dorbar and appeals against the order of the Vice-President went to the Political Agent, and then to the Chief Commissioner of Assam in Shillong.[28]

Since then, the British officers along with Manipur Lambu (peon) and some troops made a circuit to take census for the collection of house tax as no land tax and revenue had earlier been paid by the hill tribes of Manipur. The British officers had to take census personally since Manipuri Lambus were not found reliable and due to corruption, extortion and cheating. A house tax of Rs. 3/- was subsequently payable by every house in the hill areas of Manipur.[29]

In 1919, C. Crimson (I.C.S.), President of Manipur State Dorbar made a proposal to establish three Sub-Divisions in the hills in order to decentralize the amdinistration of the princely state of Manipur. Accordingly, in 1920 three Sub-Divisional offices were opened at Churachandpur, Tamenglong and Ukhrul. L.L. Peter was appointed Sub-Divisional Officer (S.D.O.) of Ukhrul on May 1, 1921, but soon Tangkhul elders filed a case against him for his indulgence in immoral character with a girl of Ukhrul. Later a son and a daughter were born to her; and consequently, he was removed from the post on 31 March 1922. on the ground mentioned above.

The British administration in Tangkhul country made some substantial contributions which is an important turning point in the history of the Tangkhuls. Before the advent of the British, no power had brought the Tangkhuls under subjugation. Life remained at its original existence. But the British colonial rule brought about a great change, and the Tangkhuls were exposed to the world outside. Life was not confined within the ambit of the village. The isolated Tangkhul villages were connected to one another and the economic changes that came with British administration further affected the village economy.

First, the British put inter-village war to an end. It was the direct contribution of the British rule in the region. Life was peaceful and people felt more ecure and happier. Secondly, through the British rule, the Gospel was preached among the Tangkhuls by the American Baptist Mission. The Tangkhuls were no more under the bondage of evil spirit and torture suffered from their belief in animism. This was an indirect contribution of the British rule in Tangkhul area.

However, the religious policy of the British Government in Manipur was half-hearted. On the one hand, they wanted to introduce Christianity in the kingdom, but at the same time, they could not pursue with the desire of preaching the Gospel for fear of hurting the feelings of Meitei Hindus. Therefore, William Pettigrew[30] who first came to Imphal for the purpose of preaching the Gospel to the Meiteis, and who already had started his work had been expelled from the capital by British Officials for fear of Meiteis. He then shifted his centre to Ukhrul and there he preached and set up a mission. Soon many came forward in response to his preaching and they were baptized. He opened a Primary School at Ukhrul and taught the new converts how to read and write the Roman script to enable them to read the Bible and sing the hymnal songs. As a matter of fact, whenever the Christian missionaries went, they carried education along with the Gospel. Therefore, the credit of imparting education to the Tangkhuls in the beginning must go to this British missionary of the American Baptist Mission rather than the British Government. It, however, may be noted that, progress and development in Tangkhul region under the British rule was insignificant. The pace of development was slow. In 1914, one Middle English school was established at Ukhrul, and again, in 1924, a health centre was opened.

By late 1930s, red blankets were issued to 21 Tangkhul Awungas,[31] as a symbol of recognition to local and tribal chiefs. Many Naga chiefs, including the Tangkhul Awungas were given large red blanket which became symbols of authority as agents of British Raj. This position changed the status of the Awungas, from one where they did not owe allegiance to any one to recognizing their continued status came from British rule. They collected house tax, dispensed justice and acted as the peoples' representatives. Apart from these, there was no other commendable development in Tangkhul region. There was no motorable road throughout the length and breadth of the country. The villagers were compelled to carry the British officer on tour on a litter from village to village. They were more concerned in collecting house tax from people than their development and welfare.

However, when the danger of World War II was imminent, the British concerned much for the frontier defence of North-East British-India that a motor road was constructed from Imphal to Kongkan Thana and joined it with Burma via Shangshak. Another road was diverted to Ukhrul Headquarters.

But the great achievement of the British authorities in the field of administration of justice is commendable. The secret of success of the British administration lay in the understanding and efficiency of the British colonial officials. Therefore, Alemchiba rightly said,[32]

> Every officer posted in Naga Hills tried to understand the people by minute study of their way of life, their culture, custom and manners. They lived with the people, ate with them and walked with them, worked with them and sometimes tested their temperament.

As a matter of fact, they meant business and quality of the business to produce the best form of administrations. When they found that these institutions worked well, they retained them and pursued with them for the success of their administration. Thus, they upheld the importance and necessities of retaining the post of Awunga and Hangva and the customary laws of the people intact. In this matter, the control of the British over the Tangkhul villages was indirect.[33]

As the internal administration or villages rested in the hands of the Awunga and Hangva with the customary laws remaining in force, the British rule did not affect the original judiciary of the Tangkhuls. All quarrels and disputes were settled by the Village Council according to customary laws. But those serious issues which were beyond the ability of Village Council; or the divergent customs of different villages or tribes, or customs which appeared legally unacceptable were settled by the British Officers. Also in cases where Naga customary laws were derogatory to humanism or to modern advanced culture, scientific legal system was applied.

The British officers also administered oaths as the last resort for deciding some difficult issues which was practised by the Nagas.In this way, they brought about efficient administration and justice, and created peaceful atmosphere for the Nagas. Their efficient administration is admired by the Nagas who witnessed the British rule. The credit of the improvement of Tangkhul judicial system with modern legal system goes to the British administrators.

Administration After Independence

Subsequent to British power exercising its influence over Manipur after 1891, it exercised its indirect administrative power over the hill areas of this native state. However, paramount power did not unduly interfere in the criminal and civil administration of the various hill people of Manipur state. It was inexpedient to interfere. The best recourse was to allow the existing judicial system of hill people to continue. They only intervened in cases of heinous crimes in which event, the British made thorough enquiries and dispensed justice. However, the local courts could seek redressal to the British authorities as and when it felt the need for it. This, in short, was the judicial system of hill areas of Manipur until independence.

Four months before the Independence of India, the Naga inhabited hills of Manipur was transferred to the Maharaja-in-Council in April 1947. Perhaps, by this, on the lapse of the British rule from India the independence of Manipur was restored to the state again. The Act which effected the administration of the hill peoples of Manipur state is known as "The Manipur State Hill Peoples (Administration) Regulation, 1947." By this, the administration of hill people, which was formerly in the hands of the British passed to Maharaja-in-Council.[34]

This Act was not a complete departure from the administrative system of the British in the hill areas of Manipur state. However, some modifications were made and the process of administration of justice was made elaborate in more detail. The post of Awunga was retained and a Village Authority was incepted which was consisted of the Awunga, nominated Village Authority members and the Council of elders of the Awunga, if any as per Section 6 of the Regulation.[35] The Village Authority was empowered to administer criminal justice in cases such as mischief, theft, assault etc. An appeal against the order passed by the Village Authority lay with the Circle Bench, then Hill Bench, Imphal; and finally to the Chief Court of the State (Manipur) for the trial of Hill cases under the Manipur State Court Act, 1947.

The Manipur State Hill Peoples (Administration) Regulation, 1947, was in force for nine years. However, the Regulation did not work to the satisfaction of the people as much as the British colonial rule and their administration of justice the new system had achieved. This is because, encroached on the original administrative system of the Tangkhul village states and caused extensive erosion to the powers and functions of the Awunga and Hangva. Further, the Regulation stripped them of the powers and functions of the Awunga and Hangva in the administration of justice. The new system did not fit in into the minds and culture of the people. This was the beginning of administrative failure of the new republic of India in the Tangkhul hill country.

After the merger of Manipur state into the Union of India in 1950, when it became a Union Territory under the Indian Union, a new Act was passed in 1956, for the administration of Hill Areas of Manipur. This Act was known as "The Manipur (Village Authorities in Hill Areas) Act, 1956." This Act made a complete departure from the original administrative system of the Tangkhuls except the retention of the post of Awunga which, being hereditary by nature, could not be eliminated. Rather, it was a recognition to the hereditary system of the Tangkhul Awunga.

However, the existence of traditional Village Council called Hangva and its powers and functions had been completely changed. The institution of Hangva which was represented by clan chiefs, and nominated members, apart from the clan chiefs, according to the size of the clans was completely changed. In place of this institution, 'The Village Authority' was constituted. The membership in the Village Authority had also been changed from traditional practises. Five members were to be elected in a village where the tax paying houses were 20 but not more than 60; seven members from 61 to 100 tax paying houses; ten members from 101 to 150 tax paying houses in a village. Representation by clan was ignored by the Act.[36]

Again, instead of the nomination system making a balance of representation of all clans in the Hangva, the new Act provided election system on the basis of adult suffrage. All the seats of the Village Authority consequently were captured by the clan(s) having the highest majority population in the village. Being the largest in the membership of the village and Village Authority, they started to manipulate the village affairs, and corruption set in. Favouritism and prejudice in delivering verdicts came into being. Justice was replaced by nepotism and party spirit. Customary laws were little honoured and revered. Fear of violation of customary laws and traditions disappeared. The result was a complete failure of the new administrative machinery of the Village Authority, and the corresponding breakdown of law and order situation in the villages. Life was no more safe and secure. Justice became expensive from grass root level of the Village Authority to the higher court of the land. People longed for the earlier administrative system of their ancestors - so cheap but effective, full of justice and peace, making it available to all alike regardless of rich and poor, high and low, great and small.

The original Tangkhul democracy was far more successful than the modern Indian democratic system. Here, one of the highest figures of Indian politicians said:[37]

> The enactment of provisions for the governance of a district area peoples by persons who are somewhat alien to the traditions and history of the rest of India must necessarily raise some problems.

Surveying the overall functions and achievements of different administrative machineries and agencies of hill areas of Manipur, it is found that there was and is a complete failure of the new system. No recent Act or Regulation of modern administrative ideas could bring about a successful administration in the hills of Manipur and Naga Hills. The Nagas being a tradition-conscious people, found the newly established judicial system strange and repugnant, and thus they hardly take recourse to the Government law courts which by-passed their time honoured laws and traditions.

When people realized that there is a serious failure in the administration of justice in Tangkhul villages, leading to social degeneration, the Tangkhul Long (Tangkhul Tribal Council)"[38] felt the necessity of having a Tangkhul Tribal Court which should be based on customary laws of the people. It came into being immediately with the compilation of *Shiyan-Tanza* (Customary Law) in October 1988. Since then, it exists parallel to the established courts of Sub-Deputy Collector, Sub-Divisional Officer and the Deputy Commissioner of Ukhrul District. Most of the appeals from the decisions of the Village Authority go to this Court.[39]

Although we cannot ascertain the date of the start of the Tangkhul Long, due to absence of written record, yet its formation had been as old as the settlement of the Tangkhuls in their present habitat. In a society of constant inter-village feuds and warfare where bringing human heads home as trophies was considered prestigious, it was considered necessary that life should be guided by a refined war discipline and principle. This could be enforced and implemented by a well organised and competent body which led the Tangkhuls to form an organization called the

Tangkhul Long, which is the Tangkhul Tribal Council.[40] It has been called the "Commonwealth of Independent Tangkhul Villages."[41] Details of the Tangkhul Long will be discussed in the concluding chapter.

The most important function of the Tangkhul Long is the judicial administration, and thus maintenance of justice. It strictly enforced Raiyan, "law of conduct of war" and other laws of justice. Whereas the 'Range Council' is known as Lungphang (Branch Council), the Tangkhul Tribal Council is called Longrei i.e., Great Long. These Councils are still in existence in a modified form to suit the changing situation. It receives both original and appellate cases of the Tangkhuls of all forms.

NOTES & REFERENCES

1. Verrier Elwin (ed.), *The Nagas in Nineteenth Century,* p. 100.
2. M. Alemchiba, *A Brief Historical Account of Nagaland,* p. 162.
3. M. Horam, *Naga Polity,* p. 79.
4. Jyotirmoy Roy, *Hisory of Manipur,* p. 193.
5. Apart from the maintenance of village defence force, the erection of forts as defensive measure was very important. Stone boulders, spikes, thorny-creepers are used around the village. Natural forts like cliffs render good defensive measure. The erection of village gates with big beams was essential for the safety and security of the village.
6. M. Horam, *op. cit.,* p. 90.
7. The Naga custom and spirit of generosity does not warrant plucking of fruit of any kind in its harvest season as a serious crime. A hungry man may pluck and eat the fruit of his neighbour in the field. Stealing from the granary is considered a serious crime.
8. J. H. Hutton, *The Sema Nagas,* p. 164.
9. T. C. Hodson, *op. cit.,* p. 110.

10. Haimendorf, *op. cit.,* p. 23.

11. Godwin Austen, "The Nagas and Neighbouring Tribes," in Verrier Elwin (ed), *The Nagas in Nineteenth Century,* p. 111.

12. Haimendorf, *op. cit.,* pp. 73-74.

13. J. H. Hutton, The Angami Nagas, pp. 157-158.

14. R. R. Shimray, *op. cit.,* p. 96.

15. *Ibid.,* p. 71.

16. In a "Declared War", the number of human lives or heads to be taken was fixed and the party which took the said number of heads first was declared right and winner of the case. After that, peace must be established between the two warring parties.

17. J. H. Hutton, *op. cit.,* p. 109. He wrote this warfare was prevalent among the Angamis in early days.

18. The sound of the Log-Drum has its own significance. There are different sounds produced by the drum and villagers then know how to prepare themselves accordingly.

19. R. R. Shimray, *op.cit.,* p. 77.

20. M. Horam, *Social and Cultural Life of Nagas,* p. 92.

21. Y. K. Shimray, *op. cit.,* p. 21.

22. M. Horam, *Social and Cultural Life of Nagas,* p. 98.

23. J. Johnstone, *Manipur and the Naga Hills,* p. 36.

24. C. Furer Haimendorf, *Naked Nagas,* p. 140; Piketo Sema, *British Policy and-Administration in Nagaland,* p. 61.

25. Jyotirmoy Roy, *History of Manipur,* p. 135 Shri J. N. Das, *A Study of Land System of Manipur,* p. 10; Naorem Sanajaoba, *Manipur: Past and Present,* pp. 106-109.

26. Jyotirmoy Roy, *op. cit.,* p. 137.

27. Manipur State Archives, *Administrative Report of A.W. Davis,* Political Agent of Manipur, 1908.

28. *Ibid., Administrative Report of J.C. Higgin,* Political Agent of Manipur, 1913.

29. *Administrative Report,* J. Shakespear, Political Agent and Superintendent of Manipur, 1904-05; J. N. Das, *Study of Land System of Manipur,* p. 10; *Naorem Sanajaoba, Manipur: Past and Present,* pp. 106-109.

30. William Pettigrew was first a missionary Christian of the Anglican Church, and worked in Dacca. Later he joined the Arthington Aboriginese Mission. Then he joined the American Baptist Mission. The bloody war of Manipur, 1891, drew him to preach the Gospel in Manipur which he started in 1895.

31. Manipur State Archives, Adininistrative Report of C.W.L. Harvey, President, Manipur State Dorbar, 1931-32.

32. M. Alemchiba, *op. cit.,* p. 133.

33. Indirect British administration was a popular form of administering hill and tribal people of India, Africa and Malaya. The local conditions were suited for application in the administration. Some studies on this form of administration are Margery Perham, Native Administration in Nigeria; M. Fortes, *African Political Systems;* Michael Crowder, *West Africa Under Colonial Rule,* and J. S. Furnivall, *Colonial Policy and Practice.*

34. G. K. Gori, *Changing Phase of Tribal Area of Manipur,* pp. 11-12.

35. Sanajaoba, *Manipur: Past and Present,* pp. 287-388; *Manipur Gazette,* Extraordinary Publication, Manipur State Hill Peoples (Administration) Regulation, 1947, p. 71.

36. Manipur Gazette Extraordinary, No. 6 E-4, 11th April, 1957, p. 108. "The Manipur (Village Authorities in Hill Areas) Act, 1956" became an Act immediately after the notification in the Office Gazette by Central Government.

37. M. Hidayatulla, *The Fifth and Sixth Schedules to the Constitution of India,* p. 69.

38. Shiyan-Yanza was prepared by the Tangkhul Long (Tangkhul Tribal Council) based on the traditional laws of the Tangkhuls to settle their own disputes.

39. M. Horam, *Naga Polity,* p. 116.

40. R. R. Shimray, *op.cit.,* p. 98.

41. A.S.W. Shimray, "The Tangkhul Long: Its Judicial and Arbitrating Functions," Paper read at the XV Annual Session of North East India History Association held at Arunachal University, Doimukh in December 1994. The term 'independent' however, cannot be applied to the present Tangkhul Long.

6

TANGKHUL RELIGION

Religion was, and still is, the centre of Tangkhul life since all activities are linked with it. There is no venture of life—social, economic, political and other domestic and household activities in the life of the Tangkhuls without first performing religious rites, ceremonies and sacrifices to their deity. No morsel of food is taken without first offering it to God. Every day to day business is undertaken after performing rites and offering prayers to God asking His blessings. The culture of the Tangkhuls is also basically religious in character without the sanction of which a practice cannot be incorporated in their culture. Ventures of any form undertaken by the Tangkhuls without performing due religious rites were believed to meet the failure and to bring about calamity to the society as a whole. These beliefs have made them staunch religious people. Therefore, religion comes in the forefront and occupies the predominant place in the life of the Tangkhuls. Regarding the religious life and belief of the Nagas, Tuisem A. Shishak wrote,[1]

> Among the Nagas, then, to be religious means to be true to the traditions of the tribe, every thing in the routine of life is bound up with some belief, tradition or superstition, which is an integral part of their religion. A Naga's life, in all its aspects, is guided by his religious belief and practices.

> The religion of the Nagas is intensely practical. They performed their rites lest mysterious powers about them bring calamities to their door. . . . Indeed, it is the physical necessity of protecting man from bodily harm and of getting food in abundance that dictates in large measure the substance of religious observances. The observances to this and are not dependent upon some individual, but the entire social unit, the village joins in it.

Again, it is to be noted with great interest that, the Tangkhul religion is a corporate religion where the entire village community participates in religious rites and ceremonies equally, and the same village taboo binds one and the whole village community.[2] In Tangkhul religion, the sin of one individual adversely affected the entire village population, because, the Tangkhuls had a corporate religious life, and the whole village was a religious unit as well as a social, political and economic unit. The breach of time-honoured custom of the Nagas was regarded as sin. Here Hodson rightly remarked: "Sin in their view consists primarily of breaches both by accident and by intent of the unwritten laws of society."[3] Setting aside personal liberty and interest, every individual had to be religious and obedient to the command of social and religious practices of the village community.

Missionaries and other writers have branded the Naga and Tangkhul religion as animism, paganism, or heathenism.[4] Whatever the case may be, the Nagas are not idolatrous-worshippers of graven images or idols, nor worshippers of animals. Here Hutton forwarded his argument, "Politheist, Pantheist he may be, but he is no idolator."[5] The Tangkhuls believe in the existence of a Supreme God whom they call by different names such as Kasa-Akhava (Master of Creation or Creator), Varivara (Source of Peace), Kazingpa (the one who dwells in heaven/dweller of heaven) and Reisang-Chonmi. With the advent of Christianity in Tangkhul hills, their God was also called Kahuiya Akhava (Master of Salvation, Saviour), a name simultaneously used with the name, Varivara. This shows the monotheism of Tangkhul religion.

The Tangkhuls also believed in the existence of the spirits around them who are capable of creating harm to men such as disease and sickness, calamities, and even causing men to death by their supernatural powers. They are called by different names such as Chipee (satan). Kameo, Rengpa (owner or master of the land) because, he dominates the world and became the ruler of the earth. With regard to the religious belief of the Nagas, Elwin described:[6]

> . . . and although they have a name for God, they do not seem to worship a supreme being . . . certain it is that their belief in the existence after death of the freed spirit is not uncommon, if not general. . . . Whatever may be their belief in a god or a future state, it is certain that they believe in the infinity of evil spirits or demons. Each disease is supposed to be in the immediate keeping of some particular demon, who travels about dealing out sickness and death at his caprice, and to propitiate these many demons is their care.

The demons are malevolent spirits and so the relation of the Tangkhul with the spirits is rather negative. Therefore, they have to propitiate the spirits by performing religious rites and sacrifices in order to ward off their sufferings. Though the Tangkhuls believed in a Supreme deity, their sacrifices were directed towards the malevolent spirits. If the spirits who were propitiated did not response to the sacrifices, the Tangkhuls would then turn to their benevolent God. They defied the demons and uttered words of rebuke, "Hey, you Satan, although you are treating us in this way, be it known to you, God is above you." So their ultimate belief and worship is to God who is in heaven.[7]

Again, it is generally believed that, the Tangkhuls believed in ancestor worship—worship to the spirit of dead. This is a wrong notion. The rituals they performed were a token of their love to the dead and also it was seasonal, not permanent. It began from the day a person died and continued till Thisham, a festival celebrated to bid farewell to the dead. In those days, the living members shared their food and drink to the soul of the dead and kept it somewhere in their house. However, human faith and religious belief is rather permanent—not seasonal—since God or spirit whom they worship is a supernatural being and immortal. Therefore the Tangkhuls out of their extreme affection and attachment to the dead, refused to accept or conciliate the demise of their dear ones and still take him/her as alive in their imagination sharing with the life of the living in the family. Therefore, it cannot be taken as ancestor worship in the way many other societies do.

Another characteristic of their religion is the dominance of superstition. Constant fear of evil spirits led them to perform divinations, rites and ceremonies; and their predictions were strictly and faithfully executed either to proceed with the plan or withdraw from it. This involves both in individual or communal affairs Here, they used different methods of divination in order to see omens such as Kapa Khayang (bamboo divination), Hara Khayang (egg divination), Harkho Khayang (cock divination) etc. Household omens were consulted by the head of the house whereas the community divinations were performed either by the village priest or some village elder. The detail process was meticulously observed and prediction of the omens was made accordingly.

In Kapa Khayang, a bamboo slit is divided into two, and if they are slit into two equal parts, the omen is considered good and the result of the venture is likely to be positive. In Hara Khayang, an opening is made on top of the egg, boiled on heated ashes and the cooking process is observed. In Harkho khayang, preferably a white cock is strangled to death and its legs are examined. If the right leg is placed on top of the left slightly crossing, it is a favourable omen and good for a venture.

Further, in consulting omens, the natural agents such as dreams, squirrel crossing the path against the journey of a person, deer and tiger barking in front of the way and certain kind of birds shouting on the left side of the road are considered bad omens. In such cases the person is to return home though he may already have been far advanced in the journey. Otherwise, the journey, it is believed, is bound to meet in failure, even to the extent of misfortune on the wayfarers.

Another belief of the Nagas is the existence of lycantrophy, Khangayei in Tangkhul language, a man possessed of evil spirit (Rai Kaphung) and the art of performing black magic. In lycantrophy,[8] the spirit of a man turns into tiger or snake, or any form of animal depending on the nature of the spirit; and it roams about in the jungle and executes the exact life of the animal while the person himself is at home or in a trance. But the man will die when the spirit animal is killed by the hunter or otherwise. This will take place in few days time after the spirit animal is killed. As for possess of evil spirit (Rai Kaphung) Vampire, it enters into the body of a sick or healthy man and gives severe pain, even causing death. This vampire sucks the blood of man. The attacked person produces the exact voice of the person whose spirit attacks him.[9]

Some people use black-magic which their spell casts on a person or enemy causes sickness and death. In such cases, people seek a man who possesses more powerful magic to cast out the spell which had attacked him. Sometimes, some medicine men possess this power and cure the sickness by their spells. But the Tangkhuls consider possessed of evil spirit (lycantrophy), and black magic as the acts of demons, which is considered sin. They curse such people calling the name of God to punish them. Some people were even expelled from the village for doing such sinful acts. Some other people use poison which they mix in food and drinks and cause unfortunate person who eats or drinks death.

They believe that this kind of act brings good harvest or plentiful store of paddy in the granary.

Another feature of the traditional religion of the Tangkhuls was the practice of necromency.[10] Here a priest or priestess falls into a trance and the spirit goes to the land of the dead called Kazeiram (to be discussed later) which is known as 'visit to the land of dead'. The spirit of the oracle (priest/priestess) contacting the spirit of dead receives reports which again, they tell to the emissaries about their future. At times the necromancer brings some articles, as they say, from the land of the dead. In this way, people are induced to consult the necromancers about the life of their future with their problems and solution to their difficulties.

The Nagas also believe in the magical power of 'luck stones' called talismans. They are stones of luck and prosperity. According to J.P. Mills, the Rengma Nagas treasured them, and timely cleaning was a must by the priest or priestess.[11] Black or white, stones of bright shining polished colour of different sizes which they believed possessing magical powers of luck and prosperity are kept at home or at an important place of the village. There are luck-stones of individuals as well as of the village community. They are also of different types—good harvest, games, war, cattle, and so on as the ease may be. Those who possess any of those stones are believed will be rich in the particular objects.

A community deity-stone of a particular composition was kept at a distant place—a few miles away from the site of the village settlement, and buried by wrapping it with pig's fat killed for its sacrifice. Only the Awunga and his heir can approach the stone and offer prayers and sacrifices. This takes place only once or twice in his life or at times of dire necessity when the village is visited by some misfortune. Only village male elders accompany the Awunga. Awunga asks blessings and power in order to ward off the community calamity. Whenever the Awunga offers prayers and sacrifices to the village deity stone, he does it for the peace, prosperity and good health of the people; and for the victory of the village asking more heads of the enemy heroes and prominent people of the enemy villages. For the commoners, to come near the stone is a taboo except at the cost of their lives.

In the remote past, when one of the clans of Tangkhul called Shuingtuidang with a subordinate clan moved from Imphal valley to hill countryside in order to find settlement, the leading clan found a small stone having all kinds of animal hair growing over it. To their surprise the small stone grew bigger and bigger and reached the size of a buffalo. Being unable to carry it any longer, they suggested to break it into pieces for convenience of carrying. So they applied wax and burnt it. One half of the stone was broken into small pieces and scattered, whereas the other half still remains at the very place where they broke it. This stone is called Lungning. It is believed that the magical power of the stone also had disappeared along with the broken pieces. Till today, Tangkhul Nagas who have not embraced Christianity[12] perform rites and offer eggs, heads of eels and other sacrificial articles to the stone invoking the stone to give rain at the time when draught affects cultivation. The half portion of Lungning is still revered as a historic stone of the Shingtuidang clan.[13]

Religious Organisation and Functionaries

Although a Naga village is a religious unit, there is no common worship of the villagers nor any structure of religious prayers. Again, there is no regular worship services of the village community. Further, a written code of established theological principles and beliefs are absent in the religion of the Nagas. It is also worth mentioning that there is no priestly class of the Nagas as those of other religious groups to look after the spiritual growth of the village community. In this regard, W. Robinson wrote in the middle of the last century, "The Nagas have no established form of worship; they have no temples erected in honour of their deities, and no ministers peculiarly consecrated to their services."[14] This led people to think that the Naga religion is unorganised, devoid of theological and ecclesiastical formation.

Notwithstanding the above observations, it is to be noted with serious consideration that the religion of the Nagas is a 'Corporate Religion', and no corporate religion can stand without formal faith and proper establishment. As the Naga religion is the centre of all activities of their life, they have their own surviving religious philosophy from very early times. Traditions, culture and practices are also incorporated in the religious laws of the Tangkhuls that Horam wrote of the Tangkhuls that they attributed all kinds of sickness to evil spirits for violation of taboos and other social laws and as a result the anger of the spirits came upon men.[15] Further, they have their own custodians of their religion. Though there is no regular worship services as such, the regular seasonal and yearly festivals, rites, ceremonies and sacrifices are conducted and performed by those people who are the priests of the village.

In every Naga village, there are priests and priestesses. But most of the Tangkhul priests and priestesses are village medicine-men and medicine-women and magicians. Therefore, they conducted and performed religious rites and sacrifices to placate the evil spirits to ward off their sufferings and calamities; and also invoke prayers for successful warfare, hunting and prosperity of the village, as the case may be. They cure diseases of sick people by herbal medicines as well as with their magical powers. They are also consulted for rituals and sacrifices for the many festivals and other important activities of the village.

At the apex of the religious organisation of the village is the Awunga. Normally, though he is the head of the Tangkhul village state, or a secular head, yet he has wide and extensive religious functions. He is the only competent authority to come near the village stone-deity for offerings and sacrifices and to offer prayers as mentioned above. According to T.A. Sh ishak, the village chief automatically becomes the head of religion and the leading religious leaders of the Tangkhuls are indispensable officials of the chief.[16] In this connection, Hodson also remarked: "His authority in their eyes is religious in origin and nature."[17] These statements are supported by Tangkhul scholars.[18]

In the same manner, there are priest and medicine-men of the clans in the village. They can be either the head or the eldest of the clan or any one who has the requisite qualification, who is well versed in customary laws, religious practices, medicinal knowledge and possessed of magical power. The function of clan priest is confined mostly to religious rites, ceremonies, sacrifices and taboos of the clan. The domestic priest, the (male) head of the family, is the father or eldest male. He does all religious functions of the house, although in some other cases, he can employ the service of a priest or physician who is more efficient in this respect depending on the circumstances and nature of the case.

Regarding the execution of religious functionaries, all important village festivals and ceremonies such as Luiraphanit (New Year festival), Mangkhap Phanit which is a special thanksgiving after arduous work of seedling or transplantation, Chumphut (opening of granary after harvest), Thisham (farewell feast to the spirit of the death), Feast of Merit which also marks the end of the year and other festivals of important recognition of the village are declared by Awunga in, or without, consultation with the village priest and fixed the date or days for the particular feast. Labour of any kind on these festival days is a taboo. The Awunga inaugurates the function by performing rites and ceremonies. Sometimes, the village priest performs it at the behest of the Awunga, but the presence of the latter is required without which no ceremony is valid and complete. The birth of a child or death of a person, visit of epidemics, famine, draught etc., are also declared as days of Shar that is solemn days where no form of labour is allowed in the village.

In big villages with large population, the solemn days on account of death, or the birth of a child are observed clanwise since such events are phenomena of daily occcurrence which involvement of the entire village is too great a loss for agrarian society like the Nagas. Sometimes; a single family alone observes Shar when sickness occurs in the house. The head of the family offers sacrifice and propitiates the spirit to release the person from his sickness.

Although, the inauguration of Feast of Merit, games and sports and other festive activities are not necessarily of the same kind of religious observances, the presence of the Awunga is necessary, and he occupies the prominent seat in public where the priest grace the function. In this case doing private business is not a taboo.

But whatever the case may be, when a Shar is declared, whether of the village or a household, the village gate or the door of the house is closed to the outsiders. In the same way, the inmates are also not allowed to leave the village, which is a taboo. Whenever this rule is violated, heavy fine is imposed and it was used for a sacrificial article and renew the Shar again.

Unnatural death of any form, sudden visit of calamities like fire disaster, storm destroying crops, epidemics both to men and animals are consequenced by the observance of a solemn day popularly called Genna.[19] Here, the village priest or the chief-cum-priest performs rituals to please the harmful deities or spirits by offerings, prayers and sacrifices. After this appeasement ceremony, the people feel a sense of relief. All kinds of negative events, say, natural calamities and the works of demons are together attributed to the latter which urge the people to perform rituals which indeed was an unwarranted expense.

Apart from observing solemn days under the circumstances mentioned above, no Shar day is ever declared for the purpose of community worship and prayers. As a matter of fact, no evil spirit is worshipped by the Tangkhuls except to appease them by offerings of meat and other food items which is done out of fear. In this respect Horam remarks: "his idea of worship and adoration cannot find a place in this sort of religion. The joy which should follow praise and worship of one's deity are also naturally absent. No day in a week is specially set aside for religious observances."[20] But one important characteristic of Naga and Tangkhul Shar is that it is a collective observance in uniform without exception of any individual regardless of his religiosity. This is an important criterion which brings about the religious cohesion and social solidarity of the Naga village, and it disciplined each individual to develop the spirit of oneness of the village society. In return, he gets security and protection of the society. Again, this uniformity in observing such days and religious taboos make the Naga equal believers; and there is no room for renunciation of the world and live an ascetic life of any individual as is found in some other religions.

Concept of Heaven and Life After Death

The Tangkhuls believe in the existence of the realms of the spirits or spirit beings. Therefore, they believe in the existence of heaven which they simply called Kazingram meaning sky or heaven. It is the dwelling place of God situated in the sky above. The other realm of spirit is called Kazeiram. It is the place of the spirits of dead. According to their belief, Kazeiram is situated in the heart of the earth, and therefore, an underground world. The spirits of those who were not righteous while they were living on this earth go to Kazeiram and Kokto, king of the dead rules over them. They believed that the spirit leaves the body immediately when a man dies, but it hovers round the house of its family and rests even in the house that the household members prepare a place for him and share their daily meal to the spirit of the dead. This continues till a farewell ceremony for the spirit is performed at Thisham as mentioned earlier. At the underground world, the rich remain rich and the poor, poor as much as they lived on this earth.

The religion of the Tangkhuls does not indicate or bring salvation to men. They believe life after death in the underworld. However, they also believe that those who live a righteous life on this earth will go to heaven after death and live with God full of bliss and happiness. Though the idea of dividing the righteous and unrighteous living is not given in their religion, the ethical rule and the aspiration to live a happy life in heaven makes a Tangkhul live a life above reproach when they are on this earth. This concept had been found in the belief of the Tangkhuls even before the advent of Christianity in their land. Here Hodson remarks,[21] ". . . I was told that, the good go to heaven above but the bad are consigned to an abode beneath the earth. What exactly constituted goodness and badness was not explained to me." In Tangkhul religion, ethical principles form religious principles as well.

Disposal of the Death

Different ways of disposal are adopted for the dead body among the Nagas. Some tribes like the Aos, Konyaks and the neighbouring tribes exposed it on raised platforms with some belonging of the deceased. The body is allowed to waste away with nature. The Tangkhuls and their neighbouring tribes like Maos, Kabuis and Anals bury their dead. Every household has its own grave in which all the dead bodies from the ancestors are buried. However, if any death occurs due to war or accident outside the village the corpse is buried outside the village gate. Whenever a death occurs in a village, a public solemn day is declared and when engagement of work is prohibited. For the family or relatives of the dead, this may continue for days as per their desire and necessity.

An animal is killed in honour of the dead, whether big or small according to the ability of the family; and the meat is shared among the relatives and those who worked for the burial of the dead. A special portion goes to the Sharra (priest) for sacrificial rites. A portion of the belongings of the dead are also buried along with as they believe that those things are used again by the spirit of the dead in Kazeiram as he used on this earth. The comfort of life after dead partly depends on the preparation of the family for the dead.

Some special ceremonies were performed for the burial of the Awungas. The activities might have been more expensive with more meat, singing, dancing and challenging the spirit of dead for taking away the life of their Awunga. Some powerful Awungas demanded human sacrifice to enable them to recover from sickness or for sacrifice at their burial. In early days, as the story says, the Awunga of Mapum village was sick to death, and the people of the village brought a boy from Ningthi village. Surprisingly, the sickness was over when the boy was brought. There he remained and grew up along with the village boys and girls till he attained teenage, and he was loved by a girl of the village. The Awunga became sick again later. The villagers planned to sacrifice the boy for the recovery of the Chief. When the arrangement for the human sacrifice was being made, the girl disclosed it to the boy who escaped and reached his Ningthi village. Out of fear of Mapum village, he then went to Nampisha village—the second camp village, of the Tangkhuls when they came out of Samsok—and he remained there till he died. He married and got children the descendatns of whom are still living in this village.[22]

Advent of Christianity and Its Impact

With the expansion of the British rule over Naga territory, the Christian missionaries approached the British authorities to grant permission to work among the Nagas. At first, the approach was turned down fearing that it might hinder the work of the British administration and further expansion of territory in Naga country. But when independent Nagas resisted the advent of British colonial rule, they utilized the service of different Christian organisations to tame the Nagas. An authority on Christianity in North East India writes:[23] "The earlier motive of those officers who supported missionary work (other than personal religious conviction) was that it would help 'civilize' the hill tribes and hence contribute to their pacification." As we have seen, the warlike habits of the hills people especially when they led raids upon the administered territory in the plains was a serious problem for the government throughout the nineteenth century. They hoped that they could be pacified without the expensive imposition fo direct administration. Missionary activity help this objective.

Realizing the ethnic, cultural, traditional and customary peculiarity of the Nagas from the plain people of India, Johnstone, the British Political Agent in Manipur, wrote about the need of Christianising the Nagas to save them from the invasion of corrupt culture. Here, this rather long quotation which follows though mentioning the Angamis only, may be applicable to other Naga tribes.[24]

> A fine interesting race like the Angamis, might, as a Christian tribe, occupy a most useful position on our Eastern Frontier, and I feel strongly that we are not justified in allowing them to be corrupted and gradually 'converted' by the miserable, bigoted, caste-observing Mussalman of Bengal, men who have not one single good quality in common with the manly Afghans, and other real Mussalman tribes. I do not like to think it, but unless we give the Nagas a helping hand in time, such is sure to be their fate. . . .

He continued:

> Properly taught and judiciously handled, the Angamis would have made a fine manly set of Christians, of a type superior to most Indian native converts and probably

> devoted to our rule. As things stand at present, I fear, they will be gradually corrupted and lose the good qualities, which have made them attractive in the past, and that, as time goes on, unless some powerful counter influence is brought to bear on them, they adopt the vile, bigoted type of Muhammadanism prevalent in Assam and Cachar, and instead of becoming a tower of strength to us, be a perpetual weakness and source of annoyance.

According to Horam, the religious policy of the British administrators in Nagaland who employed Christian missionaries was guided by political interest. He wrote,[25]

> When the British established their authority over that Nagas, they favoured the missionaries in many ways—not because of any sympathy with their missionary work, but because they thought that their influence would be of service to the British administrators in their campaign against the Naga dissidents.

The American Baptist Mission was allowed to go to Naga Hills, Garo Hills and Assam valley. Major Francis Jenkins supported the efforts of Rev. Nathan Brown when he arrived in Assam in 1836. Before long there were many foreign missionary organisations working in North East India. In 1894, Rev. William Pettigrew came to Imphal for the same cause. He was the first foreign missionary to have worked in Manipur.

His first objective was to Christianise the Hindu Meiteis of Imphal valley, and accordingly for this purpose, he opened a school at Moirang-Khong at Imphal, the capital of the kingdom. Six months later, Major Maxwell, president of the Dorbar ordered him to close it down lest the missionary activities provoke the orthodox Manipuri Hindus.[26] However, he was allowed to work among the people of the hills. In 1895, he came to Ukhrul and got permission from the Awunga of the village to build a house for his living. It was the beginning of missionary settlement and their work in Tangkhul.

The first task of Rev. Pettigrew was to convince the people that the missionaries were not the paid agents of the Government.[27] They had come for the service of the people to enlighten their physical, intellectual and spiritual growth. For this purpose, his second important task was to educate the people in order to enable them how to read and write; and then thirdly, to preach the Gospel of salvation through the spread of education. For hygiene and physical growth, and ultimately for the end of his missionary work, he did not under-estimate the importance of medical service, for which a dispensary was attached to his residence at Ukhrul. Many diseases which could not be cured by the traditional appeasement to the spirits were cured by the application of modern scientific medicines of the missionary. This convinced the ignorant people to come forward and cooperated with the missionaries which brought about great changes in the life of the Tangkhuls physically, intellectually and spiritually.

In 1896, a primary school was opened at Ukhrul where 30 students attended. Later, it became a Middle English School in 1897 and the number of students increased further. Soon parents realized the advantage of sending their children to school getting the facility of employment under either the mission or the Government. Their suspicion at the appearance of the foreigners melted away gradually.

However, it was not until 1901 that converts were made. In that year, 12 students who attended the mission school were converted and got baptism. By 1907, the membership rose to 70, but most of them participated in their traditional festivals, dancing, singing, even in drinking Naga rice-beer, which according to western missionaries, were activities connected to spirit worship. Therefore, W. Pettigrew drew up a list of rules for the new converts to follow strictly. Here many rebelled against the rule and withdrew from the line put up by the missionary except 7 dedicated Christian students. Then, Pettigrew along with the seven students established a separate church at Ukhrul. This was the first Christian community and Church in Manipur and continued to be the only Baptist church in the state till 1916.[28] By 1911, the church membership grew to 28 strong drawn from Ukhrul and neighbouring villages. These people, in turn served as the nuclei of Christianity among the Tangkhuls and they worked devotedly with the missionaries which brought about great achievements in their mission works.

The British political agent of Manipur restricted the movements of missionaries to different parts of Tangkhul area. Therefore, the missionary activities were confined within the periphery of Ukhrul and neighbour villages. However, in 1911, the British Government wanted to take census of the state and W. Pettigrew was appointed Superintendent. He made good use of this opportunity and with some of his students, visited different villages of Tangkhul area and studied the culture of the people for further propagation of the Gospel. Soon much of the Tangkhul land had come under Christian influence. The Tangkhuls of Somra Tract which is beyond the frontier of Manipur state also had missionaries visit their hill. In 1948, the Golden Jubilee of Manipur Baptist Convention was held in Ukhrul. Thousands of Christian from all over the state gathered there for the occasion.[29]

In the beginning the spread of the new faith was not without severe opposition. In the first place, the Tangkhuls were religious people and their traditional religion was deeply rooted and well established in their faith for generations. Therefore, they could not be easily convinced of the doctrine of new faith. Secondly, by the feature of corporate religious life, one individual could not be converted apart from the other members. Thirdly, those who embraced the new religion were discouraged to take part in keeping village festivals, solemn days and other communal activities that the advent of Christianity brought about disunity in Tangkhul villages. People were afraid of the wrath of god for violation of the village solemn days and other religious and customary observances that the presence of Christian missionaries and their spread of the new faith was behemently opposed. At times, there were threats of physical assaults to the missionaries and their families.

Despite all these oppositions, the growth of Christianity could not be arrested. It grew significantly and in course of time even those who opposed Christianity became ardent Christians. There were several factors for the wide-spread and progress of Christianity. First, was the spread of education. Wherever the Christian missionaries went, they established schools to enlighten the minds of the people and those who had the knowledge of reading and writing were employed either in Government offices or missions which ultimately enhanced their living standard. Secondly, the mobile dispensary of Pettigrew and later by other missionaries attracted the ignorant people many of whom had deadly diseases. They found that by mere offerings and sacrifices they could not be cured. The medicines of the missionaries on the other hand had results.[30] This convinced the people to come forward to Christianity. Thirdly, during the World War I, 1200 Tangkhuls went to France as Labour Corps. This was the first time Nagas had personal contact with the world outside. They could see things for themselves. Their outlook was broadened. When they returned home, they became better tools of Christian missionary for the propagation of the Gospel.[31]

Before long, the advent of Japanese forces into Manipur during World War II seasoned and sharpened the minds of the Nagas to their already acquired knowledge. Lastly, the relentless efforts of the missionaries, their persuasive approach and demonstration of a true Christian life convinced more people. Revival movements, to), brought in large number in the faith. Today, there are more than 92% Christians in the Tangkhul area.[32]

Again, though the Nagas believed in eternity of soul and life after death either in heaven or Kazeiram, the Naga concept of heaven is vague. Further, their traditional religion and faith in the existence of heaven does not offer salvation.

When the Christian missionaries preached their religious belief, it so convinced the Tangkhuls that they readily embraced Christianity leaving the fear of demons. They were tired of offering sacrifices to appease the evil spirits and they wanted to be free from the torture of superstitious fear. These were important factors for their embracing and becoming members of the church.

Impact of Christianity

The tremendous achievements brought about by the spread of Christianity among their people cannot be overlooked. Much of the present progress and achievements of the Nagas in their social, political, economic and religious life are the direct and indirect contribution of the new faith spread by the American Baptist Mission along with the establishment of the British rule in Naga country. The Nagas were set free from superstitious fear and cumbersome worship and sacrifices to demons. They did not grope any more in spiritual darkness. Modern hygiene and education and humanitarian services are the contribution of Christian Missionaries. Education, in turn, helped the development of political consciousness and nationalism. One of the greatest achievements of the Christian missionaries was the end of intra-village and tribal welfare. Here Alexander MacKenzie commented the missionary work of Clark: "His labours are apparently bearing fruit in leading to the settlement of blood-feuds, and a desire on the part of those villages which have neighbours."[33] Inter-village war and constant psychological fear of war ruled no more in the minds of the people. Superstition gave way to reason. Human outlook widened and standard of living was elevated.

However, the advent of Christianity among the Tangkhul Nagas is not without its adverse effects on the society. The reverse effect of the spread of Christianity must be mentioned. Whereas the Gospel concerns for salvation and spiritual well-being of a person or community, the early Christian missionaries attacked all the activities of the Nagas regardless of whether these activities had their origin and connection with religion or not. Therefore, M. Horam remarks: "Christianity did not bring unmixed blessings, it did a lot of damage."[34] The new converts were not allowed to associate themselves with those who were not Christians. Their participation in the traditional festive activities like singing and dancing were prohibited. Naga customs and culture were points of attack and damnation. Early Christian missionaries and converts failed to distinguish culture, customs and other social practices from religion. Rather, they demanded that the converts should adopt western culture. The valuable Naga usages and practices were condemned as satanic elements even by the new converts who learnt it from the missionaries. Therefore, Haimendorf wrote:[35]

> Seeing his own customs condemned by the missionaries, he learnt to despise his own tribe and cultural inheritance. Christianity and Naga culture seemed to him opposite poles, and on the side of the missionaries, there had indeed been few attempts to bring the two into harmony and build on that which was valuable in tribal life.

As a result, there was a wide gap between the converts and non-converts, and enmity developed within the circle of the village community. Many families were broken. The original village government of the Nagas—strong and stable—was threatened. Often villages divided into two: Christian villages and non-Christian villages. Naga history which was handed down from generation to generation through oral tradition, dance, poetry and songs sank to oblivion. The existence of Naga culture was threatened when the new converts adopted western culture and condemned their own culture which is inalienable identity of the tribe.

Impact on Awungaship

It may not be out of place to mention that one important impact of Christianity fell on the powers and functions of the Tangkhul Awunga. The time honoured position, powers and functions of the Awunga, well-tried and accepted without reservation, which was rather strengthened by British rule as medium of effective administration in Tangkhul country was seriously eroded by the spread of Christianity. When Christian missionaries brought the new faith with its established theological principles and introduced western culture, it produced serious effects on the stagnant culture of the Tangkhuls. The devotion of the new converts to the new faith and their desire for higher life-style also affected their honour and loyalty to the Awunga. Two opposing religious beliefs began to exist in parallel within many a village.

This led to the decentralisation and reduction of the powers and functions of the Awunga and the Hangva. The new converts felt that, they did not fall within the purview of old village administration. For any dispute or issue that occurred within the village, they would go to the church authorities for settlement instead of going to the court of the village Awunga and Hangva. Again, for the dispute between a Christian and a non-Christian, the former wanted to go to the court of the British officials ignoring the existence of the village court of Awunga and Hangva. However, the British officials recognized and honoured the tradition and successful administration and judicial system of the village chief and Hangva. Therefore Rev. Clark remarked with regret:[36]

> Their village government is a government much higher even from the civilized nations. To build another village separate from the other for the sake of the Gospel creates division. This new religion should not disturb their village government system . . . had I knew it before, I would never had built a new (Molung-yimsen) village.

In course of time, even the Awunga and others were also not free from the influence of the new religion. Despite their initial and bitter opposition to the new faith, and their hatred and suspicion to the rpesence of the alien people in their soil, they themselves also embraced Christianity. For instance, Raihao, the Awunga of Ukhrul was one of the 12 students who first attended the mission school at Ukhrul. Later, he was converted and baptized. He was also the interpreter of the Christian missionaries in the class. The conversion of the village Awunga helped the missionaries to get better foothold in the village and got more freedom to preach in the entire village community. It was soon followed by many more conversions.

Another important impact of Christianity on the Awunga is that, often his conversion into the new faith led him to be more mindful of the new religion, faith and salvation than as he was mindful of his secular business before. This made the Awunga less autocratic and more liberal. He had to compromise his old ways of chieftainship to the changing modern form of administration. He would incorporate the two administrative systems into his old office of Awunga.

Whatever changes may have been brought about by the advent of Christianity there is not denying the fact that, the post of Awunga remains unchanged. Even with the change and erosion of the powers and functions of the Awunga, his post stands as ever. This is one distinct feature regarding the post of Tangkhul Awunga. Further, through modern education, people realised that this traditional office of the village Awunga should be maintained and strengthened with some improvement to suit the present situation.

The overall survey of the influer.ce of Christianity shows that the benefits gained through the spread of the Gospel and new faith far outweighed the disadvantages. Had it not been the Christian missionaries and their incessant efforts to enlighten the Nagas, the people would have much slower progress.

No doubt, the Christian missionaries attacked the culture of the Nagas and were in large measure agents of change for western culture on the converts. On the contrary, the Nagas, with the help of modern education, through the spread of Christianity, have started to revive their culture recently and traced back their history through the elders of the villages, and from the non-Christian Tangkhuls who are now, the custodians of the Naga folk-songs, folk-dance and customs of the tribe. The need of the hour is a revival of the Naga culture which is indeed a matter of great urgency. In this connection, Horam remarks:[37]

> . . . the Nagas must realise that once the alien culture is allowed to establish its root in Naga soil, Nagas will be reduced to a second class citizen in their own territory; and I cannot resist the conviction that when Nagas yield to outside pressure, Nagas are lost beyond hope.

NOTES & REFERENCES

1. Tuisem A. Shishak, *Principles Underlying the Socio-Religious Practices of the Tangkhul Naga Animists,* pp. 90-91.
2. The word "Genna" popularly used by many writers for 'taboo' simply means forbidden or prohibited from. Therefore, a 'taboo' means prohibition from doing any form of work on a particular day or days when it is set aside as a solemn day for the purpose of worship or performance of religious rites or ceremonies. This is the "Sabath" of the Nagas called Shar in Tangkhul. Another meaning of 'Taboo' is prohibition from doing anything against the custom, tradition and culture of the Nagas. E.G., 'Incest' is a "taboo" according to the culture of the Tangkhuls. So also 'War Dance' performed by women is a 'taboo'.
3. T.C. Hodson, *The Naga Tribes of Manipur,* p. 163.
4. M.M. Clark, *A Corner in India,* p. 3; M. Horam, *The North East India,* A Profile, p. 191.
5. J. H. Hutton, *The Angami Nagas,* p. 177.
6. Verrier Elwin, *The Nagas in Nineteenth Century,* p. 57.
7. The Tangkhuls use the word Kazingram for both heaven and sky. They believe that the Kingdom of God or His dwelling place is

situated somewhere above in the sky. But He knows everything happening on this earth, even the thoughts of men, hears the prayers of men and receives their sacrifices. God intervenes when the demons torture men.

8. J. Hutton, The Sema Naga, p. 201; J. P. Mills, *The Ao Nagas,* p. 247; *The Rengma Nagas,* p. 228; Asoso Yonou, *The Rising Nagas,* p. 30; Ursula Graham Bower, *Naga Path,* p. 20.
9. R. R. Shimray, *Origin and Culture of Nagas,* p. 232.
10. *Ibid.,* p. 131.
11. J. P. Mills, *The Rengma Nagas,* p. 229.
12. The large majority of the Tangkhuls today are Christians. But there are still a group of Tangkhuls who retain their old belief. According to S. K. Gori, the Christians of Manipur East District shown by 1981 Census is 92 per cent, *Changing Phase of Tribal Areas of Manipur,* p. 112.
13. Lungning still remains three miles from the village settlement of Ningthi in the South-West from where present researcher hails. The non-Christians of the village still make offering to this stone and keep it with great reverence.
14. V. Elwin (Ed.) citing W. Robinson, *A Descriptive Account of Assam,* in The Nagas of Nineteenth Century, p. 503.
15. M. Horam, *North East India: A Profile,* p. 193.
16. Tuisem A. Shishak, *op. cit.,* p. 323.
17. Hodson, *op. cit.,* p. 79.
18. Horam, *Naga Polity,* p. 81; Shimray, *op. cit.,* p. 53.
19. The term Genna is not a Tangkhul word, which had been explained in a preceding chapter. It is preferred to use the Tangkhul word such as Shar.
20. M. Horam, *Naga Polity,* p. 120.
21. T. C. Hodson, *op. cit.,* p. 161.
22. The story was narrated to the researcher by his father and this story is still in the memory of the village elders.
23. F.S. Downs, *History of Christianity in India,* p. 56; Piketo Sema, *British Policy and Administration in Nagaland,* pp. 59-67.
24. J. Johnstone, *Manipur and the Naga Hills,* pp. 43-44.
25. M. Horam, *Nagas Old Ways New Trends,* p. 85.
26. Rev. Champhang Jajo, *Christian Life in a Tribal Context,* p. 20.
27. William Pettigrew, *40 Years in Manipur,* Assam, p. 6.

28. F. S. Downs, *op. cit.,* p. 109.
29. Rev. Champhang Jajo, *Christian Life in a Tribal Context in Manipur,* p. 55.
30. F. S. Downs, *op. cit.,* pp. 80, 177.
31, Rev. Champhang Jajo, *Christian Life in a Tribal Context in Manipur,* pp. 37, 38.
32. G. K. Gori, *op. cit.,* p. 112.
33. Alexander MacKenzie, *North East Frontier of India,* p. 99.
34. M. Horam, *North East India: A Profile,* p. 207.
35. Christoph von Furer Haimendorf, *op. cit.,* p. 49.
36. Panger Imchen, cited in *~~Ancient~~ Ao Naga Religion and Culture,* pp. 156-7.
37. M. Horam, *Nagas: Old Ways, New Trends,* p. 116.

7

THE TANGKHUL AWUNGA AND THE TRIBAL CONGLOMERATION

Though the Nagas are living in a compact area, they are divided into a number of tribes. Because of their common origin from the Tibeto-Burman race, they have certain common traits in their social, cultural, economic and religious life. Politically also, every Naga village was an independent unit having its own independent policy of war and peace, law making and administration.

Despite all these common features of the Nagas, there are and unique forms of their government, among different tribes. The comparative study of the governance of various tribes of the Nagas shows that there are different forms of governments and both monarchical form of government and republican form of government are practised by the Nagas. Also while we find the forms of democracy in some Naga tribes, there is also found existence of extreme form of autocracy or despotic form of government on the other hand. Again, in some other Naga tribes, we find the existence and practice of both republican and monarchical forms of government depending on the leadership, personal qualities, abilities, wealth of the leader concerned, and his son who would succeed him.

Further, in most of Naga societies, the jurisdiction of the Naga chiefs is limited to their own villages and does not extend beyond it. However, some exceptions are found in the chieftainship of the Konyaks and Maos where their sway extended over some other villages as titular chiefs without interfering in the internal administrations of those villages they dominated.

Such are the wide variations in the forms of the village states of different Naga tribes that it is worth studying these variations. In all the tribes, we find the existence of village councils which is the most important organ of the village state. Except in the autocratic government of the Konyaks and direct democratic government of the Angamis, the councillors are all-in-all in making policy of war and peace, law making and administration of the village state. Sometimes, they act as a check to the autocratic tendency of certain powerful Naga chiefs. The nature of the Naga state governments of some selected Naga tribes is discussed below.

Angamis

The extreme form of democracy or direct democracy which is also known as pure democracy is being practised in Angami society. In early days, Angami democracy was practised in such an extreme form that they did not have permanent village chiefs except in the form of religious leaders called Kemevo, who held loose secular and religious functions. This independent minded spirit of the Angamis appeared to make the Angami village without a leader or a chief. Assessing the nature of the Angami village state, Haimendorf writes:[1]

> The Angamis were never ruled by chiefs, and no one individual seems ever to have had authority over an entire village community. Wealth and prowess in war gave a man a good deal of influence, but the villages were run on strictly democratic lines and no one could command his neighbour.

In this Horam writes, "The Angami is independent minded and one Angami is as good as another."[2] Without a chief in a village, it is most likely that there was no village government as such. Therefore, Visier Sanyu is of the opinion that, "In the pre-colonial period, it is historically inconceivable to think of the Angami villages as the form of state at any level. . . ."[3] Rather, the practical administration was found in the clans of the Angmis than in their village.

Although an Angami village may be regarded as a political and religious unit, the village settlement was divided into Khels of different clans. They were clearly demarcated and fortified. The leadership of the clan chief seemed to be more effective over the clan than the leadership of the village chief, who was chosen at the time of necessity casually. In Angami society, the clan is the real social unit. Within the village, it formed almost a village, and at times, the inter-clan feuds led to severe quarrels almost amounting to bloodshed and war. Therefore, the clan gates were kept closed from dusk to dawn. This is a peculiar feature of the Angami Naga society. Therefore, one anthropologist wrote:[4]

> Although the village may be regarded as the unit of the political and religious sides of the Angami life, the real unit of the social side is the clan. So distinct is the clan from the village that, it forms almost a village in itself, often fortified within the village inside its own boundaries and not infrequent of variance almost amounting to war with other clans in the same village.

Another peculiar characteristic in the social life of the Angamis is the absence of village councils which is found in almost all other tribal communities. Therefore, whenever there was a quarrel or dispute, one village elder, most possibly the Kemevo, opens the proceeding, joined by all adult males having their own right to speak, in order to settle the issue.[5] However, in the midst of charge and counter charge, and the people shouting in favour of their respective clans or relatives, the eloquent village elder sought out a solution. Their decisions were always respected by the people. If this could not bring about the issue to an end, it was decided by the strength of first-one party against another, one Khel against another Khel. Sometimes, it led to bloody quarrel as mentioned above. In this connection, Hutton wrote again:[6]

> Before the Deputy Commissioner's court was available, when settled at all, were probably settled by a sort of informal council of elders who would discuss the matter under dispute with one another, the parties and the general public at great length, until some sort of agreement was arrived at. . . . Regular customs with regard to the manner of dealing with offences certainly existed, and in the absence of any higher authority, there is no doubt but that the elders manage to arbitrate after some fashion or other in most disputes.

But it will be fairly wrong to think that Angami villages were and are devoid of village government and leaders. It was a political and religious unit having its own chief under one religious taboo.[7] For example, when the village was under the threat of hostile village, or when the former was to undertake raid against the hostile village, naturally, the village elders met and selected a person to be the chief who could lead the war and bring glory to his village. But in the next raid, others could take over the office. Succession to this post by his son depended on the personalities, prowess, physical strength and influence of the latter on the village community.

Further, it is to state that the whole village was under the religious taboo at the headship of the Kemevc who belonged to the family of founding village. The post is hereditary. He announced all religious festivals, ceremonies and religious solemn days where the entire village community had to observe strictly without exception. This was one criterion of the village unity. However, it can be well assumed that the practice of extreme democracy stood on the way to village and inter-clan cohesiveness in normal situation where everyone followed the dictate of his own sweet will. Here we may quote Hutton again:[8]

> Every man follows the dictate of his own will, a form of purest democracy which is very difficult to conceive of as existing even for a single day; and yet that it does exist here is an undeniable fact.

Again, it is to state that, the Angami village state exercised the republican form of government, and thus, the post of the village chief was not hereditary. Therefore, a person did not require this post by chance, but rather he deserved it by his personal ability and capacity. For this, he did not require divine sanction either as practised by the Tangkhuls.

Konyaks

The Konyaks had two types of government. One is the republican form of government, and the other one is despotic monarchical form of government. The Upper Konyaks (those who are living in Patkoi range and are neighbours to Phom, Chang, Khiamnungans etc.) practised democratic and republican form of government; whereas, the Lower Konyaks (those who are neighbour to Assam valley) exercised despotic and monarchical form of government. According to Shimray, when the Konyaks migrated to Chui village, which was the oldest Konyak village, they held a council to decide whether they should have Ang system or not.[9] Those who favoured monarchical form of government settled in the lower part of their country, whereas the other group who commended republican form of government migrated to upper part of their country.[10]

The leadership of the Upper Konyaks rests on the wealth, personal prowess, influence, ability, skill in war and the one who can command the obedience of the people. Therefore, this post is not hereditary, but his son can succeed the office provided he possesses those qualities. The village chief is assisted by a Council of Clan Elders in the administration of the village state.[11] Again, the post of councillor is also not hereditary. At his retirement, or death, he could be succeeded by the most capable person of the clan.[12]

Other important social groups which assisted in the administration of the village are (a) Hambu, (b) the Eyang, and (c) the Longwang.[13] A Hambu is a warrior class, leader of war and expedition. An Eyang is normally a religious leader who occupies important social position. He is taken from the senior clan only, who is also senior most of the clan responsible for worship, rites, sacrifices and festivals of the village. In this, care should be taken since any mistake calls down the wrath of the spirit with the punishment of severe diseases, even death of the Eyang. Therefore, it is not an enviable job; but this post is hereditary. The Longwang is the representative of the clan in the village council. Each clan sends one or more Longwangs who are intelligent, diplomatic and well versed in tribal customs and traditions. They discuss all issues, problems, plans and disputes of the village together. The decisions they arrived at are final and binding. Sometimes, all the villagers joined in decision making of the council. Chaenkajimpu is the head of Chaen (Morung) who is responsible for the maintenance and decorum of the Chaen. However, no woman shares any leadership and responsibility in the administration of these village states.

The Lower Konyaks practised monarchical form of government. Their Angs were very powerful and despotic. They married as many wives as they could afford to maintain. The Angship of the Konyak villages are undisputable. Their persons and offices are sacred, and no common people should approach the Ang upright. For instance, the servants of the Ang of Sheengha have to croach or creep whenever they passed him or offered some gifts to the Ang. Indeed, the autocratic Ang demanded such a high courtesy from the subject people.[14]

The first son of the chief wife alone has the right to succeed the office of the Ang. Again, they are so despotic that what they say is the law, and no one can question the action of such a powerful Ang. They exercised their autocratic power over the bodies and properties of their subject people at their own sweet will. Therefore, Haimendorf remarked:[15]

> Most of the 'Great Angs' in the still unadministered territory were, at the best, rather autocratic, and at worst, definitely tyrannical, commandeering the labour, property, and last but not the least—many pretty daughter of their subjects.

Some powerful village Angs extended their sway over the neighbouring villages and exercised their powers as overlords that they are called 'Great Angs' as mentioned above.[16] However, internal administration of the dominated villages remained unaffected. They had their independent policy and administration of their own under their respective village Angs. The Angs of Mon, Chui and Wakching were the most powerful 'Great Angs' of Lower Konyaks who exercised their overlordship beyond their villages. Wakching was such a strong village that till recent years, it stretched its arm of dominance into the plains of Assam and exacted tributes from the cultivators. Further, some Konyak villages, as much as two day's journey, paid tribute to the Great Ang of Wakching.

Another characteristic of the Great Angs of the Konyaks is the maintenance of their persons pure from blood pollution with the woman of common origin by their marriage. This system was prevalent among the Angs of lower rank also to some extent, by which they sought brides and grooms of their sons and daughters respectively from the Ang families of equal rank. In this regard, C. Haimendorf describes thus in the following words:[17]

> The position of the so-called "Great Ang" is quite different. These powerful village chiefs, such as the Great Ang of Mon and the "Great Ang" of Chui have the sacred blood of chiefs, pure and undiluted, in their veins. There can be

> no more exclusive community than that of the great Ang class, for as the king of Egypt kept the royal blood pure by marrying their own sisters, so that the great Angs take their wives from their own great Ang class, and it is only the children of such a union that acquire the father's rank.

Still another important feature in the governance of the village state of Lower Konyaks is there is practice of oligarchical form of government, and the absence of the councillors to be taken from all clans of the village which was, and still is practised by other Naga tribes. The grown-up males of the Ang class formed the council of the Ang, and they decided all forms of quarrels, disputes and issues of any sort within the village.[18] The practice of oligarchical form of government, no doubt, strengthened the despotism of the Konyak Angs. When there is no popular council of the village, it shows that the Konyak village state was run void of democratic principles. Lastly woman played no role in the governance of the Konyak village state.

Khiamnungans

The Khiamnungans have republican form of government. Therefore, the post of the village chief is not hereditary. However, if the son of a chief possesses the qualities of leadership as the chief possesses, he can succeed to the office of the chief. Every village has its head or chief. According to Sardeshpande,[19] the chief and other leaders of the village are neither elected nor nominated. Rather, they are accepted by the people to be their chief and leaders according to their physical strength, prowess, wisdom and influence and their abilities who can bring peace, prosperity and glory to the village.

In Khiamnungans society, there are two main clans from which the chief and leaders of the village are drawn. One is called Sheev and the other is Lam. Though the post of the chief and leaders are not hereditary, and an ambitious and capable person can aspire to these posts, they should belong to either of those two clans mentioned above. The people of those two clans who belong to lower sub-clans cannot aspire to these offices under any circumstances. Common people are excluded from these posts of village administration.

Sheev is the ruling class of the Khiamnungan society and village. This clan produces warrior class called Nokpao. They protect the village from the raid and invasion of the enemy villages; fight war and bring glory to the village. However, the ruling class and warrior class of the village are taken from the two topmost sub-clans of Sheev, known as Longshen and Thai. Longshen is the highest sub-clan of Sheev and without their approval, no work or plan of the village can be executed.

Lam is a priestly class. All religious functions like the performance of rites, ceremonies, sacrifices and worship of any form are the responsibilities of the Lams. They are known as men of wisdom, knowledge and patients who produce an officer class called Petchi. The Petchi perform dual role—religious and secular. In religious matter, all rituals, sacrifices and worships of the village are conducted by them. Secular duties of the Petchis are by no means less important than religious duties. They make peace between feuding parties, examine conflicts and carry out negotiations. They act as emissaries and diplomats with the neighbouring villages. They execute the duties of judges and examine cases and other issues and pronounce judgements. The decisions made by the Petchis are approved by the Nokpaos and issue verbal orders for the punishment to be carried out on the defaulters.[20]

Customarily, both the Nokpaos and Petchis, who are the elders and wisemen and who have both the authority and wisdom are law-makers and decision makers of their village state. Their decisions are always respected by the village community. Those who oppose their decision are expelled from the village. Inter-village disputes are settled by the village elders of the two conflicting villages.[21] But under no circumstances, women can be included in the leadership of the village and its administration.

Semas

The Semas have powerful village chiefs called Akekao, and the post of Akekao is hereditary. The hereditary chieftainship and despotism of the Sema Akekao is almost the same as that of the Konyaks. Regarding the similarity of the two, Horam wrote: "A powerful village head has been known to acquire the status of a chieftain or even a king, e.g., the Konyak and Sema Nagas."[22] He continued further: "Chieftainship is hereditary, in the real sense of the term, among the Semas and Konyaks." But one peculiar chieftainship of the Semas is that, at times at the death of the chief, his younger brother succeeds him where the son of the dead-chief occupied secondary position. But when the new chief (younge. brother) is dead, chieftainship goes to the eldest son of the former chief (elder brother).[23] However, the accepted rule is that the eldest son of the original chief succeeds the father if he (son) has not founded a village of his own, and remains with his father.

Again, another featuie of the Sema chieftainship is that, when a person founded a new village and becomes the chief, his parents and elder brothers who follow him will remain there as common men under him. The chieftainship cannot go to the father and elder brother, nor to the eldest son of his elder brother.

Further, when a Sema founded a new village, then he becomes the chief and absolute owner of the land.[24] He may share portions of land to his close and prominent companions and dependents. In the rotation of cultivation of land, he procures the best area for himself. In this regard, the Sema chiefs are similar to Kuki chiefs as well. The remaining land, he parcels out for the cultivation of his subject people. He exacted free labour from all grown-up adults including his own brothers to work in his field for four to sixteen days a year. Some powerful chiefs demanded much more than sixteen days. Sometimes as a token of appreciation, the chief shared portions of meat and salt to the villagers.

A Sema chief has two fold functions—secular and religious.[25] As a secular chief, he directs the village in war and decides matters by himself or sometimes in consultation with the village elders (Chochomi). However, consultation with the village elders depends on the personal character of the chief. Some powerful chiefs ignore the village elders in making decisions. But in the settlement of disputes and the question between his own village and the neighbouring villages, the village elders come into prominence as it is a known fact that the elderly people are more conversant in customs and tradition than the younger people. It is also the responsibility of the chief to entertain distinguish strangers and see to their safety.

The religious duty of a Sema chief is to announce the village gennas and festivals and to issue orders early in the morning before people scatter. In this matter, the chief shares religious functions with the priest (Awou). A person who cannot give warning of gennas in the proper way can never take the post of chief.

In the administration of the village state, the chief is assisted by a village elder called Chochomi. The chief employs him as a herald and sends him to other village as his emissary. As the deputy of the chief, in the absence of the latter, he manages the reins of the village administration, or otherwise entrusted. However, in order to assist the chief in settlement of disputes and to know the opinion of the village community, a number of Chochomis are appointed by the chief from different clans. Sometimes, the Chochomis become very powerful to the extent of controlling the chief though such incidents are very rare. However, some Sema chiefs are so powerful and autocratic that the office of Chochomi is even non-existent. Generally, the post of Chochomi is secondary in the polity of Sema village.

Another functionary in Sema village is the office of Awou. He is the principal religious official selected and appointed by the chief and his elders. From religious ceremonial point of view, he is the most important person in the village. When a new Sema village is founded, the house of Awou is first built, and then the house of the chief. He is also entitled two days free labour from the community of the village. Though the chief share some religious duties as mentioned above, all rites and ceremonies are performed by the Awou. He also annnounces agricultural gennas.

However, the Sema Awou's post is not a coveted one and unpopular as it is believed that he is liable to die early. According to their superstitious belief, during jhum cultivation, if the sap of trees spray on his body, it is taken as spitting and a curse on him which causes his early death. Therefore, naturally, poor people are selected to occupy the post with the benefits of remuneration mentioned above.

Lothas

The Lothas have a republican form of government. The Lotha village chief is called Ekyung. Shimray mentioned that the one who is intelligent, influential, wealthy-throwing feast of merit; physically the strongest and brave in war who can bring trophies of heads can attain the post of chief.[26] However, according to the version of Mills:[27]

> In the days when villagers were constantly at war, each village was ruled by a chief (Ekyung) assisted by an informal council of elders. The chieftainship was hereditary in the family of the man who originally founded the village but did not at all necessarily pass from father to the son. The most suitable man became chief by force of character.

However, if the son of the chief possesses the qualities of chieftainship, his succession to the office of the father is accepted by the people. In this case, the Lotha chieftainship is hereditary to some extent. In the same way, any member of the village community who has the traits mention earlier can aspire the office of the chief.

According to Horam, the main function of the chief was to lead people in time of war and settle disputes of the village with the council of elders.[28] Inter-village war among the Lothas was rare. Womenfolk are debarred from the polity of the Lothas. All important issues and disputes are settled by the chief and village elders. British rule brought about a great change in the powers and functions of the Lotha village chief and elders. The British officers installed Gaonbura instead of the former chieftainship and some village elders were also appointed to assist the Gaonbura who had to exercise power at the direction of the British officials. This new system was introduced to suit the colonial policy of the British. The Gaonbura was entrusted to collect taxes and settle disputes as the agent and representative of the people. As a recognition to the chieftainslup of the Gaonbura, a red blanket was issued to him which was a symbol of honour and position.

Rengmas

In the governance of Rengma village states, the republican form of government was and is prevalent. It is almost the same as the pattern of Lotha village government. The head of the village is called Khokhiigii and Lekho-ong by the western and eastern Rengmas respectively.[29] The office of the chief is hereditary in the clan, but not necessarily in the family. The most suitable person in the clan has the right to succeed the office of the chief. However, the eastern Rengmas admitted their inability to trace the nature of hereditary chieftainship in their society. Rather, they agreed that their villages had been run by a man of influential character who could rule over the village community, and settled the disputes of the village.[30]

In Rengma village polity, the chief is assisted by prominent leaders of the clans as advisors. It was the custom and tradition of the Rengmas that the village chief made truce and alliances with the friendly or warring villages as the case might be. There are several instances where southern Rengmas made alliance with the Angamis whereas, western Rengmas aligned with the neighbouring Lothas. In olden days defiance to the chief was punished by destroying the house of the offender. Violation of the village gennas and customs was also punished severely even to the extent of expulsion from the village. However, the chief could be removed in case of misrule and oppression. It happened in Tseminyu village in early days.[31] By virtue of the office, the chief has religious function as well. All the village gennas are announced by the chief, and performed religious and agricultural ceremonies of the village.

By the advent of the British rule, a complete change of the village government was brought about. In this, Mills lamented, "British rule has put an end to the power of the chiefs, to the great loss of the tribe, and it is probably impossible to revive it."[32] The habit of rushing to the court of the British officers was developed, which the latter did not possess clear knowledge of the customary laws of the people. Thus the independence of the Rengma village state and the power of the chief came to an end.

Aos

The Aos also have republican form of government and the government of village state is guided by the principles of democracy. Every Ao village has its chief called Ungr by the Chonglis and Sungba by the Mongsen group. The post of chief is not hereditary. A person of high calibre possessing wealth and riches, good physic, dominating personality, brave in battle, intelligent power and kindness to the subject people are the requisites of a leader.[33] But any citizen of the village who commands those qualities cannot simply become a village chief. According to Lima Imchen,[34] the chieftainship is exclusively for the Pongeners of Chongli group and Imchens of the Mongsen group. They are the chief councillors holding the political powers in their respective group. Therefore, succession goes to the most capable person of these two clans in these two language groups of the Aos. Again, there are assistant chiefs called Tanglu and Chongnu in Chongli and Mongsen groups respectively. In the word of Mills, "All meetings are held in, and all animals are killed in front of his house. He gets the head.... Ungr's assistant ... gets a head if several animals are killed at the same time."[35]

In the village polity of the Aos, there exists a council of the village elders called Tatar chosen from all clans residing in the village. They are the representatives of the people of their respective clans. There is a corresponding way of selecting the Tatars with that of a village chief. However, normally, the fittest elder who can speak boldly for the interest of the clan is chosen by the clansmen. The Tatars assisted the chief in the governance of the village, but at the same time, they remained as a check or controlling power to the authority of the chief from absolutism.

According to Horam,[36] the terms of the chief and Tatars are for a period of three to five years, at the expiry of which new chief and members of council are elected again. But in the method of electing or selecting new members, Mills wrote: "Usually all the clans in the village are represented in each meeting ... selection is by general consent. There is nothing in the way of formal voting."[37] He further said that since no one wishes to quit the office within such a short period, there was always a quarrel between the old members and the new aspirants. However, no one can be re-elected however influential he might be. But exception to this rule is found in the society of the Mongsen group. Unlike the Chonglis, it is not necessary for Mongsen elders to relinguish the office at a time. The period of election is also different one from another - five years for Chongli and six years for Mongsen.

All disputes and cases of both civil and criminal are heard and decided by the councillors. The cases within a clan are settled by the clan elders amicably as far as possible. However, according to Ao custom, the offences of under-age children before they became members of Morung are not taken as crime and their parents cannot be fined for the offences of such a child.

But in olden days when the village councillors failed to settle disputes of any form, they referred the matter to a powerful chief of other village for arbitration whose decision was hardly evaded in order to end litigation. Yimsingangba of Ungma village was a model of it. "Despite his crude methods people flocked to him from all over the Ao country, probably because, even if they did not get justice, they got a decision of some sort which put an end to litigation of which every one was heartily sick."[38]

Normally, the retired councillors, and in some cases, village elders are taken for village priest known as Putir. Here also public opinion is sought for the selection of the village priest. Whereas less important rites and ceremonies are performed by the priests in term, the bigger rituals and festivals require the presence of all priests. Taboos and rituals of fishing, hunting, war, agriculture of the village are conducted by the village priest. They also shared some portion of meat as remuneration of their service to the village community.

Maos

The Mao Nagas, like some other Naga tribes, practised monarchical type of government. Therefore, the post of the chief is hereditary by nature. According to Jyotirmoy Roy,[39] there exists 'democratic village council' among the Maos. Their chiefs therefore, are not despotic like the chiefs of Konyaks and Semas. From remote past till very recently, there existed sixteen villages[40] of the Maos each having its own chief with independent administrative policy. However, one peculiar characteristic is that, the chief of Pudunamai extended his power over the sixteen villages and collected tributes from them as overlord. Another important feature is that the entire sixteen villages fall under one religious genna; and the chief of Maikhel village is the custodian of Mao-genna. It may be recalled that according to legend, Maikhel village is the place where the Nagas separated.

The chief of Pudunamai enjoyed certain privileges.[41] He had the right to keep one runner as a messenger under him. His house should be built by the villagers in two days. The community granted a terraced field for the cultivation of the Chief, and he was entitled to get one leg of the animal killed for the feast of Merit. Every household should give him one basket of paddy at harvest time. In social functions, he seated himself against the main pillar of the house and tested the rice-beer and meat before others touched it. His death was observed by the entire community of sixteen villages for several solemn days. For the Maos, he may be likened the king of sixteen villages.

As the Mao chief had several rights and privileges, there are several taboos binding on him. His wife was also under certain taboos being the wife of the chief. For instance, the chief should not go out of the village during the days of taboo, even to the field except for the performances of sowing and harvest rituals. He should not take bath and wash cloths during village taboo days. In those days, he was not allowed to sleep with his wife. Some food taboos are also binding on him. When the village was under taboo, his wife should expose paddy in sunshine. He announced the village gennas and performed rites, ceremonies, and sacrifices; and offered prayers for the peace, prosperity and welfare of the village community.

The Mao village chiefs are assisted by a council of elders chosen from each clan residing in the villages. Normally, the eldest ones are chosen. The post is not necessarily hereditary. It can go to the next oldest man of the clan after him. The chief presides over the village council meetings held in his house and the councillors decide disputes, make rules and policies of the village. Usually, the chief is the commander in war though the most able warrior leads in the battle. Differences between two or more villages are decided by the elde s of the villages concerned. Till today, most of the disputes and quarrels of the Maos are handled by themselves and the cases are decided and settled according to Mao customary laws. Their management of the cases is so effective that the present set up of governments have nothing to do in most of Mao issues. Some cases of serious issues concerning a village or more when the concerned parties cannot arrive at a decision are referred to the elders of the sixteen villages and their decision is always respected.

From early days, the sixteen villages formed a loose federation of the Maos; and most of the difficult inter-village issues are referred to, and are, settled by the elders of this federation. No woman membership in their village council was allowed. Sometimes, there are occasions of the general assembly of the whole grown up males of the village to decide some important village issues and plans for the security and defence of the village.

Marams

The Marams are a group of Naga people living in present Senapati District of Manipur. The Maos are of the opinion that the Marams are a class of Mao group.[42] But the Marams do not subscribe to this view. Linguistically there is wide difference between the two. However, they are close neighbours.

The Maram villages have their village chiefs called Sugong which the post is hereditary based on the principle of primogeniture. The eldest son has every right to succeed the father. According to Hodson,[43] in early days, a Maram village, which is now known as 'Maram Khunjou' consisted of 900 houses exercised great influence over a large number of villages extending as far as Mayang Khong in the south, and collected tributes from them. The chief has both secular and religious functions and is under certain taboos which he is supposed to observe in a very strict way. He is assisted by a council of elders taken from all clans residing in the village. This post is also hereditary within the family. All quarrels and disputes and important matters are deliberated, discussed and decided by the village council. The Sugong announces the village gennas but the important religious rites, sacrifices and worship are done by the village priest.

Kabuis

The Kabuis are another major tribe of the Nagas. They live in Manipur and neighbouring hil's of Nagaland and Assam. Tamenglong District is regarded as the central habitat of the Kabuis, and from that area their settlements have spread. The other name of Kabui is known as Rongmei, meaning man of south. According to legend, the ancestors of Zemei, Liangmei and Rongmei descended from one patriarch. The first group live in northern side of their habitat. Hence the name Zemei; the second one at the middle who are now, the Liangmeis and the Rongmeis occupied the south. The first two are known to the Britishers by the name Kacha Naga, whereas Kabui is a combination of Rongmei and Impuimei. All these sub-tribes have their own village chiefs. The polity of these tribes are also the same, the only difference is in magnitude. Therefore, the study of the Kabui chieftainship will enable us to understand the polity of two other allied tribes mentioned above.

The Kabuis have hereditary chieftainship called Guang and succession to the post is on the principle of primogeniture. The village chief is called Khallakpa by the Meiteis. He is assited by two officials called Luplakpa and Khunbu.[44] Regarding the village administration of the Kabuis, Mingthoi Thaimei wrote:[45]

> Usually every K: bui village is a self-ruled and self-administered tiny world—so far as its internal administration is concerned. . . . In the administration of the village, Nhanpou-Nhanpei (founder members) has greater weight and all other members of the council are helpers of them only.

According to Hodson,[46] besides the hereditary officials, other councillors are elected. The wealth, riches, success in war and faculty of speech of the chief influence the council in the administration of the village state. However, there is erosion of the religious power of the chief since elders of the village perform religious functions which were elsewhere responsibility of the chief. According to Thaimei, "One of the distinct features in public life of the Kabuis is the predominance of the aged men:...."[47] All important issues and plans of the village are discussed and decisions are made by the village council. Sometimes, some serious problems need to call the general assembly where all grown up males should take part in the deliberations and decision making.

Quarrels, disputes, theft or cases of both civil and criminal are settled by the village council according to their customs and traditions. For cases beyond the comprehension of human knowledge, they seek divine guidance through ordeals. Generally, the decisions of the village elders are respected and obeyed since they are final and binding. If any party refuses to accept the decision made by the council, that particular person or persons is/are boycotted and excommunicated by the village.

Cases between two villages or more are decided by the elders of the parties concerned. In order to avert bloodshed, they always resort to oath-taking which ensures result of serious consequence. However, if they fail to come to any agreeable point, the trial by strength determines the issue. During war, the most successful warrior becomes the leader rather than the chief. This leads a person to social recognition. A successful warrior is always respected by the people and such a person has a place in the village council or general assemblies.

Other Naga tribes of Manipur, like the Anals, Marings, Mayon and Monsang also have hereditary chieftainship and council of elders, usually taken from different clans residing in the village. Since the council of their village elders are represented by clan chiefs, their posts are also hereditary. The Mayon village headman who is known as Erungpa is responsible for both social and religious functions of the village. This characteristic of the village state is found in all Naga tribes because of which the Naga chiefs are responsible for the declaration and observances of gennas and also for the performance of rites, ceremonies and sacrifices which are related to entire village community.

In village chieftainship of the Anals, a complete change has been taken place. K.B. Singh described the changes brought about in the village polity of the Anals:[48]

> Every Anal village has a chief known as Khureng.... Headship was hereditary in the past but it is not so now-a-days and if a suitable person from Sinrung sub-clan is not available, headship will go to any suitable person from other sub-clan.

Tangkhuls

The polity of Tangkhul village state had been discussed in the preceding chapters — *Chapter II 'The Early Village State'* and *Chapter V — 'Political and Judicial Organisation'*. By assessing various forms of village states of different Naga tribes, some unique features are found in the formation and functions of Tangkhul village states. Unlike the Mao Chief of Pudunamei and the Great Angs of the Konyaks, the sway of the Tangkhul village chiefs was limited within the territory of their respective villages. Colonisation and domination over the smaller and weaker villages by the stronger ones did not occur in the history of Tangkhul polity. In case of inter-village war because of some issue of serious matter, when they could not find amicable solution and resorted to war, the more powerful villages came out victorious. Then they were satisfied with a few heads of the enemies. The vanquished village was never dominated and colonized by the stronger village. The spirit of co-existence was always respected. Thus, small villages were not left at the mercy of the stronger and more powerful villages.

Similar to the loose federation of sixteen villages of Mao, the Tangkhuls had a loose organisation of areas or ranges called Longphang which is a branch of Longrei meaning the great Long which the latter is the organisation of the whole Tangkhul community. Cases of serious disputes between two or more villages were referred to Longphang and it tried those disputes amicably. If any party became aggressive and refused to accept the verdict of Longphang, the aggressive village was warned with dire consequences of combined raid. In early days, Longphang was more effective in dealing with local issues than Longrei since the former was an organisation of a smaller group which was more acquainted with the local situation. By the presence of Longphang, the powerful villages could not exploit the weaker villages without commendable reasons. People hardly took their cases to the court of Longrei for the reason given above. Again, in those days, common feeling and spirit of communalism were not strong by the nature of polity of the time. Therefore, when the *Meitei Raja* raided Tangkhul villages, there was no common contingent of the Tangkhuls to fight against the enemy. Rather, the Meitei Raja was resisted by individual Tangkhul villages.

The Tangkhuls of Somra Tract in Burma also practised the same form of village government. They have hereditary post of the Awunga and council of elders (Hangva) as those of the Tangkhuls living in present Manipur state. However, the Tangkhuls of Upper Chindwin District had undergone a complete change since their assimilation to Shan culture and adoption of Buddhism. This brought about the change of their village government from original Tangkhul polity. However, the practice of maintaining the Council of village elders is still retained. They have the authority to decide village disputes, theft, and other cases of both civil and criminal, according to the customs, usages and tradition.

Assessing various forms of the village states of different Naga tribes, we find the existence of extreme democracy and republicanism of the Angamis to absolute despotism of the Konyaks; and both hereditary and elected chieftainship of the Aos, Lothas and Rengmas to hereditary chieftainship of the Maos, Marams, Kabuis and Tangkhuls. However, despite variations of the governments of Naga village states, we find some common features in the polity of the Naga tribes. First, there is the council of elders to assist the village chief in his function of administration. Secondly, the laws of village states are based on customs, usage and traditions. Thirdly, by nature of Naga animism and superstition, religious principles form an important part of their laws. Therefore, the village priests also played important role in village administration in determining the dates of village feasts, taboos, rituals and sacrifices.

However, one exception can be seen with regard to the making of law where autocratic Angs of the Konyaks were so powerful that their words became law. Further, we find the existence of limited form of colonialism in the polity of the Maos and Konyaks. Their chiefs exercised their sway over certain villages and collected tributes from the dominated villages. However, the internal administration of those villages were left entirely in the hands of the conquered chiefs. Here, the colonial chiefs were titular heads over the vanquished villages.

NOTES & REFERENCES

1. C. F. Haimendorf, *Naked Nagas*, p. 13.

2. M. Horam, *Naga Polity,* p. 78.
3. Visier Sanyu, "The History of Village Formation Among the Angami Nagas", p. 198.
4. J. H. Hutton, *The Angami Nagas,* p. 109.
5. M. Horam, *op.cit.,* p. 85.
6. J. H. Hutton, *op.cit.,* p. 143.
7. The village issues were taken up by the Kemevo who did not have as important a status as the Awunga. For instance, these days, Angami villages are governed by the Gaonburas.
8. J. H. Hutton, *op.cit.,* p. 143.
9. Ang is the title used to the chief or ruler of the Konyak village. It is an hereditary post. Some powerful Angs exercised their sway over some other villages as overlord. They are known as "Great Angs".
10. R. R. Shimray, *Origin and Culture of Nagas,* p. 56.
11. S. C. Sardeshpande, *The Patkoi Nagas,* p. 112.
12. *Ibid.,* p. 33.
13. *Ibid.,* pp. 132-134, 140-141.
14. C. F. Haimendorf, *op.cit.,* p. 37.
15. Ibid., p. 104; Sardeshpande, *op. cit.,* p. 135.
16. C. F. Haimendorf, *op. cit.,* p. 35.
17. *Ibid.,* p. 94.
18. *Ibid.,* p. 94.
19. S. C. Sardeshpande, *op. cit.,* p. 21.
20. *Ibid.,* pp. 21, 39, 40.
21. *Ibid.,* pp 39-40.
22. M. Horam, *Naga Polity,* p. 77.
23. J. H. Hutton, *The Sema Nagas,* pp. 148-149.
24. *Ibid.,* pp. 144, 47.
25. *Ibid.,* p. 150.

26. R. R. Shimray, *op. cit.*, p. 57.
27. J. P. Mills, *The Lotha Nagas*, p. 96.
28. M. Horam, *op. cit.*, p. 77.
29. J. P. Mills, *op. cit.*, pp. 139-140.
30. *Ibid.*, p. 140.
31. *Ibid.*, p. 138.
32. *Ibid.*, p. 139.
33. M. Horam, *Naga Polity*, p. 75.
34. An interview with Dr. Lima Imchen, Reader of NEHU in Sociology Department on 4th September 1994. He belongs to the Ao Naga tribe.
35. J. P Mills, *The Ao Nagas*, p. 183.
36. M. Horam, *Naga Polity*, p. 79.
37. J. P. Mills, *op. cit.*, p. 183.
38. J. P. Mills, *op. cit.*, p. 192.
39. Jyotirmoy Roy, *History of Manipur*, p. 193.
40. (1) Pudunamei, (2) Punanamei, (3) Rabunamei, (4) Kalinamei, (5) Songsong, (6) Chawainu, (7) Mao-Pungdung, (8) Chawainamei, (9) Chakamei, (10) Makhan, (11) Tadubi, (12) Sajouba, (13) Maikhel, (14) Tabufu, (15) Kaibi, (16) Etufu.
41. R. R. Shimray, *op. cit.*, pp. 54-55.
42. Hodson, *op. cit.*, pp. 84-85.
43. T. C. Hodson, *op. cit.*, p. 83.
44. Sipra Sen, *History of Manipur*, p. 50.
45. Cited in K. B. Singh (ed.), *An Introduction to Tribal Language and Culture of Manipur*, p. 46.
46. T. C. Hodson, *op. cit.*, p. 102.
47. K. B. Singh (ed.), *op. cit.*, p. 48.
48. K. B. Singh, "The Anals of Manipur" in *Introduction to Tribal Languages and Culture in Manipur*, p. 88.

8

CONCLUSION

From the stage of migration to their present settlement in Naga Homeland, the Nagas have travelled a long way in terms of time and space. Their society has undergone a number of changes during this period. But the most significant changes came towards the end of 19th century and the first half of 20th century with the impact of British administration and the spread of Christianity. Despite the Tangkhul Nagas coming under the native state's administrative jurisdiction, this Naga tribe has undergone similar changes like the large Naga community.

Whatever waves and directions of their migration might be, at the last stage, the Nagas could come and live together in one compact area now called Naga Homeland. However, surprisingly enough, the Nagas remained isolated—one tribe from another, even one village from another within the same tribe. This is still prevalent in certain corners of the Naga inhabited areas. There were several factors for the isolation of the Naga villages. First, remoteness of the Naga inhabited area made then untouched to the non-Naga people and civilization around them. Secondly, the physical terrain and difficulty of access to their villages retarded free access of the people, and vice versa. Thirdly the hostilities of different Naga tribes and villages made them isolate themselves from one another. Fourthly, the economic self-sufficiency required the Naga villages a limited contact with the world beyond their hills for commercial intercourse. Most important of all, the independent nature of the Nagas did not allow any outsider to enter into the territory of their villages. Any kind of movement and access to a village without proper reason was suspected and checked. The Nagas lived a primitive life till recently.

However, with the advent of British rule and spread of Christianity, great changes has been taken place in the social, economic, political, cultural and religious life of the Nagas. The actual administration of the British in Tangkhul country commenced after 1891, and it continued till 1947. This was the beginning of changes that had taken place in the area. Tangkhuls started to make contact with other people which widened their outlook.

Apart from the British colonial rule and spread of Christianity, which changed the life of the Nagas, the impact of World War I and the World War II enhanced the changes. Nagas fought the Wars together with the Allied Forces,[1] Japanese forces[2] and the forces of Azad Hind Fauz.[3] For that, they crossed the sea and landed in France as Labour Corps. During the Second World War, the Naga Homeland became the battle ground of the two greatest forces. The development and civilization in the world outside and the new war technologies brought new ideas of progress and development in the minds of the Nagas. They were no longer isolated from fellow human beings and their cultures.

The changes affected all fields of Nagas life from their village administration to the present political and judicial system. Through modern education and science, the spirit of village state had been done away with. Political consciousness led to the development of nationalism which removed the narrow clanism, village oriented isolation and tribalism. Nagas started to be restive about their future and political integrity of the Naga inhabited areas and for their future territorial independence. Soon an organisation called Naga Club was formed (1918) to look after the interest and welfare of the Nagas.[4] It submitted a memorandum to the Indian Statutory Commission headed by Sir John Simon on 10 January, 1929. A new organisation called Naga Hills District Tribal Council was formed again, which again turned into the Naga National Council in February 1946.[5] The Naga National Council declared the political independence of the Nagas on the eve of the departure of the British from India. When the problem turned out to be more tense and serious, the Nagas submitted the case in the General Assembly of the United Nations Organisation in 1947 for its intervention and solution of the problem.[6]

India refused to honour the declaration of the Nagas of their political rights and duties. By force, the Indian administrative control penetrated into the territory of the Naga inhabited area; and along with it, there was an inflow of both administrative officials and businessmen from India. New commercial goods dominated the poor market of the Nagas. Money economy came into being. Nagas became more conscious about money and its value. Money became everything to them than the inborn quality and culture of the Nagas. It adversely affected Naga handicraft and weaving. They started to shirk physical labour and dignity of labour is avoided. The money-minded Nagas want to imitate the life-style of the rich though there is no means to meet this end.

It was typical of the British rule in North East India that their chief concern was law and order. Taxes were collected such as Rs. 3/- per house from Tangkhul villages, which was meant for contributing towards the expenditure of amdinistration and not for the development their area. To the Tangkhul Nagas, such a contribution was difficult to pay since money circulation was at initial state. The British administration over the Naga inhabited areas of Manipur did not make much progress in development of roads, schools, agriculture and industries. These developments, if at all, had to come from the people themselves. Consequently, the economic development of the Tangkhuls was extremely backward. Manipur state of today does not appear to have made any serious effort to improve the living condition of the Nagas. The village in the remote areas remained untouched with the political and economic developments of the period—1940 to 1950.

These broad changes had their effects on the Tangkhul society. We have in earlier chapters made reference to the Naga society which was an open society. Other than the Awunga and his associates, the Naga tribesmen were equals. The only exception to this was that the Tangkhul womenfolk, like their counterparts of other Naga tribes, have a position subordinate to their menfolk. There has developed a wide gap between the haves and have-nots, between the educated and the unlettered. Educated Nagas have shunned the village life and have contempt life for physical labour. The full significance of the social differences is being felt, but has not been fully studied.

Today, well-to-do Naga families and educated employed Nagas usually live in urban areas, away from their villages. Whereas, their lives have advanced materially and they have concern more for the furtherance of their own living condition, they cannot contribute to the upliftment of their society in the villages. They hardly visit their village except in the festive seasons and marriages of their near ones. The result is more isolation of the villages when people are looking for urban life, the villages are left undeveloped and uncared for. This is the reason Naga villages remain much backward. Japanese war veterans who fought the World War II in early 1940s visited Manipur in 1980s to pay homage to those who laid down their lives. They were surprised to find the Tangkhuls in the same backward condition. The footpath which they followed remained unchanged and the trees under which they took offensive and defensive position remain standing as they saw in those days.[7] This rather simply testified to the undeveloped and backward condition of Tangkhul villages.

Another aspect of change is witnessed in the religious life of the Nagas by the spread of Christianity. However, the dimension of change brought about by Christianity is found not only in the religious outlook of the people. As a matter of fact, the changes brought about by Christianity is found in all aspects of the life of the Nagas. First, it removed undue fear of the spirits and unwarranted expensive sacrifice to propitiate the evil spirit which was a big and unavoidable burden in animism. Secondly, the people were relieved of the binding and torture of superstition. They have nothing to consult the spirits or observe divination and different signs to carry out venture of the day. The dreaded inter-village war, heinous chopping of heads and psychological fear of warfare of the time have been done away with. Peaceful atmosphere has set in the Nagas society and they have nothing to fear one another.

The peace that prevails wrought free access and contact which widened the outlook of the people. The mind of the people are not confined within the village but they can now looked beyond it to the world outside. Education has spread and people have learnt more about hygiene. By the nature of new creed, those who embraced Christianity felt a solace from the bondage of sin, and salvation was assured to them. In short, Christianity brought about all round development in the life of the Nagas, and the Tangkhuls in particular. Had Christianity not been preached in Tangkhul area, it would have taken decades, perhaps a century, for the Tangkhuls to reach such a state of life as they live today.

But the spread of Christianity is not without its adverse effects in the life of the Nagas. The early Christian missionaries and their new converts failed to distinguish the social customs and culture of the Nagas from religious and spiritual ills of Naga animism. Therefore, they attacked the social customs and culture of the Nagas regardless of their origin and relation with the religion. They did not spare their attack even on the costumes of the Nagas which was the lone cover of the bare body of the people. The result was almost a complete annihilation of Naga culture among the Christian population of the Nagas.

However, thanks to the progress of education, people realised the necessity and importance of their culture as their national identity. Attempts for the revival of their culture is very strong but not at the cost of Christianity. Social evils had been already discarded by the Nagas, not on the basis of Christians principles only, but also by the realisation of modern rationalism. Therefore, all social practices of values are being traced and preserved.

In the midst of all these changes in the total life of the Nagas, the post of Awunga remains though there had been some changes in the administrative set-up like the formation of Hangva being replaced by the introduction of Village Authority and its new administrative system. Rather, the recognition that the post of Awunga is hereditary has strengthened the post in Tangkhul village polity. The office of the Awunga, we may say, continues to be one important link between traditional Tangkhul society and the rapidly changing modern times. Therefore, the office of the Awunga still stands and is respected by the people even today. It has to continue in the future, too, since it is the office created by the people and sanctioned by their tradition.

As proverb says, "Two are better than one", the administration of Awunga is always assisted and supported by the Hangva. As a matter of fact, the Hangva is the main organ and functionary of the Tangkhul villages. No doubt, it is the executive body to carry out the functions of the village. However, under no circumstances, a Naga woman can take part in the administration of the village. According to a Naga oral tradition, 'A woman has no real place'. She may be born here in a village and remains there as a citizen of the village today. But tomorrow, she may go to another village and be there as its citizen by her marriage. Therefore, neither woman nor the 'slavery'[8] class has the right to rule over free citizens and their land. Further, sometimes, the Awunga with the heir (in certain cases, with the members of Hangva) had to approach the village deity and offer sacrifices for the peace, prosperity and well-being of the people. But the approach of a woman to the village deity is forbidden, it being a taboo to the Tangkhuls. Therefore, the inclusion of woman in the administration of the village does not arise at all.

The Tangkhul villages, being a political, social, economic and religious unit, the Awunga of a village has manifold rights and duties. As mentioned above, in order to offer sacrifices and perform rituals, the Awunga has religious functions as well. Being the head of the village and priest, Hodson said, "He cannot refuse to act; or he may not depart from the line of action sanctioned by long custom."[9] Therefore, the religious duties of the Awunga is as much important and inalienable as the secular duties. In this agrarian society of early days, all social and religious activities were well-linked with agriculture, and therefore, the Awunga as the chief of the village had manifold duties both secular and religious.

However, modern election system on the principle of adult suffrage has affected the village administration of the Awunga and Hangva. Though the post of Awunga has not been changed to an elected post, the members of Village Authority, a substitute of the Hangva, have to be elected as mentioned earlier. This change of system has naturally affected the powers and functions of the Awunga. Because, the membership of the Village Authority has not been nominated clanwise to represent all the clans residing in the village as practised from early days. Rather, it was by the system of majority votes that the biggest clan ultimately has got the opportunity of capturing the entire seats of the village body.

The limitation of the post of Tangkhul Awunga in the system of permanency and hereditary is that without question, the eldest son of the Awunga is entitled to succeed the post regardless of his inability and inefficiency for the post. Except for a few, most of the Awungas of today are uneducated and lack administrative ability; and therefore, are unable to shoulder the administration of the village entrusted to them. They occupy the post only by virtue of being the successors of the post. It is, therefore, felt, and is the need of the time, that the Awungas should acquire education in order to accommodate modern administrative principles so that their village administration may be in conformity with the changing situation of today. This will improve the position of the Awunga, and ultimately bring about desirable administration of Tangkhul villages.

While our study is primarily centred on the role of the Awunga in the village affairs and the system which continues today, over-arching the Tangkhul Awungas is the Tangkhul Long. A Tangkhul Long does not in any way weaken the position of the Awunga. Rather, it strengthens its position, because, today issues might arise which requires a collective decision of the Awungas.

However, much earlier to it, there had been the Tangkhul Long: Longrei, Longphang, a loose federation of the Tangkhuls. Longrei means the 'Great Long' or the 'Great Council' which is Tangkhul Long itself and its jurisdiction covered the the whole territory of present Ukhrul District. Longphang means 'Branch Long' or 'Branch Council' covering a certain range. There are several Longphangs in Tangkhul region. The function of the two Longs was for the peaceful co-existence of Tangkhul villages. In early days, when a certain powerful village raided a weaker village, the latter usually appealed to Longphang for justice. The case which Longphang could not solve was referred to Longrei. The aggressive villages were warned by the Long of dire consequence of common raid.

In recent times and especially after the establishment of British rule in the Tangkhul hills, although there was no such raid or aggression by the powerful village into the territory of a weaker village, the people felt the necessity of continuing the function of the Tangkhul Long as a social organization for the progress, development and welfare of the people. Thus, it came into its complete form today. Apart from the function for the welfare of the people, it raises its voice as a mouth-piece of the Tangkhuls against the exploitation and atrocities of the people by the forces of any form.

The village Awungas form the General Assembly of the Tangkhul Long.[10] They are represented by virtue of their office. The General Assembly of the Tangkhul Long has an elected president and other functionaries who hold office for a term of five years. The president and other office bearers need not be any Awunga, but another elected Tangkhul elder.

However, the Tangkhul Long is not the dominating power and organisation over the Awungas of the Tangkhul villages. By the formation of the Tangkhul Long, the village Awungas do not surrender their rights and duties to the authority of the Tangkhul Long. Rather, it is the commonwealth of the Tangkhul villages to see for the betterment of the Tangkhul villages and the people. Further, it does not override the powers and functions of the Tangkhul village Awungas.

However, realizing the expensive litigation in the courts of modern established government and that also without proper judication of the cases according to the taste of the people, the Tangkhul Long felt the need and necessity of establishing a court of justice to try and settle cases pertaining to Tangkhuls based on the customary laws of the people. When various customary laws of the people (Tangkhuls) were collected and compiled, it became the Customary Laws of the Tangkhul Long known as Shiyan-Yanza in 1988.[11] It has both original and appellate powers of cases. It is a parallel court existing side by side with the courts of the Deputy Commissioner, Sub-Divisional Officers and Sub-Deputy Collectors of present Ukhrul District of Manipur State. However, the court of Tangkhul Long does not eclipse the existing office and court of the village Awunga nor has ruling power over the verdicts made by the court of Awunga and Village Authority.

From the facts discussed above, we may conclude that the establishment of the court of the Tangkhul Long based on customary laws is a recognition of, and gives importance to, the customary laws for the governance of the Tangkhul in which the Awungas are the guardians. The establishment of Tangkhul Long and its court is an illustration of the Tangkhul Nagas' respect for tradition in spite of modern changes and innovations. It has confirmed the Tangkhul Nagas' desire not to make a breach from the past. They have seen the value of traditional justice and have confidence in its function. Certain cases, particularly between two or more villages, question of land etc. are settled amicably through the Tangkhul Long.

NOTES & REFERENCES

1. During the World War I, the native state of Manipur raised 2,000 Labour Corps of which the Tangkhuls alone contributed 1200, and the rest from other tribes of Manipur. They worked with the Allied Forces, witnessed the warfare by themselves and learned the use of modern war weapons. Again, in the World War II, the British raised V-Force (Volunteer Forces) from Naga population, and a good number of the Nagas fought with the Allied forces against the Japanese.
2. In 1943, when the Japanese forces reached Tangkhul country, they employed a good number of the Tangkhuls as their guides and interpreters. Among them, Rev. Ringshi of Bungpa village and Miss Salengla of Nampisha village were prominent. The former was caught in Burma and went along with a Japanese general till the battle at Kammon, one of the heaviest battles in Tangkhul hills.

General Kutoku, Commander of 31st Japanese Division was led by Ringshi, whereas Miss Salengla led Khongsang, a Liaison Officer of the Japanese forces. This story has been narrated by A. S. Vashi.

3. The Azad Hind Fauz came in Manipur with the Japanese forces. They closely worked with the people of Manipur including the Tangkhuls. A good number of them were captured by the British at present Phungyar S.D.O. Headquarters in Ukhrul District. Their story was narrated by A. S. Hongvaileng, father of the author.

4. Initially the Naga Club was a social and cultural forum. But the political developments taking place in India later forced the Club to look into the political problems of the Nagas arising out of the departure of the British. This Club was formed with the cooperation of the British officials of Naga Hills. Details may be read in *A Brief Historical Background of Naga Independence,* a Federal Government publication of Nagaland; P. Sema, British Policy and Administration in Nagaland 1881-1947; V. K. Nuh, *Nagaland Church and Politics,* p. 81; Amalendu Guha, *Planter Raj to Swaraj,* p. 322.

5. In 1945, during the time of C. R. Pawsey, Deputy Commissioner of Naga Hills, Naga Hills District Tribal Council was formed with the view of uniting the various Naga tribes. However, in 1946, the Naga tribal representative changed it into Naga National Council which ultimately became the parent political body of the Nagas.

6. *A Brief Historical Background of Naga Independence,* pp. 14-15, printed by the Federal Government of Nagaland Press, 1968. In this regard, a cable was sent to the Government of India and the United Nations Organisation which the UNO was kind enough to send the acknowledgement; V. K. Nuh, *op. cit.,* pp. 102-106.

7. The heaviest Anglo-Japanese battle was fought at Shangshok village in Ukhrul District which the British soldiers called it "bloody battle." A good number of casualties occurred on both sides. The Japanese soldiers have visited the village to perform formal rituals of homage to those who had been killed in the battle.

8. This term has been explained earlier.

9. T. C. Hodson, *The Naga Tribes of Manipur,* p. 185.

10. According to Census of Manipur (1971) published by H. Ranbir Singh, Directorate of Census Operation, Manipur, the villages in Ukhrul District were divided in language-wise, and there were 168 Tangkhul villages in the District with a population of 51,356 in numbers. However, Census of India (Manipur) 1981, Directorate of Economics and Statistics, Government of Manipur and Census of India (Manipur), Series 1, Final population totals Paper I of 1992,

Vol. I, II by Amulya Ratna, do not give the population of Ukhrul District in language wise, Zingkhai N, Longwui Pangsin Lairik, makes an attempt to put in written form the functioning of the Tangkhul Long.

11. "The Tangkhul Naga Shiyan-Yanza" is the "Tangkhul Customary Law." It is a collection of the Tangkhul customary laws and compiled by the Tangkhul Long which was approved by the Tangkhul Naga Long in the General Assembly on 13th October 1988. Since then, it came into force. Some detail of this use of customary law is published by Ako Shaiza, *Tangkhul Wungram Shiyan Chikan.*

APPENDIX - I

DECLARATION OF REVIVAL (PAREIHANBA)

I, the king of Manipur, Okendrajit, son of (Late) King Budhachandra, do hereby exercise my power, authority, rights on the religion, custom of my beloved people of the country to safeguard the extinguishing ancient culture of my Motherland, that from today the 23rd April 1992, (the 21st of Shachibu), one time suppressed and subdued religion, culture, custom and tradition of Meitei Eenaat, i.e. "The Lainingthou Sanamahi Pakhangbaism" is restored and revived from conversion and adoption of Hinduism since the 18th century by "The Maharaja Pamheiba (Garibaniwaz) and Maharaja Chingthangkhomba (Bheigyachandra) from today effect. I, declared, "PAREIHANBA" once it was done by the then aforesaid kings of the country as "PAREILEISINBA' in the interest of the people of the country. I open the Lubaak Taabu and abandoned Hinduism as state religion and recognition is hereby withdrawn from the Royal Customary Law of the country, instead, "The Royal Customary Law revived the Lainingthouism as State Religion and do hereby given recognition as State Religion."

Further, along with the revived "Lainingthouism", all the properties either in kind or customary courts which were annexed with Hinduism and Govinda cults are again restored to the Pakhangba Customary Court, all the Hindu names placed on the deity gods and goddesses of the country are again restored to the original names of the particular gods and goddesses, e.g. Mahabali into Mongba Hanba .... Hiyangthang Lairenbi, Baruni Mahadeva into Nongpok Ningthou Apaanba, Thangjing Mahadeva into Thangjing Lainingthou, Jivistha into Pakhangba, Visnu into Lainingthou Sanamahi etc. All the traditional and customary functions of the Deity Gods and Goddesses shall be performed into Meitei Laining Law by the Meitei devotees only.

The Declaration covers the revival of the Unitary body of the Hill and Plain people which was once divided by the Hindu pandits. There shall be no question of touchability and untouchability among the Hill and Plain people which was forced by the Hindu cult. Hence those who want to suffix the title "HAO" (tribal) in their Yek, he is to choose and shall include in the 6th Schedule of the Constitution of the Indian Union and shall recognise constitutionally.

The Kangla is the Holiest Place for the Meitei Laining, it opened to all the believers and devotees of the Meitei Laining and awarded to function and celebrate all kinds of religious rites and performances according to the Meitei cult, and awarded to reconstruct the lost and damaged structure in the Kangla and all its related places.

From today, the country shall have a Royal Court as it was in the past. It is highest in its form, no judicial court of the country shall hold trial regarding tradition and religion and moreover, the verdict of this court is final, even the Supreme Court cannot interfere regarding the religious matter.

I swear in the name of the Almighty Pakhangba that I shall abide by the revived custom and religious law of the Meitei Eenaat and shall act without fear and favouritism. I will do for the just cause of the people of the country for the future betterment of the people and the country.

Hence, I did PAREIHANBA according to my authority given by the Holy Spirit of the Almighty the Creator and the people of my beloved country as their own trusted King of the country. This Declaration brings our spiritual and physical unity of the Hill and Plain people and remain as one unique body.

We were one and shall be one, no more division shall be allowed.

Thanks

Ningthourel Okendrajit
Meitei Ningthourel Yaiphaba
Langon Ningthou Apannba,
Sana Konung, Imphal

23/4/92

APPENDIX - II

OFFICE OF HIS HIGHNESS THE MAHARAJA
MANIPUR PALACE, IMPHAL

Dated, Imphal the 8th Nov. 1892.
No. P-6/H.H/CUS-92
ROYAL EDICT
(Free English)

I, hereby, make it to know to the Hundung King Wungnaoyo (Thawaijao), and to all the hill people of Hundung that the hillsmen and plainsmen have been brothers since time immemorial. Lest we forget that we are one, and following His Exalted Highness King Churachand, and my father, His Divine Highness, Budhachandra, who both erected a memorial stone each, I, Preihanba, the' King, on this Sunday, the 8th of November 1892, at 10.00 in the morning, also put up a stone which carries my footprint and another stone upon which is inscribed the sacred alphabet, as a token of remembrance between the hillsmen and the plainsmen; and further send a sacred female buffalo.

May this sacred beast which I have sent bear offsprings and live long; and should any one kill or devour the flesh of this sacred beast, let these acts be similar to consuming my own flesh, that of the king. May that person receive the retribution of divine Grand father Pakhangba.

Sd/-

Written by: T. I. Meitei
the King of (Houleipak)
Manipur, 8.11.1892

H. H. PAREIHANBA/P. S. to
OKENDRAJIT
Ningthourel (Houleipak)
Manipur

APPENDIX - III

PRESIDENT, MANIPUR STATE DARBAR (HILL)

Standing Orders No. 12 of 28/3/1941
Memo No. 4375/Hill of 10/3/1945

The following order is passed to guide officers when disposing of disputes between Christians and non-Christians concerning Separate Pattas, the right of Khulakpas, and the Civil duties of both Christians and non-Christians.

(1) Amongst Tribes in which the post of Khulakpas is hereditary, the post of Khulakpa and rights pertaining there to be hereditary in the future.

(2) A villager, simply becoming a Christian, cannot be allowed to divest himself of his civil duties unless the performance of those duties is obnoxious to the Christian religion.

(3) The present practice of allowing Christians to live separately will continue, but no new Pattas will be given unless circumstances made it highly desirable to do so.

(4) Separate Pattas already given to Christians will continue providing things run smoothly.

Sd/- R. H. Show
S.D.O–E
17/3/45

Sd/- T.A. Share, ICS, 20/3/41
P.M.S.D. (HILL)

BIBLIOGRAPHY

PRIMARY SOURCES: 'A' ARCHIVES

Manipur State Archives, Imphal, Manipur, *Administrative* Reports.

Deputy Commissioner's Office, Ukhrul, Manipur State.

Sub-Divisioner's Office, Ukhrul, Manipur State.

Assam State Archives, Dispur, Assam.

PRIMARY SOURCES: 'B' REPORTS, GAZETTEERS ETC.

Austen Godwin, H. H. "Report on the survey Operation in the Naga Hills and Manipur During the Field Season," General Report on the Topographical Survey of India for the Season, 1872-1873.

Brown G.E.R. Grant, *Burma Gazetteer,* Upper Chindwin District, Vol. 'A', Superintendent, Government Printing and Staty., Union of Burma, Rangoon, Reprint, 1960.

Brown, G.E.R. Grant, *Burma Gazetteer,* Myikyina District, Vol. A, Superintendent, Government Printing and Staty., Union of Burma, Rangoon, Reprint, 1960.

Grierson, G.A. *Linguistic Survey of India,* Vol. III, Part I, II, Motilal Banarsidas, Delhi, 1903.

Census of India, 1981 (Manipur), *Statistical Abstract of Manipur,* Directorate of Economics and Statistics, Government of Manipur, Imphal, 1981.

Census of India, (Manipur), Series I, India, Final Population Totals, Paper I of 1992, Vol. I, II; Amulya Ratna Nanda, Registrar General and Census Commissioner of India.

Singh, H. Ranbir, *Census of India, 1971,* (Manipur), Directorate of Census Operation, Manipur.

Singh, R.K. Birendra, *Census of India, 1981,* (Manipur), Director of Census Operation, Special Tables for Scheduled Caste and Scheduled Tribe.

The Imperial Gazetteer of India, Vol. XVII, XVIII, Reprint Edition, Today and Tomorrows Delhi.

Manipur Gazette Extra-ordinary Publication, The Manipur State Hill Peoples (Administration) Regulation, 1947, 1957.

SECONDARY SOURCES

Alemchiba, M. A *Brief Historical Account of Nagaland,* Naga Institute of Culture, Kohima, 1970.

Bower, Ursula Graham, *Naga Path,* Butler and Tanner Ltd., London, 1950.

Bertram S. Carey and Tuck, H. N. *The Chin Hills,* Firma K.L.M. Pvt. Ltd., Calcutta, 1976.

Cantor F. Norman, *Western Civilization: Its Genesis and Destiny, From Pre-Historic Era to 1715,* Vol. I, Foresman and Company, Illinois, 1969.

China Reconstruct, Vol. XXX, No. 10, October, 1981.

Christoph von Furer-Haimendorf, *The Naked Nagas*, John Murray, 50 Albamarie Street, London, Reprint, 1996.

Clark Mary Mead, *A Corner in India*, American Baptist Publication Society, 1907.

Crowber Michael, *West Africa Under Colonial Rule*, Hutchinson and Company (Publisher) Ltd., London, 1973.

Dev J. Bimal and Dilip K. Lahiri, *Manipur Culture and Politics*, Mittal Publications, Delhi, 1987.

Das, J. N. *A Study of Land System of Manipur*, (Sponsored by N.E.C., Shillong, 1989), Law Research Institute, Eastern Region, Gauhati High Court, Gauhati, Assam.

Desai, A.R. *Social Background of Indian Nationalism*, Bombay Marg Popular Press, Bombay, Reprint, 1994.

Downs, F.S. *History of Christianity in India*, Oxford University Press, Bombay, 1969.

Downs, F.S. *The Mighty Work of God, A Brief History of the Council of Baptist Churches in North East India: The Mission Period, 1836-1950*, Christian Literature Centre, Gauhati, 1971.

Dutta, Pural, *The Singphos*, Directorate of Research, Government of Arunachal Pradesh, Itanagar, 1990.

Elwin, E. (Ed.), *India's North East Frontier in the Nineteenth Century*, Third Impression, 1972.

Elwin, V. (Ed.), *The Nagas in the Nineteenth Century*, Oxford University Press, Bombay, 1969.

Federal Government of Nagaland, A Brief Historical Background of Naga Independence, Printed by the Manager, F.G.N., 1988.

Frank M. Lebar, Gerald C. Hickey and John K. Musgrave, *Ethnic Groups of Mainland South East Asia*, Human Relations Area File Press, New Haven, 1964.

Furnivall, J.S. *Colonial Policies and Practice: A Comparative Study of Burma and Netherlands,* India, New York University Press, 1956.

Guha, Amalendu, *Planter Raj to Swaraj, Freedom Struggle and Electoral Politics in Assam,* 1826-1947, People's Publishing House, Delhi, Reprint, 1988.

Gori, G. K. *Changing Phase of Tribal Area of Manipur,* B. R. Publishing Corporation, Delhi, 1986.

Hodson, T. C. *The Naga Tribes of Manipur,* B. R. Publishing Corporation, Delhi, Reprint, 1974.

Hodson, T. C. *The Meitheis,* London, Second Edition, 1975.

Hutton, J. H. *The Angami Nagas,* Oxford University Press, Second Ed., 1968.

Hutton, J. H. *The Sema Nagas,* Oxford University Press, Second Edition, 1968.

Horam, M., *Naga Polity,* D. K. Fine Art Press, Delhi, Reprint, 1992.

Horam, M. *North East India: A Profile,* Cosmo Publication, Delhi, 1988.

Horam, M. *Social and Cultural Life of Nagas,* B. R. Publishing Corporation, Delhi, 1977.

Horam, M. *Naga Old Ways New Trends,* Cosmo Publication, Delhi, 1988.

Hidayatula, M. *The Fifth and Sixth Schedules to the Constitution of India,* Asok Publishing House, Gauhati, 1979.

Hutton, J. H. *The Mixed Culture of the Naga Tribes,* Reprinted from the *Journal of the Royal Anthropological Institute,* Vol. 96, Part I, 1965.

Imchen Panger, *Ancient Ao Naga Religion and Culture,* Har Anand Publication, Delhi, 1993.

Johnstone James, *My Experience in Manipur and Naga Hills,* Simpsonlow, Mersten and Co., London, 1896.

Johnstone James, *Manipur and Naga Hills,* Manas Publications, Delhi, Reprint, 1987.

Jajo Champhang, *Christian in Tribal Context in Manipur,* Swapna Printing Works Pvt. Ltd., Calcutta, 1990.

Kabui, G., *Anal, A Transborder Tribe of Manipur,* Mittal Publications, Delhi, 1985.

Kabui, G. *Genesis of the Ethnoses of Naga and Kuki-Chin,* Published by Naga Students Federation, 1993.

Leach, E. R. *Political Systems of Highland Burma: A Study of Kachin Social Structure,* The Athlon Press, University of London, Reprint, 1970.

MacKenzie, Alexander, *The North East Frontier of Bengal,* Mittal Publications, Delhi, 1989.

Mills, J. P. *The Ao Nagas,* Oxford University Press, Bombay, Reprint, 1980.

___. *The Rengma Nagas,* Spectrum Publication, Gauhati, Reprint, 1980.

___. *The Lotha Nagas,* Macmillan and Company, London, Reprint, 1980.

___. *The Effects on the Naga Tribes of Assam of Their Contact with Western Civilization.*

O'Malley, L.S.S. *Modern India and the West,* Oxford University Press, London, 1968.

M. Fortes and E.E. Evans-Prichard, *African Political System,* Oxford University Press, Reprint, 1973.

Maiya Gachui, *Hao Mi-un Ngashan Kala Tangkhul Khararchan, (History of Tangkhul),* Goodwill Press, Imphal, 1986.

Nagas '90', *A Souvenir,* Kohima, 1990.

Nuh, V. K. *Nagaland Church and Politics,* Kohima, 1986.

Perham Margery, *Native Administration in Nigeria,* London Oxford University Press, New York, Toronto, Rpt., 1962.

Pettigrew, W. *40 Years in Manipur,* (Ed., Jonah M. Solo and K. Mahangthei, Modern Press, Imphal, 1986.

Robert, L. Tignar, The Colonial Transformation of Kenya, The Kamba, Kikuva and Maasai From 1900 to 1919, Princeton University Press, New Jersey, 1976.

Roy, J. *History of Manipur,* Imphal, 1973.

Roland, K.Y.L., *Tangkhul Naga History,* Maikhel-Tungam Zimik Group, The Manipur Stationery and Printing Industries, Imphal, 1976.

____. *A Comparative History of the Nagas, From Ancient Period Till 1826,* Inter-India Publications, Delhi, 1988.

Shimray, A.S. Wungnaoyo "The Tangkhul Long: Its Judicial and Arbitrating Functions," *Proceedings of the North East India History Association,* Fifteenth Session, Doimukh, 1994.

Shimray, R.R. *Origin and Culture of Nagas,* Samsok Publication, New Delhi, Revised Edition, 1986.

Sema, H. *Emergence of Nagaland,* Vikas Publishing House Pvt. Ltd., 1986.

Sira, K. L. Hao Khararchan, Published with the Assistance of the Government of Manipur.

Shaiza Ako, *Tangkhul Wungram Shiyan Chikan (Tangkhul Customary Law),* The Eagle Press, Dimapur, 1983.

Shimmi Roland Y.L. *Identity of Nagas,* Published by the T.K.L.I., Tangkhul Katamnao Long, Imphal, Manipur, S.M. Press, Imphal, 1993.

Sen, Sipra, *Tribes and Castes of Manipur,* Mittal Publications, Delhi, 1992.

Sardeshpande, *The Patkoi Nagas,* Daya Publishing House, Delhi, 1981.

Singh, K. B. (Ed.), *An Introduction to Tribal Languages and Culture of Manipur,* Manipur State Akademy, 1988.

Sema Piketo, *British Policy and Administration in Nagaland, 1881-1947,* Scholar Publishing House, New Delhi, Second Edition, 1992.

Sanajaoba, Naorem, *Manipur: Past and Present (The Heritage and Ordeal of Civilization,* Vol. I, History, Polity and Law, Mittal Publications, Delhi, 1988.

Samuel Enoch Stumpf, *Socrates to Sartre, A History of Philosophy,* McGraw-Hill Book Company, New York, 1966.

Tajenyuba Ao, British Occupation of Naga Country, Published by Naga Literature Society, Mokokchung, Western Printing Press, Dimapur, 1993.

Thapar, Romila, *From Lineage to State,* Oxford University Press, 1984.

Yonou Asoso, *The Rising Nagas, A Historical and Political Study,* Vivek Publishing House, Delhi, 1974.

Zingkhai N. Longwui Pangsin Lairik, Modern Press, Imphal, 1974.

SECONDARY SOURCES—UNPUBLISHED

Sanyu Visier, "History of Village Formation Among the Angami Nagas, A Case Study of Kohima and Khonoma," A Doctoral Thesis, Department of History, NEHU, 1989.

"The Tangkhul Naga Shiyan-Yanza," (Tangkhul Customary Law), 1990, A Mimeograph.

Tuisem A. Shishak, "Principles Underlying the Socio-Religious Practices of the Nagas," A Thesis submitted to the Faculty of the Graduate School of State University of New York, at Buffalo in Partial Fulfilment of the Requirement for the Degree of Master of Arts, 1970.

Vashi, A.S. *"The Naga Kingdom"*, a Mimeographed.

INTERVIEW

The Researcher made a number of visits to Ukhrul District of Manipur and Imphal, and had discussions with the following persons, the contents of which has been used in the Thesis, though not necessary in the footnotes.

Ramnganing Muivah, Deputy Commissioner	Ukhrul	20-12-1992
Stephan Angkang	Imphal	14-10-1993
Prof. Horam	Imphal	14-10-1993
K. K. Hugh	Imphal	15-10-1993
Prof. Gangmumei Kabui	Imphal	15-10-1993
R. Silas	Imphal	16-10-1993
K. Prongo	Imphal	16-10-1993
Wungnaoyo Zimik	Hundung	18-10-1993
Nganingkhul Zimik	Hundung	18-10-1993
Ramyo Luikham	Ukhrul	19-10-1993
Peter Advocate	Ukhrul	19-10-1993
Y. K. Shimray	Ukhrul	19-10-1993
Rashing Shangjam	Ukhrul	20-10-1993
Machihan Sasa	Nungui	25-10-1993
Lima Imchen	Shillong	4-9-1994

R. N. Ngaleithang	Dimapur	9-10-1994
Lanu Aier	Shillong	27-4-1994
A.S.H. Shimray	Ningthi	1986
A.S.V. Shimray	Ningthi	1992-1994

•••